D0255911

COUNSELLING IN CONTEXT

THE REV. DR. DAVID ATKINSON is Chancellor of Southwark
Cathedral and Canon Missioner in Southwark Diocese.

He was for some years Fellow and Chaplain of Corpus Christi
College, Oxford, and lectured in pastoral theology at Wycliffe Hall.

He helped found the Oxford Christian Institute for Counselling.

David is married to Sue and they have two grown up children.
He is author of a number of books including several titles in the
Bible Speaks Today series (IVP) and *Pastoral Ethics* (Lynx, 1994).

THE REV. DR FRANCIS BRIDGER is vicar of Woodthorpe, Nottingham. He has served in an inner-London parish and as a lecturer
in ethics and philosophy at St John's College Nottingham, where
he was also Director of Studies and where he currently teaches
part-time. He is married to Renee, an Anglican priest, and they have
three adult adopted children.

Francis has written or edited a number of books and articles on
practical theology, including *The Cross and the Bomb* (Mowbrays
1983), *Videos, Permissiveness and the Law* (Grove Books 1984) and
Children Finding Faith (Scripture Union 1988). He also served from
1987 to 1991 as a councillor on Broxtowe Borough Council.

Books available
in the same series

GROWING THROUGH LOSS AND GRIEF

Althea Pearson

Forthcoming titles

FOR BETTER, FOR WORSE

Mary and Bruce Reddrop

FAMILY COUNSELLING

John and Olive Drane

FREE TO LOVE

Margaret Gill

SETTING CAPTIVES FREE

Bruce Stevens

HANDBOOKS OF PASTORAL CARE
Series Editor: Marlene Cohen

COUNSELLING IN CONTEXT

Developing a theological framework

FRANCIS BRIDGER
AND
DAVID ATKINSON

HarperCollins*Publishers*

HarperCollins*Publishers*
77-85 Fulham Palace Road, London W6 8JB

First published in Great Britain
in 1994 by HarperCollins*Publishers*

1 3 5 7 9 10 8 6 4 2

Copyright © 1994 Francis Bridger and David Atkinson

Francis Bridger and David Atkinson assert the moral right
to be identified as the authors of this work

A catalogue record for this book is
available from the British Library

ISBN 0 551 02732-0

Phototypeset by Harper Phototypesetters Limited,
Northampton, England
Printed and bound in Great Britain by
HarperCollinsManufacturing Glasgow

CONDITIONS OF SALE
This book is sold subject to the condition that it
shall not, by way of trade or otherwise, be lent, re-sold,
hired out or otherwise circulated without the publisher's
prior consent in any form of binding or cover other
than that in which it is published and without a
similar condition including this condition being
imposed on the subsequent purchaser.

All rights reserved. No part of this publication may be
reproduced, stored in a retrieval system, or transmitted,
in any form or by any means, electronic, mechanical,
photocopying, recording or otherwise, without the prior
permission of the publishers.

CONTENTS

SERIES INTRODUCTION

The demand for pastoral care and counselling in churches has increased to record levels and every indication is that this trend will continue to accelerate. Some churches are fortunate to have ready access to professionally trained and qualified counsellors, but in most situations this onerous task falls to pastors.

Some pastors* are naturally gifted for the ministry of counselling. Some receive training before ordination and then seek to extend this as opportunity permits through the years. Others have the task of counselling thrust upon them. Most seem to feel some sustained demand, internal or external, to be competent in the field. This series aims to address some of the gaps frequently left in theological training. It is intended to offer support to those entrusted with responsibility for the care and well-being of others.

Comparative studies of healing agencies were pioneered in the United States. As long as thirty years ago The Joint Commission on Mental Illness reported that 42 per cent of 2,460 people canvassed would go first to the clergy with any mental health problem.

Of course there may be reasons other than overtly religious for a preference for clergy counselling. There may seem less stigma in seeing a pastor than a psychiatrist. Also, viewing a problem as a

---

* The term 'pastor' is used generically here, to include all who have a recognised pastoral role within a local church or Christian community.

primarily spiritual matter may preclude taking some degree of responsibility for it and for examining its depths. And, of course, clergy visits are cheaper! Unfortunately there can be the additional reason that parishioners feel an inappropriate right of access to their pastor's time and skills. God's availability at all times is sometimes confused with ours, as is divine omniscience.

Being a front-line mental health worker can put a pastor under enormous and inappropriate strain. Counselling is becoming the primary time consumer in an increasing number of parish ministries.

Feeling unsafe and inadequate in any situation inevitably produces some form of self-protective behaviour, unless we can admit our inadequacy while retaining self-respect. Religious professionals who are under pressure to function as counsellors but know their skills and knowledge to be in other areas may understandably take refuge in various defences, even dogmatism. The term 'religious professional' is more familiar in some countries than in others. The clerical profession actually preceded all others, in status and in time. 'But what are we professional *at*?' can be a difficult question to answer. This is especially so when clergy are driven to believe that anything short of multi-competence will let God down.

One pressure is that graduates of some theological colleges have actually been taught that ordination will confer counselling skills. 'We must insist upon the idea that every man who has been called of God into the ministry has been given the basic gifts for . . . counselling' (Jay Adams, *The Christian Counsellor's Manual*, 1973, Presbyterian and Reformed Publishing Company; Part One, Page 20).

Equating a ministry calling with being a gifted counsellor could be seen to involve some leaping assumptions. These are becoming more apparent as we distinguish what we used to call 'the ministry' from God's calling of *all* believers into ministry. As more work is done on what we mean by 'ordination' more clergy can be released into those areas of ministry for which they are clearly gifted and suited.

Belief that counselling skills are divinely bestowed in conjunction with a ministry 'call' will probably not issue in the purchase of this series of handbooks! Other pastors who believe or fear that neither counselling nor any other skills can be taken for granted, are possibly conducting their ministries under some heavy burdens. This series is written with a concern to address these burdens and to redress some erroneous equations that relate to them. Each author has extensive experience in some avenue of ministry and is also trained and experienced in some aspect of counselling.

These Handbooks of Pastoral Care are designed to aid pastors in assessing the needs of those who come to them for help. The more accurately this assessment can be made the more confident the pastor can be about the form of ministry that is required in each instance. Sometimes pastors will decide to refer the matter elsewhere, but on other occasions there can be a prayerful assurance in retaining the counselling role within their own ministry.

Marlene Cohen
Oxford, March 1994

AUTHORS' INTRODUCTION

This book is born out of a profound desire to see counselling and pastoral care by Christians develop in ways which are honouring to God, true to scripture and informed by Christian theology. We believe that the present counselling scene, while containing many good features, is also fraught with potential and actual dangers. It is with these in mind we have written.

Counselling in Context is therefore aimed at three kinds of reader:

those who are Christian ministers, lay and ordained, with responsibilities for pastoral care;
those who are in training for such ministry;
those who are interested in counselling.

Although we make certain assumptions about the level of knowledge possessed by the reader, we have minimised technical counselling language so as to make the argument as widely accessible as possible. Moreover, we deliberately do not seek to discuss particular approaches or techniques since there are already a number of books from this perspective to which we have referred at various points.

Rather, we are concerned to set out what we believe to be a number of fundamental issues for Christians involved in pastoral care and counselling and in doing so to challenge several commonly-held assumptions. The book is consequently organised into three parts.

Part 1 looks at the broad features of counselling with a view to offering a reasoned critique of some of the key presuppositions behind current practice, especially that of Christians. In particular, the notion of contexts is examined as a way of sharpening the debate and suggesting the kind of developments we would wish to see.

Part II moves on from critical analysis to construct a model based on Trinitarian theology. We should stress that this model is first and foremost a **theological** construct. It is not designed to be another example of clinical technique. The reader will search in vain for the kind of model which offers 'five steps to successful counselling'. Our concern is to establish the essential principles on which good practice should be based.

Part III, which is much shorter than the previous two, rounds off the discussion by considering the idea of hope. Our initial drafts contained this in Part II but further reflection led us to offer the chapter as a conclusion to the whole book rather than as one component of an earlier section. In our view, the message of hope contained in the Christian gospel makes a fitting ending to the arguments we advance in Parts I and II.

For those who are interested in source criticism, Parts I and III were written by Francis and Part II by David. We both, however, 'own' all three parts, even though our styles may slightly differ. We are grateful, moreover, to Christine Smith at HarperCollins for her willingness to accept a joint contribution to the series and to Marlene Cohen for her support and encouragement as series editor.

Finally, it goes without saying (but we will say it nevertheless) that our families have provided the most important context in which we have been able to write. Without them we would not have got thus far. To our respective wives, Renee and Sue, we record our thanks.

Francis Bridger
David Atkinson
Advent, 1993

Part 1

A CONTEXTUAL
ANALYSIS

CRISIS OR CROSSROADS?

Is Christian Counselling in Crisis?

It may seem strange to think of such a widespread and popular ministry as counselling as being in crisis. The starting point for this book is that in important respects Christian counselling has reached just such a state of affairs. The enthusiasm for counselling which runs through Western churches masks fundamental problems which have yet to be faced. The failure to acknowledge these constitutes a dangerous trap into which the Christian counselling movement has already begun to fall. Nothing less than a ruthless appraisal is necessary if Christian counselling is to be saved from being absorbed into a general mêlée of competing therapies which rob it of its distinctiveness and authenticity.

All this no doubt seems apocalyptic. However, it is the view of both authors of this book that urgent thinking is necessary. The notion of crisis can be interpreted in several ways. [1] In ordinary language, it refers to something sudden and dramatic which portends disaster: the news media daily thrive on political crises, economic crises and national crises as events which undermine our stability and threaten collapse. Crises are something to be avoided or swiftly solved before they destroy us.

A second, not unconnected, meaning identifies crisis with the idea of a critical moment or turning point. 'She has reached a critical stage in her recovery,' we say of someone who has been seriously ill. 'This experiment has reached a critical juncture,' remarks the scientist. 'Pearl Harbour marked a critical point in World War II,' writes the historian. What all these descriptions signify is the idea of decisive moments which affect a train of events so that a once-and-for-all change takes place.

But, theologically, crisis can be construed in yet a third way. The Greek *krisis* literally means a judgment. The conquest of Israel by the Babylonians or the fall of Jerusalem in AD 70 were both interpreted by the biblical writers as a *krisis*, a judgment from God.

Our modern notion of crisis, however, owes more to the first two meanings than to the third. The term crisis is reserved for events which are sudden, threatening and decisive. These are not generally seen as divine judgements, at least in the West. Yet it is a different matter with personal crises, where individuals frequently ask the question 'What have I done to deserve this?', implying, perhaps, that somehow God has punished them for previous wrongdoing.

The Three Types of Crises

At first sight, we may wonder how any of these definitions can be applied to Christian counselling. The counselling movement hardly seems in danger; even less is it perceived as a danger to others. Nor is it immediately obvious that counselling stands at a turning point in its own development or in relation to the Christian church. And to think of counselling as somehow related to divine judgment seems self-evidently absurd.

Our contention, though, is that all three senses of the term crisis are applicable. In the first place, as a number of studies have shown and as we shall argue in a later chapter, the uncritical adoption by the Christian churches of models of counselling based upon the assumptions of humanistic world views has severely undermined the historical tradition of Christian pastoral care on which the church's ministry has been based for nearly two millennia. (In using the term 'humanistic' we refer both to the therapeutic school of that name and to the wider philosophy of humanism in which it has its roots.) This in turn has reduced much of what passes for pastoral practice to a state of theological and practical incoherence, more so as post-Freudian assumptions and practices have been accepted as if they represented a new gospel. [2, 3, 4]

In the second place, Christian counselling is in crisis because it has reached a decisive point in its relationship with pastoral theology. Leading writers such as Thomas Oden and Stephen Pattison are now questioning how much longer Christian ministry can survive without rediscovering its historical and theological roots which go back well before the Freudian revolution. It is not simply that the adoption of the humanistic models of counselling has threatened historical models: rather it has produced a totally new paradigm for pastoral ministry. [5] The church must choose how far it will permit this model to dominate. A critical moment is already with us.

Thirdly, although it would be too strong to view the counselling movement as a judgement on the church: there is a sense in which we need to ask whether God is standing over and against contemporary trends in Western Christianity, especially where a humanistic worldview has been uncritically absorbed. If so, how far should we think of counselling as one such trend? We would argue that the matter is not simple. It is the essence of every crisis that it is ambiguous to interpret. And so the same is true of counselling. It contains aspects about which one can only rejoice: its capacity to free people from all sorts of slavery, is but one example. Yet at the same time it also contains profoundly disturbing aspects, not least the absence of any real role for theology or Christian philosophy in most counselling approaches. [6, 7] As they say in the USA, 'The jury is still out.'

So where does this leave a series such as this? Although in our view the Christian counselling movement stands at a crossroads, we do not believe it has yet irretrievably committed itself to a wrong path. Moreover, we shall be concerned, especially in the second part of this book, to sketch a positive approach which we hope will set a framework by which to develop counselling models which are genuinely based on Christian theology and are not just attempts to clothe secular models in Christian garb. Before we can reach that point, however, we must in the first part analyse more deeply the nature and roots of the present situation; and so we begin with the three aspects of crisis of which we have already spoken.

1 An Identity Crisis

There is a certain irony in describing counselling as being in the throes of an identity crisis. Yet, irony aside, this would not be an unreasonable characterization. The fundamental problem is that it is difficult to know whether counselling is to be regarded as:

merely *one* aspect of Christian pastoral care in conjunction with others;

an *alternative* form of pastoral care (as is widely assumed and practised);

a *rival* to pastoral care.

The widespread acceptance of psychotherapeutic models suggests that, at the present time, the second and third of these hold sway though there are signs that this may be changing.[8]

Whether or not this is the case, we need to recognize that at the popular level, Christian counselling has taken its identity firstly from the Freudian and post-Freudian therapeutic revolution and only secondly from the Christian pastoral tradition. This has meant that its roots are confused and its assumptions frequently in contradiction. The consequence is that both counselling and pastoral care suffer from a problem of self-definition.

A major feature of this confusion is the difficulty in defining the relationship between theology and psychology. How theology and psychology are to relate to each other is perhaps the most problematic question facing Christian counsellors today and the last 20 years are littered with attempts to define the relationship in terms which do justice to both disciplines.

On this issue counsellors generally fall into four camps (see Chapters 2 and 3). Firstly, there are those who accept the importance of insights from both theology and psychology but who give priority to theology. In a clash between psychological and theological findings, theology would always win. Secondly, there are those who assign a comparable priority to psychology. They admit the validity of theology but maintain that the controlling discipline must be psychology. Thirdly, another group argues that theology and psychology represent differing but equally valid perspectives so both must be taken into account in equal measure. In a clash, neither must be allowed to overrule the other *a priori*. Lastly, some counsellors simply believe that theology and psychology refer to such different ways of thinking that they have nothing to say to each other: let each rule its own roost – separately.

2 A Crisis of Truth

Hand-in-hand with confusion about the relationship between psychology and theology has gone the neglect of theology and philosophy. A significant aspect of this has been the uncritical acceptance of non-Christian humanistic presuppositions. Although we need to see all truth as God's truth, it remains the case that much counselling that calls itself Christian amounts to little more than an attempt to dress up therapies which in their fundamentals run contradictory to Christian theology. As Howard Clinebell and Gary Collins respectively have pointed out, the Christian scene is dominated by all kinds of eclectic approaches which collapse under the weight of their internal contradictions when subjected to scrutiny.[9] The uncritical acceptance of presuppositions drawn with little questioning from a variety of sources simply stores up trouble until it can be avoided no longer. That moment has now arrived.

It is important to realise that we are not arguing here for a *rejection* of non-Christian ideas. Far from it. Christians do not hold a monopoly of wisdom or truth. The point we are making is that Christians must exercise discernment in choosing counselling models and methods and must subject each to critical scrutiny. This will involve evaluating not just therapies themselves but their underlying beliefs in the light of a Christian worldview.

In a scramble to develop methods which bring therapeutic success, Christian counsellors have too often found themselves without a distinctive theologically-based philosophy by which to evaluate those methods. The consequence has been that, with some notable exceptions (the early work of Frank Lake and Bob Lambourne in Britain and some Christian counsellors in America, for example) the criterion for testing clinical approaches has largely been that of therapeutic outcome: if it works it is acceptable.

But this is clearly not adequate. No counselling method can be taken for granted simply on the say-so of its proponents, even if favourable outcomes are the result. There are wider issues of coherence with Christian truth which must be considered. Questions of purpose, meaning, suffering, hope and freedom lie at the heart of counselling and require theological and philosophical discussion. They are too important to be left to one side. We shall see later (chapter 4) how, in recent writings, leading counselling theorists are now coming round to this view and how genuinely effective counselling demands that the counsellor also face such questions of truth.

3 A Crisis of Practice

One of the most disturbing features of Christian counselling practice is its preoccupation with individuals. Christians have swallowed, more or less without question, the assumption that counselling should be primarily concerned with repairing individuals so that they can become better adjusted to cope with life's difficulties. It is easy to see how this goal has become paramount, yet in its simple and unqualified form (which is the most prevalent) it is nothing short of insidious.

We shall argue strongly that this kind of individualism is anti-biblical, anti-Christian and therapeutically undesirable. At its worst it has merely endorsed the narcissistic selfism represented in the psychobabble of the affluent and self-indulgent middle classes of the Western world. Even at its best it has reinforced the Western view that ultimately it is the autonomous, abstract individual rather than the individual-in-community who counts most. But either way Christian counselling has, by and large, colluded with a profoundly anti-social gospel. If *krisis* is to be interpreted at any point as judgment, it must surely be here.

In subsequent discussion, therefore, we shall focus on two aspects of the crisis of counselling practice. Firstly, the way in which it has engendered a therapeutic method which leaves largely unanalysed the impact of social forces and structures upon individual psychology. Secondly, the way in which it has ignored the role of community, especially the community of faith in the healing of the individual. This in turn leads to the issue of the church's corporate role in counselling.

So what should be the relationship between counselling and the pastoral ministry of the people of God as a whole? Such is the mystique and power of counselling that both ministers and laity increasingly judge themselves inadequate to carry out the pastoral task without recourse to some kind of professional training in counselling technique. Given that the Christian church has survived and grown for the best part of 2000 years without such professionalisation, this would be faintly amusing if it were not so disturbing. The sad fact is that we feel naked unless covered with the Emperor's therapeutic clothes.

Yet, as we shall argue, although there *is* a place for counselling within the ministry of the whole church, it is a place different from that often accorded to it at present. The division between professional clergy and laity which has been problematic in ministry for so long has been replaced by a division between the professional counsellor and everybody else. It is imperative that this be replaced by a theology of ministry in which all members of the body of Christ are seen as sharing in pastoral ministry. This alone will provide an adequate foundation for specialist counselling.

Facing the Crisis

When Karl Barth and his contemporaries found themselves challenging the theological *status quo* after World War I, they developed what came to be known as **crisis theology**.[1] Their fundamental contention was that the church needed to face the uncomfortable fact that liberal theology had failed and that radical action was needed. The church faced a crisis both in the sense of having reached a turning point and in the sense of facing the judgment of God.

The argument of this book is that the church now faces a comparable crisis in its understanding of ministry and that at the heart of this lies a faulty understanding of Christian counselling. The three areas we have outlined are the components of a much more general situation which the reader will find developed throughout the chapters which follow.

Despite all that we have said so far, however, we should say that we do not believe the situation to be completely pessimistic. Good counselling practice has been enormously helpful to many people. Moreover, there are some signs that the sort of rethinking to which we have alluded has already begun in some quarters.[3-5, 8, 10] Nevertheless, much work remains to be done if the crisis which afflicts both pastoral ministry and counselling is to be adequately faced. Counselling *can* be lifted out of crisis: it remains to be seen whether the church has the will to do so.

Why Contexts Matter

When we examine the threefold crisis of Christian counselling we find that we cannot escape the importance of contexts. The context in which counselling takes place is crucial. For counselling never takes place in a vacuum. It is not an activity abstracted from real life but is always rooted in it. Moreover, everyday life does not comprise merely one context but a series of overlapping contexts: home, work, leisure, family, political, social and so on. The counsellor has to take account of all these and more. To see how this is true, we shall look at four examples, each of which is based on fact:

Example 1 Lisa

Lisa is 14 years old. She is a bright, outgoing girl with plenty of energy and ingenuity. She is of mixed parentage, her mother being white and her father black. She was born while her mother was still in her teens and unmarried. Although Lisa's mum has since been married and divorced, this was not to Lisa's biological father. In fact, Lisa has never been told who her father is and although she has asked her mother several times, she can get no response.

When Lisa was two, her mother gave birth again - this time to a boy who was wholly white. A year later, a second brother was born, also white. Lisa's mum was now 22 and married but her husband was not the biological father of either of Lisa's brothers.

As the marriage steadily deteriorated, Lisa was exposed to violence between her parents. Although they were never seriously violent towards her, it had a profound effect on her nonetheless. One of Lisa's early memories was of her mother's husband slapping her mother viciously around the face and throwing her into a corner.

Even at an early age, Lisa had responsibility thrust upon her. By the time she had begun school, she had a third brother and was expected to look after him along with the other two. Some days her mother would keep her away from school so that she could babysit while her mother went out. Lisa's first year at school was severely disrupted.

By the age of seven, Lisa's home situation had become even worse. Teachers began to notice signs of bruising around her shoulders and legs. When asked, Lisa replied that she had fallen down the stairs but this was widely disbelieved. At the same time, the health visitor warned that the ability of Lisa's mother to look after her children was in question. They did not seem to get enough food or clean clothing and the frequency of medical attention was increasing.

Finally, following a particularly violent incident, social workers intervened to place Lisa and her brothers in temporary care. This, however, was to prove far from temporary. Over the next three years, Lisa's parents divorced and her mother was happy to leave her children in a children's home since it relieved her of responsibility for them. On several occasions, the authorities tried to link the four children with long-term foster parents but at every attempt Lisa's mother made so much trouble that prospective foster parents were frightened off.

When Lisa was ten, foster parents were at last found who were prepared to foster Lisa and her brothers. Although they were white, they loved Lisa as much as the boys and were sensitive to her feelings.

Lisa, however, was badly torn between feeling the warmth of her new-found security and her sense of loyalty towards her natural mother. This was made worse by a sense of guilt on Lisa's part that somehow she had been to blame for the collapse of her mother's marriage and the placing of her brothers and herself into care.

By the time she was thirteen, Lisa was full of rage, fear and resentment as she struggled to find her identity. Slowly she began to turn against her foster parents. Step by step she came to reject their beliefs, their values and finally, themselves. To her, *they* were to blame for her being taken away from her mother. *They* were the ones who stopped Lisa getting in touch with her. (In fact, Lisa's mother had never replied to attempts by her foster parents to establish regular communication with her children.) *They* were the ones responsible for her feelings of rejection. And so it went on in Lisa's distorted mind.

This anger resulted in malicious acts both at school and at home. Several times Lisa's foster parents were warned that she would be suspended or expelled for vandalism and theft. At home, it was no different. Lisa stole regularly from her foster parents (who were powerless to stop her) and even once deliberately smashed the car windscreen in a rage. She spent all her time in her bedroom, except for meals which were eaten in silence. Lisa had come to hate her mother, her foster parents and herself.

During this time, there had been repeated visits by a school counsellor and social worker but all to no avail. In the end, the situation deteriorated to such an extent that Lisa asked to return to a community institution where she would not have to cope with the demands of family life. Her foster parents, heartbroken, agreed. Their early hopes had been completely shattered.

Example 2 Eddie

Eddie is a family man in his late thirties. He has a daughter Tricia who is 19 and has left home to live with her boyfriend and their baby, and a son Terry who is 10 and suffers from severe behavioural problems.

Eddie is unemployed. Since he is an unskilled labourer, he is unlikely to find work in his town which has a male unemployment rate of more than 40 per cent. He has tried to move to a more prosperous area but for Eddie it is all but impossible. Eddie's lack of a job means he is trapped. He and his wife Pam are nearing despair.

Their problem is made worse by their sense of failure towards Tricia. They blame themselves for Tricia having 'kicked over the traces' (as they put it). They now look back on their own beginnings as a couple and wonder if the fact that they were living together without being married when Tricia was born has anything to do with her attitude.

Then there is the problem of Terry. He was born in difficult circumstances and almost did not live. At one time it was thought that he might have suffered brain damage but mercifully that was not the case. Nevertheless, Pam coddled and cosseted him throughout his childhood and while Eddie was in work made sure that Terry got all he wanted.

Now Terry is in constant trouble. The most recent example concerned damage to a neighbour's garden gate. According to Terry, it was an accident. But the neighbour contends that he saw Terry deliberately kick holes in it. At first, Pam and Eddie thought the dispute could be sorted out amicably. But the neighbour demanded the price of a new gate which turned out to be far more than they could afford. When the neighbour resorted to law, Pam could cope no longer and suffered a nervous collapse.

Fortunately, their local minister suggested they contact a friendly lawyer who was able to persuade the neighbour to drop the complaint and settle for a much lower sum in compensation. Although the matter was resolved, Pam and Eddie were left with the bitterness of soured relations and the humiliation of being dependent entirely on welfare benefits for all they had. Their earlier despair was now reinforced by a loss of dignity.

Terry, meanwhile, was sent away to stay with Eddie's brother and his wife. Significantly, he showed no signs of misbehaviour when with them but as soon as he returned home all the old troubles reappeared.

Eddie and Pam are nearing the end of their mental and emotional resources. The future looks utterly bleak and nothing in their lives offers any hope. They are not simply despairing, they are literally hope-less.

Example 3   Michael

Michael is unlike most men: he holds a commission in the Army. He was initially attracted to the forces while at a private school where he enlisted as a cadet. Michael's family approved of his decision to make the Army his career, not because there existed any strong tradition of service in his family but because Michael's parents believed the disciplined structure would be good for character.

Michael went straight from school to an Army college where he graduated with honours. After some further training he was posted to Germany for three years. While there, Michael met and married a German girl named Lisel. They returned to England with a baby girl. A year later, Lisel became pregnant once more but early tests revealed that the foetus was suffering from Downs syndrome. After much heart searching Michael and Lisel decided to terminate the pregnancy. However, the abortion was not straightforward and as a result, they will never be able to have children again.

Emotionally the experience has brought their marriage to the brink of collapse. Lisel is a Roman Catholic who agreed to the termination only because she could not face the prospect of moving around the world with a handicapped child and a husband who would be away much of the time.

Michael is distressed by the fact that he cannot now father a son and heir. The tradition of his family places great stress upon this and he feels he has let them down. The problem is complicated, morever, by Michael's emotional introversion. His upbringing and training have taught him to be stiff upper-lipped about the emotional side of life and to cope with tragedies and hardships without flinching. He is therefore unable either to help his wife in her distress or get in touch with his own feelings. He has nobody to whom he can turn since his family have made it a virtue never to show emotion and his fellow officers have been trained according to the same code of conduct.

Michael's grief is consequently driven underground. He refuses to acknowledge its existence and wonders why is is permanently depressed. He has begun to drink heavily since this is the only 'manly' way he knows of coping with his sorrows. Michael feels, therefore, as if his life is in ruins. His marriage has been all but wrecked, he cannot now have a son and his career no longer seems attractive. There appears little point in continuing. He keeps on telling himself to pull himself together but this does not help. In fact, it makes things worse.

Example 4 Ada

Ada is a senior citizen. She was born 74 years ago in Hackney in the East End of London, where she has lived most of her life with her family, including five brothers and one sister. As the eldest of seven, Ada found herself expected to look after her younger brothers and sister and to take responsibility within the home.

Ada's mother was a large woman with a kindly heart who took in washing to supplement the family income. Ada's father was a docker. Unfortunately, he was an oppressive husband and father who did not hesitate to beat his wife and children, especially when drunk (which was quite often).

Ada's brothers and sisters were warm and friendly but suffered from learning disabilities. These were later diagnosed as hereditary but Ada's father did not see it like that. He blamed his children for their lack of mental ability; so they were made to feel worthless for most of the time. In a way this was worse for the boys since their father held a low view of women and therefore did not expect his daughters to be more than skivvies. But he was deeply disappointed in his sons and frequently told them so.

When Ada was 23, her father was killed in a dockside accident. Immediately, all the children over the age of 14 were sent out to find work. Only Ada, her sister and one of her brothers were successful. Eight years later, Ada's sister married and moved away. By this time her brothers had all found menial jobs but these were low paid and insecure. At the first sign of economic recession, they were the first to be made redundant.

For another twenty years Ada continued to support her mother and brothers, none of whom married or moved away from home. Ada's mother died at the age of 61, worn out and poor. Within the next decade, the hereditary condition which seemed to run in the male line brought about the early deaths of all but one of Ada's brothers, Roy. At the same time, Ada rarely heard from her sister.

By the time she was sixty, Ada had never known anything but hardship, poverty and responsibility. Marriage had passed her by, as had deep friendships, and her health was beginning to fail. In all this she tried to keep cheerful 'for Roy's sake' but in truth there was little to be cheerful about. When she saw the area in which she had been brought up transformed into a high-price ghetto for the well-off, she wondered what she had done to deserve a life of poverty. Ada was no better off than her father and mother sixty years before.

From Crisis to Context

Counselling never takes place in a vacuum. Many of the problems in Christian counselling have arisen because Christians have failed to recognize the broad context in which the Christian counselling movement has developed. In this section we shall be looking at three particular kinds of context which are crucial for understanding the counselling process and for developing a coherent approach.

Let's begin by going back to the four case studies we have just outlined. Suppose that Lisa, Eddie, Michael or Ada were to come to us for help. What would we do? How would we respond? What sort of help would we give? The answer would depend upon what we believed about the **purpose** of counselling. In turn this would depend upon the **context** we had decided was important in defining the counsellor's task.

1 The Psychological Context

Counselling as it is widely practised in Christian circles has followed its secular counterparts in accepting (largely uncritically) two assumptions. It is generally assumed that:

a person's distress has an internal origin (maybe triggered or reinforced by external circumstances) which can often be traced back to childhood or even foetal experience; [13, 14]
the primary treatment or therapy which the counsellor provides should be geared to restoring internal psychological equilibrium.

The task of the counsellor on this basis is to enable the counsellee to understand and put right those negative feelings and attitudes which have been distorted by past experience.

Explicitly Christian models may (depending on their theological basis) incorporate such concepts as sin, forgiveness, redemption, restoration and salvation but even the most biblically-orientated models have usually accepted the two assumptions mentioned above. Moreover, the place of distinctively Christian resources for healing has not always been made clear. The result has been, in Michael Wilson's words:

> Styles of counselling based upon psychology and divorced from traditional resources of help such as prayer and sacraments have too often been adopted by the church without sufficient critical evaluation.[15]

We need to acknowledge, moreover, that although an understanding of the psychological context may be indispensable, there is a danger that the significance of the other contexts may be missed. By assuming that a person's distress can be explained wholly or principally in terms of psychological background, the counsellor will almost certainly devise a therapy which is inadequate. An understanding of the psychological context is *necessary* but not *sufficient*.

2 The Philosophical/Theological Context

Both philosophy and theology suffer from a bad press. They are often taken to be irrelevant to the real stuff of life. Philosophy (partly through its own obsession for much of this century with the meaning of words) is regarded as a waste of time: a pastime for eggheads with nothing better to do. Theology has become synonymous with pettymindedness and intransigence. Such characterizations are, of course, caricatures but like most parodies they contain some degree of truth.

We need to grasp, therefore, that both philosophy and theology are fundamental to good counselling practice. Each is concerned with ultimate questions of meaning and purpose – exactly the questions brought to counsellors by troubled clients. The difference between the two is that theology goes beyond philosophy in seeking to relate ultimate questions of life to God. The theological context of counselling, therefore, is concerned with ultimate questions of human existence and purpose in relation to God. We should remember, moreover, that such questions do not arise simply from the agenda brought by persons in distress. They also underlie all counselling *theories*. The task of the Christian counsellor is consequently to open up issues of meaning and purpose so that counsellors can begin to face the deep questions of life, not least the question of their relationship to God, to themselves and to the people and world that God has made and redeemed.

Significantly, those who seek counselling come already asking fundamental philosophical and theological questions (although they may not always recognize them as such):

Why am I afflicted by depression?
What meaning does life hold?
Why do relationships go wrong?

How can I know right and wrong?

Is my life controlled by inner drives and external circumstances over which I can have no control or am I really free to shape my life?

Why am I suffering?

Sometimes these questions lie deep under the surface and need to be brought into daylight. At other times they are already on the surface and arise straightforwardly. But whichever it may be, the task of the Christian counsellor must be to enable counsellors to interpret their experience in a philosophical and theological context so as to discover God-given coherence and meaning for their lives.

All four of our examples raise three kinds of questions. But how many of those who practice counselling within the churches are equipped to answer or even identify them? The need for a revisionist approach to counselling has come.

3 The Social Context

Why is the social context of counselling important? Let's go back to our examples. In each case, the part played by social conditions was crucial.

Lisa felt rejected because she was of mixed parentage when society expected her to be either black or white (preferably white) but not a mixture of both. Her colour reminds her that she is caught between two cultures. Moreover, society does not recognize foster parents as 'real' parents, so Lisa is constantly faced with the taunt that her 'real' mother is inadequate or does not want her. This leads her to question her own self-worth and in turn to project her sense of rejection onto her foster parents. There is a close connection between her social and psychological contexts.

For Eddie and Pam the connection is even more acute. Their despair arises in large part from unemployment and poverty. Any counselling strategy for them must recognise the force of their economic and social circumstances. The best that a purely psychological approach might achieve would be to give them some means of coping with the situation. But in the end, it can only be resolved by changing their conditions.

In Michael's case, the social and theological contexts are connected in two ways. Firstly, his family and friends expect him to produce a son and heir to carry on the tradition. This exerts enormous social pressure upon him so that when it seems he cannot fulfil their expectation, he sees himself as a social failure and lapses into depression. Secondly, Michael's upbringing and Army code of conduct will not allow him to deal effectively with his emotions. It is unmanly to admit grief, emotions must be tightly controlled and no one must know of his inner turmoil. He *cannot* express his desolation because socially he *must* not.

For Ada, the structure of her psychological world has been shaped overwhelmingly by social inequality. As the eldest sibling she was expected to act as a quasi-parent and therefore could find no freedom for herself. Ada's image of womanhood was taken from her mother, herself the victim of social norms and expectations. Ada's life chances, morever, were restricted by her family circumstances of which the continuous battle against poverty was the most oppressive. She has had to fight against bureaucracies large and small for everything. Now in her old age she is stressed again by the changes in her neighbourhood which threaten to destroy the small haven of security she has managed to establish for herself. Ada is perhaps the clearest example of why the social context of counselling is important.

Summary

We have looked at four examples based on real-life experiences to illustrate the argument of the ensuing chapters. This may be summarized as follows:

1 Counselling has come to be understood as a one-to-one exercise in which the purpose of the counsellor is to relieve mental and emotional distress by restoring internal psychological equilibrium.

2 Effective counselling must take account of the differing but related contexts in which human beings find themselves.

3 Within the conventional model, the counsellor's understanding of a counsellee's problem and the development of a counselling strategy has been determined predominantly or exclusively by the *psychological* context. This has centred on the counsellee's inner world rather than his or her social context.

4 Our four examples illustrate the importance of relating a person's psychological context to his or her social context. The two are interwoven.

5 Neither psychological nor social contexts can be divorced from philosophy and theology. These are fundamental to human beings. The distinctive task of the Christian counsellor is to enable a counsellee to face critical questions with theological as well as psychological resources.

These five points set the agenda for the remainder of this book. In the chapters which follow we shall follow through the arguments in some detail, not with a view to disparaging the practice of Christian counselling but with the aim of improving it. For, in the end, the counselling movement is here to stay.[16]

THE PSYCHOLOGICAL CONTEXT I

The Meaning of Counselling

So far we have written as if the meaning of counselling were crystal clear. But is it? What's more, is it legitimate to use the term 'Christian counselling' over and against counselling in general? Should we speak simply of 'counselling by Christians' which lays the emphasis upon the distinctiveness of the counsellor rather than the process or content of counselling? Or should we speak of 'counselling in a Christian context'?

The answers to these questions are of fundamental importance. Yet they are far from clear. For the way in which the term counselling is used within the Christian churches frequently disguises a lack of clarity. It can refer to activities ranging from professional psychiatric help to a listening ear offered by a pastor or a friend. In the Christian church it has been taken to mean virtually any kind of help which involves empathetic listening. As Michael Wilson has pointed out:

> There is a continuum of creative conversation which begins at one end with friendship, moves through counselling in a more formal sense, and at the other end consists of psychotherapy and more specialized treatment.[1]

The fact that counselling can mean so many things to so many people makes it absolutely vital that we gain a clear understanding of what we mean when we use the term. At the very least we owe it to those who seek counselling that they understand what kind of help is being offered and to what degree of professional expertise.

As a starting point, we may take a definition offered by Roger Hurding, a professional psychotherapist who is also a Christian. Hurding notes two elements within the practice of counselling. On one hand, he points out that the counsellor offers advice: 'Straightforwardly, to counsel is to advise.[2] On the other hand, the counsellor also offers friendship. Both elements are important: 'We might put these two strands of meaning together and say that to counsel is to befriend in order to advise or help someone.'[3] Elsewhere, he defines counselling as 'the activity which aims to help others in any or all aspects of their being within a caring relationship.'[4]

If we expand Hurding's definition slightly, we find that counselling as generally understood and practised has a threefold aspect. First there is the troubled counsellee in need of help; second there is the counsellor who is expected to bring relief and resolution of the problem; third there is the one-to-one relationship between them which is crucial to the success or otherwise of the counselling process.

We shall be discussing the nature of these three aspects at various points throughout the book. For our present purpose, however, we shall focus upon a number of definitions and characterisations of counselling put forward by leading Christian counsellors and others. In what follows, we shall use the terms counselling, therapy and psychotherapy to refer to the same process – the difference between them lying in the length and depth of treatment and the degree of professional therapeutic expertise possessed by the counsellor.

As we survey the range of definitions, we see that the threefold characteristics mentioned above occur repeatedly. A leading textbook of counselling in the United States defines counselling as 'a process that assists individuals in learning about themselves, their environment and methods for handling their roles and relationships.'[5] Gary Collins describes counselling as 'primarily a relationship in which one person, the helper, seeks to assist another human being with the problems of living.'[6] According to Lawrence Crabb, 'Counselling is centrally and critically a relationship between people who care.'[7] Howard Clinebell speaks of pastoral counselling as 'the utilization of a variety of healing (therapeutic) methods to help people handle their problems and crises more growthfully . . .'[8] Jay Adams refers to counselling as 'the process of helping others to love God and their neighbours.'[9] Frank Lake defines the task of the counsellor as helping individuals achieve change through 'listening to a story of human conflict and need.'[10] Paul Halmos, writing from a sociological perspective, defines counselling as 'the new philanthropic expertise of helping through caring-listening-prompting.'[11] Harry Guntrip characterizes psychotherapy as 'a cooperative effort of two people in a dynamic personal relationship of an analytic helping situation.'[12] Anthony Storr in the same vein defines it as 'the art of alleviating personal difficulties through the agency of words and a personal, professional relationship.'[13]

All these definitions say similar things. However, we need to recognize that within counselling as it is widely referred to and practised among Christians, there exists all too often an uncritical eagerness to apply the term counselling to all and sundry kinds of listening activity, irrespectively.

Both clergy and laity fall into this trap. A clergyman or woman who has taken a short course as part of theological training may feel himself or herself somehow to be a counsellor, when in fact all they have done is learned a few basic skills. A church may set up a counselling team which in reality consists of relatively untrained personnel who are strongly motivated and have natural pastoral qualities but whose training is minimal compared to professionals.

Our purpose in saying this is not to devalue these activities. In fact, we suspect that far more healthy pastoral care takes place without it being labelled counselling than is realised. For, as we shall argue in a later chapter, the best place for counselling is a therapeutic community (such as the church) of which the expert may be one - but only one - part.

Levels of Counselling

If we need to be far more careful in our use of the term counselling than is presently the case we need also to examine the concept of *levels of counselling* as developed by R. H. Cawley, Lawrence Crabb and others. Here we will find grounds for distinguishing between different activities which come under the general heading of 'counselling'.[14]

R. H. Cawley, who is a psychotherapist, contends that therapeutic help should be seen on four levels.[15]

Level 1 includes the kind of help given by any caring person with some life experience, whether professionally trained or not. The principal elements within this level are empathy, listening ability, support and encouragement. Simply by ventilating anxieties within a caring relationship, the troubled person may find healing.

Level 2 involves a deeper analysis and understanding of the counsellee's problems and situation. Some degree of technical understanding and training is required here. Natural qualities on the part of the counsellor are not enough.

Level 3 takes both parties into the realm of dynamic psychotherapy. Understanding the realm of the unconscious, the counsellee's past and the way in which psychological mechanisms operate plays a key part at this level. Considerable professional expertise on the part of the counsellor is essential.

Level 4 aims at thoroughgoing behavioural change through therapy in depth. This can be achieved only with the help of a skilled, trained psychotherapist.

It seems clear that much of what is loosely called counselling in Christian circles falls within level 1. Provided this is clearly understood by those who engage in it, there need be no confusion, though it might be better to call such ministry pastoral care rather than counselling. The difficulty arises, however, when counsellors or counsellees fail to acknowledge the distinction between levels or when the term counselling is bandied about without much thought. When this happens, unrealistic expectations may be generated which the counsellor is simply not equipped to fulfil. The lay counselling team in a church, for example, may be well able to meet the need for a sympathetic ear perhaps coupled with positive help and advice. Although one or two members may be trained at higher levels, the majority of the team may not be trained to go beyond Level 1 help. They will need to recognize that some problems require to be dealt with at a different, more complex, level. In such cases, they should not be afraid to refer the counsellee to a more highly trained counsellor.

Clergy in particular need not feel anxious about the principle of referral. By and large they are not trained beyond level 2 and should not hesitate to pass a counsellee on to somebody who is. There is absolutely no need for ministers or their congregations to expect that the pastor should be a psychotherapist. In most cases, he or she will have been trained for a more broadly-based calling and where specialist counselling expertise is required, referral would be regarded as normal while remembering that, as we have seen, the context for healing of individuals must always be wider than that of the counsellor-counsellee relationship. The gentle satire of sociologist Bernice Martin is worth recalling. Speaking of the confusion in modern clergy roles she comments:

> One role drawn from the modern professions, that of the pastoral therapist, does have ready appeal . . . So clergy learn less Greek, Latin, Hebrew and classical theology but more social science. They become a species of semi-professional therapist with a roving brief, generic case workers for the parish with a mildly spiritual aura.[16]

Conversely, we need to recognize that not all so-called counselling problems are a matter of deep therapy but in fact can be dealt with at level 1.

Take, for example, Peggy who showed deep distress after church one Sunday morning. She was extremely troubled. As she unburdened herself, it emerged that the root of her problem was not so much psychological as environmental. She lived alone in a flat and was suffering from severe disturbance by neighbours. Whenever she asked them to be a little quieter, she was met with aggression and abuse. The result was that she slept badly, worrying both about her disrupted relationship with her neighbours and about the noise.

What Peggy needed (and received) was a combination of sympathetic support and practical action. Fortunately her local ward councillor attended the same church and took up Peggy's cause. He was able to alert the housing department to the problem and they sent an official to talk to the neighbours. The problem was solved and Peggy's distress eased.

But was this a genuine counselling problem? According to Cawley's definition of level 1 counselling, it was. Peggy was a troubled person, finding it hard to cope with her feelings and needing help. The help she received met her need and restored her emotional and psychological equilibrium. But it did not require more than level 1 help. It amounted to counselling of the most general sort where empathetic listening followed by specific practical action was enough. Moreover, the help Peggy needed was of a particular kind: she was not in need of therapy but social action. Her subjective distress, as revealed in her psychological and emotional state, was rooted in her objective housing conditions. This demonstrates the critical link to which we have already referred: the relationship between counselling and its social context.

Turning from R. H. Cawley to Lawrence Crabb,[17] we find a more distinctively Christian analysis. Crabb shares Cawley's insistence that we have to distinguish between counselling levels. However, he goes on to set them within a more openly Christian framework. Crabb defines his own three levels.

Level A is concerned with what he calls **counselling by encouragement**. As the name implies, this kind of counselling is essentially a ministry of support and encouragement which aims at reorienting people's feelings more positively. It can be practised by all members of the body of Christ since it involves no technical knowledge or training but is simply the outworking of authentic Christian love. It is the interaction of believers in mutual care and support:

> Counselling by encouragement depends upon an awareness of painful emotions in a member of the family (of the church) and a sincere effort to understand them, growing out of an attitude of compassion and concern for the person who hurts . . . all members of the body of Christ can and should be involved in this level of counselling.[18]

Level B he describes as **counselling by exhortation**. The task here is to identify and change problem behaviour. As this requires training both in counselling methods and in theology, it will be practised by fewer people in the local church than Level A. Moreover, counsellors at this level require a thorough knowledge of biblical teaching as it relates to pastoral and ethical situations:

> Above all else counselling at this level requires a knowledge of the Bible. Counselling technique is important. An ability to establish rapport, to reflect feelings accurately (Level A) and to react sensitively to a person's needs are critical. But without a working knowledge of biblical principles of living a person simply cannot counsel at Level B.[19]

Level C is known as **counselling by enlightenment**. Here a few gifted and committed people who wish to become counsellors might undergo rigorous training of one evening a week for up to a year. The objective at this level of counselling is to restructure a counsellee's thinking so as to change the whole person in behaviour, motive and outlook. It is a deep work which Crabb recognizes is only possible by grace. In Crabb's view even the most stubborn conscious or unconscious hindrances to an individual's all-round maturity can be dealt with at this level, though he realistically recognizes the possibility of resistance and failure. The key to this is the work of God the Holy Spirit in transforming a person's *thinking:*

> I am transformed by the renewing of my mind. As **I grasp with my mind** [Crabb's emphasis] that my needs (significance and security) are fully met in Christ, then I am enabled better to conform my behaviour patterns to Christ's example and to enjoy the deep peace of a growing maturity.[20]

The counsellor's role consequently is:

> To function as an instrument through which the Holy Spirit enlightens minds regarding the truth of significance and security in Christ. And that is what counselling at this level entails – probing deeply into the hidden parts of the mind where people hold tenaciously to certain assumptions, exposing those beliefs which deny the sufficiency of Christ to meet our personal needs of significance and security, teaching that Christ is sufficient and then encouraging new behaviours in the truth that our needs are met in Christ.[20]

The picture we are left with, then, is of a much more variegated approach to counselling than has frequently been assumed. If Cawley, Crabb and others who think like them are right, Christians need to recognize that what they have to offer in the main is not professional counselling at levels III and IV but something much more akin to supportive (and sometimes challenging) friendship. In Michael Wilson's words:

> Counselling in this respect is like medicine in that you may need someone as professional as a heart surgeon; on the other hand, everyone needs to be able to take a splinter out of someone's finger.[21]

What we are suggesting is that we recognize that most of us are removers of splinters rather than heart surgeons.

However, whether we accept the analysis of Cawley, Crabb or neither, the concept of levels helps us to see that the term counselling needs considerable clarification if we are to avoid presuming too much. A clearer understanding of the different levels of counselling and the distinctions between them would enable the counselling movement within the Christian churches more readily both to discover its distinctive nature and to identify its distinctive task.

Counselling and Pastoral Care

The idea of levels of counselling needs to be set alongside a further question: are counselling and pastoral care the same thing? We have earlier suggested that to confuse the two is dangerous. If pastors are expected also to be skilled counsellors or therapists, they are in danger of being loaded with a highly unrealistic expectation which they simply cannot, and should not, fulfil. However, a further danger is that the church will lose its distinctive identity. We have seen in Chapter 1 how this is already a problem: we now turn to the issue in greater depth.

The problem can be focussed by asking a simple question: what is pastoral ministry? A common assumption among both professional ministers and laypeople is that pastoral care and counselling are completely identical. We would contend, however, that this is not so. And as the first step, we shall see how the equation of counselling with pastoral care has come to dominate modern approaches to ministry.

The reduction of pastoral care to psychotherapeutic counselling is a thoroughly modern phenomenon. According to Clebsch and Jaekle in their magisterial *Pastoral Care in Historical Perspective:*

> During recent years, counselling has been the chief locus of concern for pastoral theology . . . counselling has become

the gate through which new intellectual formulations of pastoring have entered and claimed attention.[22]

Their conclusion receives support from the American pastoral theologian Thomas Oden. In a survey of nineteenth and twentieth century writers on pastoral care, Oden notes that in modern pastoral writings the classical pastoral theologians from St Augustine to Richard Baxter have been almost totally replaced by Freud, Jung, Fromm and other assorted psychotherapists. By selecting ten key figures in the classical Christian pastoral tradition and comparing the frequency of their usage, Oden discovered 164 classical references in leading nineteenth century writers but *none at all* in their twentieth century counterparts. In contrast he discovered instead some 330 references to psychotherapists. From this he draws the conclusion that pastoral care has come to acquire 'a consuming interest in psychoanalysis, psychotherapy, clinical methods of treatment and the whole string of treatments that were to follow Freud.'[23] This is not to suggest that all twentieth-century counsellors ignore biblical and historical insights but the trend that Oden identifies is none the less widespread and should not be minimized.

So how deep or widespread has the psychotherapeutic counselling model in Christian pastoral care become? There is general agreement that until the last decade, in the United States the takeover was almost complete. In Britain with its traditional suspicion of psychotherapeutic expertise, the situation is perhaps more ambiguous. But, as Stephen Pattison has pointed out, 'there can be no doubt that over the last twenty years it [the psychotherapeutic counselling model] has become more and more influential in pastoral care in this country and continues to grow and flourish.' He goes on to conclude that 'the gospel of counselling is gradually leavening pastoral practice even at the level of general and subconscious assumptions.'[24]

We can see, then, that to understand pastoral care in terms of this kind of counselling is a completely modern development. This raises the critical question of how we should define the difference between pastoral care and pastoral counselling. In attempting to draw the distinction, it will be useful to compare the historical with the contemporary approach.

A Fourfold Approach

Clebsch and Jaekle have put forward an historical model which they claim has formed the basis of Christian pastoral care since the early church.[22] Their model echoes J. T. McNeill's verdict that mutual care and edification have been central to the church's pastoral task throughout history: they 'were principles of the Christian way of life in the New Testament and in the Church Fathers,' whilst 'the idea that every Christian is a priest toward his neighbour was one of the most vivid doctrines of the Reformation.'[25]

In Clebsch and Jaekle's view, this model encompasses four basic pastoral activities: healing, sustaining, reconciling and guiding. Although historical circumstances have led to variations in emphasis between the four and the forms in which they have been expressed have been historically and culturally conditioned, all four have nonetheless been present to a greater or lesser degree throughout the history of the Christian church.

Healing should be seen as the transformation of a person to wholeness in which physical or psychological recovery is accompanied by a new level of spiritual insight and welfare. It is important to recognize that mere recovery of psychological equilibrium is not enough: it must go hand in hand with insightful growth, otherwise it is not true healing. Psychological recovery may constitute *partial* healing but it should not be confused with healing in its fullest sense as the *shalom* of God. Thus Michael Wilson writes that 'Man's vision of his wholeness constantly breaks the shell of his understanding, disturbs his complacency and tempts him to new adventures . . .'[26] Healing in the pastoral tradition is concerned then, with the whole person.[27-29]

Turning to the activity of **sustaining**, Clebsch and Jaekle define this as 'helping a hurting person to endure and transcend a circumstance in which restoration to his former condition is either impossible or so remote as to seem improbable.'[30] The man irreparably injured in a car accident or the woman grieving for the death of her child through cancer would both constitute examples of those whose primary pastoral need is to be sustained. But as with healing, the person engaged in the role of sustainer will seek to enable the suffering individual to experience spiritual and emotional growth even in midst of tragedy. The sustaining role involves more than empathy: it requires the helper to open up new avenues of insight and meaning.

Guiding, as its name implies, entails assisting troubled individuals to choose between alternative courses of thought and action as their spiritual implications are weighed and reflected upon. Once more, the emphasis is upon opening up insights which lead to personal growth: growth of personality and growth towards God.

Clebsch and Jaekle's final category, that of **reconciliation**, is rich in theological and human meaning. It involves not only the re-establishing of broken relationships between human beings and God but also between human beings one to another. It involves confession before God and perhaps before other people; forgiveness both human and divine; and the renewal of Christian life and relationships. For this reason, moral and pastoral theology have historically been associated with each other. Moreover, when we turn to the bible we find that in St Paul's theology reconciliation is central to understanding God's relationship to the world and the world's relationship to God.[31] For in Christ, God has drawn alienated humanity to himself. Thus Paul declares:

> God was pleased to have all his fulness dwell in him (Christ), and through him to reconcile to himself all things, whether things on earth or things in heaven, by making peace through his blood, shed on the cross (Colossians 1:19-20).

Reconciliation, however, does not stop there. God has given a ministry of reconciliation to his church. To quote Paul again, 'He has committed to us the message of reconciliation' (2 Corinthians 5:19). Reconciliation is consequently not merely one aspect of pastoral ministry among many but lies instead at its very heart. The ministry entrusted by God to Christian believers is a ministry of reconciliation above all else.

From this discussion, we can see that Clebsch and Jaekle's fourfold understanding of pastoral ministry provides us with a useful model for analysing the pastoral task. In taking up this thesis, Stephen Pattison draws attention to its value in supplying an all-encompassing approach:

> Pastoral care historically seems to have consisted, to a greater or lesser extent, of individual and corporate discipline (helping Christians overcome sin in themselves and in the Christian community); building up the church community; consolation (comforting and supporting Christians during times of personal or corporate sorrow); spiritual direction and guidance about the inner life; protecting the Christian community from external threats (trying, for example, to persuade temporal rulers not to persecute or destroy Christian groups); and healing (which might include the use of spiritual, sacramental and natural methods).[32]

If we examine this statement closely we find that two features stand out. Firstly, in contrast to a narrow identification with counselling, the historical model encompasses the whole range of activities covered by the term pastoral care. If Clebsch and Jaekle and McNeil are right, pastoral ministry historically has not been confined to a particular conception of the pastor/inquirer relationship based on psychotherapeutic goals but rather has been concerned with *every* aspect of human life. There is hardly any sphere of human need with which it has not been concerned. Secondly, it seems clear that within the Christian tradition, the fundamental context for the exercise of pastoral care is not the individualistic relationship of counsellor to counsellee but the communal life of the body of Christ, the church. The pastor, although an individual, acts on behalf of the Christian community:

> First and most simply, pastoral care is a ministry performed
> by representative Christian persons who . . . bring to bear
> upon human troubles the resources, the wisdom and the
> authority of Christian faith and life.[33]

The modern notion of a one-to-one, privatized counselling
relationship in which the troubled client comes for help to the
professional expert representative of nobody but himself is in
historical terms anachronistic.

We shall consider the reasons for this descent into individualism
in a later chapter. For our present purposes we need only note the
central point which has so far emerged:

> The task of the pastoral counsellor . . . in recent years has
> tended to become that of trying to ferret out what is currently
> happening or likely to happen in the sphere of emergent
> psychology and adapting it as deftly as possible to the work
> of ministry. So pastoral theology has become in many cases
> little more than an accommodation to the most current
> psychological trends . . . with only the slenderest
> accountability to the classical pastoral tradition.[34]

It would appear, then, that we are faced with two contrasting
models of pastoral care: the counselling model and the historical
model. This does not mean, of course, that the counselling model
never pays attention to historical tradition or that the historical
model always ignores psychological insights. But the distinction
serves a useful purpose in reminding us that pastoral care existed
long before psychotherapy and that however significant the impact
of post-Freudian insights has been, the Christian model of pastoral
ministry cannot afford to ignore its own roots.

Characteristics of Each Model

It is now time to set out the central features of both of the models we have considered.

If we analyse the features of the **contemporary model** we find an emphasis on:

- the one-to-one relationship as the primary context for pastoral care;
- the importance of therapeutic expertise to the healing process;
- the expectation that the counsellor should conform to a psychotherapeutic role model;
- the adoption of psychoanalytic methods and assumptions;
- the 'translation' of traditional theological concepts such as sin, guilt, atonement and redemption into psychoanalytic categories such as failure, self-awareness, resolution and self-acceptance.

In contrast, the **historical model** emphasises:

- pastoral care as the ministry of the whole community of faith;
- the representative role of the pastor in acting on behalf both of God and His people;
- the centrality of a distinctively theological understanding of human beings and their needs;
- that pastoral practice and assumptions should never be regarded as morally neutral but as incorporating values which need to be recognized and 'owned' by the counsellor/pastor. Only then can she evaluate the motives and actions of herself and her counsellee;
- the crucial significance of theological categories such as sin, guilt, grace, atonement and redemption;
- the grounding of personal growth in Christian spirituality, based upon the historic resources of the life of faith: Bible, sacraments, fellowship, worship and prayer.

It can be seen from this comparison that the shift to a therapeutic counselling approach has entailed nothing less than a revolution. Little wonder then that ministers find themselves facing a severe confusion of identity, role and purpose.

But whatever our misgivings about the dominance of the psychotherapeutic model, it is here to stay. Given the permeation of Freudian and post-Freudian concepts, terms and practices to every level and structure of contemporary society, it is difficult to see how it could go away. We are left, then, with two questions: (a) can we legitimately speak of *Christian* counselling? and (b) how should Christian theology, especially pastoral theology, engage with the revolution in psychology since Freud? The first of these is the subject of the remainder of this chapter. The second will be taken up in the next.

Christian Counselling?

In some Christian counselling agencies there has been an ongoing debate about what we think we are doing. One clergyman expressed considerable dislike to the phrase 'Christian counselling' thus: 'Counselling is counselling is counselling,' he said, 'How can there be such a thing as *Christian* counselling?' To him it sounded as absurd as 'Christian mathematics' or 'Christian physiology'.

In our discussion so far we have indicated that in our view a distinctive Christian model for counselling is, both in principle and in practice, possible and desirable. We are not referring in the first instance to a particular technique such as prayer counselling or healing of the memories (however distinctive these may be). Nor are we saying that Christian counselling is simply counselling carried out by Christians. Rather, we are contending that what is distinctive about Christian counselling is that it does not merely conform to secular models but in fact critiques and transforms them.[35]

It does so in two ways. Firstly, by using both the tools of the human sciences and the insights of Christian theology, it offers a distinctive analysis of what it means to be human. Secondly, by offering a theological model for the counselling process to be set alongside operational techniques, it turns counselling away from the dangers of an introspective selfism towards a renewal of life in Jesus Christ. Put another way, it seeks human wholeness by shifting the centre of the human being away from the individual self to the self-in-God and the self-in-community. In doing so, it incorporates insights from secular therapies but seeks to evaluate them theologically. And although we shall see this to be no easy task, it is nonetheless essential if we are to be true to the God who has given us all truth and whose Spirit Himself is called the divine Counsellor.

THE PSYCHOLOGICAL CONTEXT II

Relating Psychology and Theology

Are psychology and theology to be regarded as friends or enemies? Should they operate in alliance or antithesis? These are questions which have proved the focus of much discussion in recent Christian counselling literature. They therefore form an important part of the current psychological and theological context of counselling. In this chapter we shall review a number of proposals put forward to answer such questions.

William Kirwan has outlined four possible positions which state the relationship between psychology and theology.[1] The first he identifies as the **'unchristian view'**. According to this, theology has nothing to contribute to therapy. It is at best an irrelevance; at worst, it might even have been a factor in producing a patient's neurosis. The two disciplines have nothing to say to each other.

The second position might be called the **'spiritualised view'**. It is the obverse of the previous view and is held by Christians who deny that psychology has any value in comparison with religion. Theology is all that is needed. Psychology is rendered unnecessary by grace: the Holy Spirit is the great psychiatrist.

Kirwan terms a third position the **'parallel view'**. Proponents of this view contend that psychology and theology are equally valid within their respective spheres but their authority is confined to those spheres. Each functions sovereignly but independently. The psychologist cannot deride the theologian and vice versa since both are dealing with separate realities.

The final position may be entitled the **integrated view**. This holds that there is no 'sphere sovereignty' in the psychology-theology relationship.[2] When each is rightly understood (a most important condition) there is no inherent conflict. In Kirwan's words, they represent 'functionally co-operative positions.'[3] Kirwan's categorization amounts to a summary of the basic positions to be found in most recent writings.

One major analysis of this kind was developed by John Carter and Bruce Narramore in 1977. This will provide a useful starting point for our understanding of the present debate.

Carter and Narramore

John Carter and Bruce Narramore of the Rosemead Institute in the United States have sought to explain the spectrum of possible relationships between psychology and theology in terms of Richard Niebuhr's '*Christ and Culture* model'[4, 5] Niebuhr first developed this model in 1951 to indicate the differing ways in which theology and human culture as a whole might be understood to relate. (It is important to realise that by 'culture' Niebuhr did not mean the arts: rather he used the term to refer to human society conceived of as a network of interrelationships and beliefs. It is this definition we shall adopt.) But because his questions paralleled those which face the Christian who wishes to understand the relationship between theology and psychology, Carter and Narramore adapted Niebuhr's analysis. Their conclusions therefore provide a useful framework for considering the central issues.

Niebuhr's original model posited three main categories for understanding possible relationships between Christian theology and the world of human affairs. Firstly, Christ could be thought of as being *over and against culture*. On this view, Christians should regard the world as alien to faith and should withdraw from it. Society has nothing of value to say to the church since it is corrupted by sin and is opposed to God. This attitude has characterized isolationist groups throughout history and can be seen among some Christians even today.

Carter and Narramore adapted this category to produce a model of the psychology-theology relationship which they term the *'Against model'*. Both disciplines must be seen in opposition to each other. The intellectual bases of psychological theories must be viewed as suspect since they are the products of unregenerate minds estranged from God. Therapies likewise are shot through with wrong presuppositions about human nature, not least in their assumption of human autonomy which by definition must be regarded as ungodly pride. Moreover, the therapeutic process itself is open to corruption since it lies in the hands of sinful and self-centred human beings. This is true both of the counsellee and of the counsellor. Both are engaged in a manipulative game which refuses to acknowledge the truth about humanity or God. The 'Christ Against' model thus sees theology and psychology as polar opposites.

Niebuhr termed his second category the *'Christ of Culture'*. Those who advocate this view lay considerable emphasis upon Christian belief as arising out of human cultures. The social context of faith is therefore all important. Both the content and shape of Christian belief are culture-dependent and culture-relative. Accordingly, God must not be seen as wholly independent of the world but rather as part of it. Our conceptions of God must be acknowledged as socially produced and therefore relative. Truth cannot be regarded as objective but must be acknowledged as subjective.

When we transpose this framework of thought to the psychology-theology relation we end up with an approach which Carter and Narramore describe as the 'For approach'. Christian theology is 'for' psychology rather than against it. (This model is the opposite of the first we considered). Consequently, the dominant mode of the relationship is assimilative: psychology absorbs theology so that theological concepts are reinvested with psychological meanings. To quote Carter and Narramore: 'Proponents of this view selectively translate or interpret various passages or concepts from the Bible for use in their particular psychology.'[6] The 'For approach' thus lies at the opposite end of the spectrum from the 'Against model'.

Niebuhr's third category is more complex. Although he terms it

'*Christ above Culture*' he further sub-divides it into three aspects: synthesis, in which both Christian belief and human culture are regarded positively; dualism, in which (rather like the 'Against model') Christ and culture occupy separate realities in permanent opposition to each other; and conversionism in which culture is transformed by Christ.

Carter and Narramore split the category Niebuhr calls the '*Above* model' into two. The first they describe as the '*Parallels* model' and the second the '*Integrates* model'. According to the first, psychology and theology can either be understood in terms of isolation, in which case there is little or no overlap between the two, or alternatively in terms of correlation in which correspondences are sought between them. These two sub-categories are similar, though not identical to, Niebuhr's dualism and synthesis.

The 'Integrates model', however, picks up on Niebuhr's notion of conversionism. It sees psychology and theology as allies not of convenience but as allies holding common goals and purposes. Moreover, since both reflect the creative activity of God, they must be regarded as related parts of a greater unity in creation which itself is grounded in the unity of God. Psychology and theology must not be considered as divergent but as complementary.

As we shall see, all four positions outlined by Niebuhr and adapted by Carter and Narramore are to be found among Christian approaches to counselling. A summary of their admittedly complex analysis, however, would look something like this[7]:

1 The *Against* model;
2 The *For* model;
3 The *Parallels* model which subdivides into:
   (a) *Isolation*;
   (b) *Correlation*;
4 The *Integrates* model.

How would we categorize Christian counsellors in terms of the Niebuhr-Carter-Narramore schema? Jay Adams would probably be the best known representative of the *Against* model. Into the *For* model would fit Leslie Weatherhead and the Westminster Pastoral

Foundation in Britain and the Clinical Pastoral Education movement in the USA. The *Parallels* and *Isolation* models are more difficult to fit names into but as far as the *Correlation* category is concerned, Frank Lake must be reckoned to be a leading exponent though he shades also into the *Integrates* category. Finally, among those who have sought to bring together psychology and theology are some of the best known counsellors of recent years such as Gary Collins, Lawrence Crabb, Donald Capps, Paul Tournier and Thomas Oden.

Lawrence Crabb

Around the same time as Carter and Narramore were adapting Niebuhr, Lawrence Crabb was writing of the relationship between theology and psychology.[8-10] Although not nearly so sophisticated, Crabb's scheme bears family resemblances to Carter and Narramore and is worth sketching, not least because of Crabb's influence in the United States.

As with many other writers, Crabb identifies four possible positions.[11] The interesting thing about Crabb is that although he believes that biblical theology should act as the gatekeeper of truth, he does not reject psychological findings *per se*. They must be taken seriously but not granted the status of ultimate or absolute truth.

Crabb labels his first position 'Separate but Equal'. Another name might be 'Compartmentalism'. But whichever we choose, the underlying idea is the same: psychology and theology relate to different worlds with their own language systems and conceptual frameworks. Both are valid but must be seen as distinct. We are back to the idea of sphere sovereignty.

Crabb entitles his second approach 'Tossed Salad'. This image is intended to convey the notion of uncritical mixing of tasty ingredients from both psychology and theology. This is the methodology adopted (in Crabb's opinion) by the majority of Christian professionals. It involves taking insights from both disciplines and blending them to create the most viable therapeutic method. Because its essential aim is synthesis, contradictions are either ignored or discarded.

A third position Crabb describes as 'Nothing Buttery'. On this model, theology refuses to acknowledge the validity of psychology. Human disequilibrium can be explained as 'nothing but' sin, selfishness, rebellion against God, family and so on. By the same token, Christian therapy must be based on 'nothing but' biblical exhortation, confrontation, and the grace of God in the gospel. Typically, this approach sees all behavioural problems in terms of personal sin.

But although Crabb identifies the *theological* version of Nothing Buttery, there is also a Nothing Buttery which operates alongside reductionist psychology. Behaviour would thus be regarded as 'nothing but' the product of instinctual drives, social conditioning or whatever. Nothing Buttery can therefore work both ways. What is common to both versions is a fundamental reductionism which excludes other insights and seeks to interpret all data according to a single paradigm.

Crabb's fourth position goes by the peculiar name of 'Spoiling the Egyptians'. Crabb derives this from the Exodus story of Israel going out from bondage in Egypt to the Promised Land. As the Israelites left they took with them goods from the Egyptians to sustain them in their journey. In other words, they spoiled (took spoils from) the Egyptians. Crabb uses this analogy to argue for accepting psychological findings provided they have been screened by theology. There is nothing wrong, on this view, with utilising insights from psychology provided they have passed the theological truth test. However, if psychological and theological findings conflict, even if the former have empirical support, they must be rejected: 'When the teaching of scripture conflicts with any other idea, the teaching of Scripture will be accepted as truth. I might add that the other idea, *regardless of its support from empirical research*, will not be accepted as truth.'[12]

Kirk E. Farnsworth

Our final example of integrational discussion is Kirk E. Farnsworth.[13] We have chosen his analysis because it exemplifies the manner in which the issue of relating psychology to theology has taken centre stage among Christian counsellors in the United States. In Britain, unfortunately, the debate has still to develop in anything like the same depth.

Farnsworth puts forward five models of what he calls 'embodied integration' which he defines as 'a process of verification, relation and application.'[14] The distinctive claim made for this approach is that it does not merely compare conceptual schemes at the level of theoretical compatibility but aims to connect theoretical integration with practical integration. It must be left to the reader to decide whether Farnsworth succeeds in this but his analysis none the less offers a suggestive framework.

His first model may be described as the *'Credibility Model'*. Here, psychological data are recognized only if they can be subsumed under theological concepts. They must be screened through a theological filter (typically Scripture) in order to make them credible. 'According to this model, no psychological finding, regardless of its empirical support, will be accepted as truth if it conflicts with the teaching of Scripture.'[15] Not surprisingly, Farnsworth cites Crabb as the supreme example of the Credibility approach.

A second model can be seen in what Farnsworth terms the *'Convertibility Model'*. This amounts to the converse of the Credibility Model. Instead of psychology being screened by theology, psychology revises theology. Theological concepts are either reworked in psychological terms or rejected.

Farnsworth's third category is the *'Conformability Model'*. According to this, the guardian of truth is still theology but not narrowly confined to Scripture alone. Rather, psychological findings are reconsidered from the general perspective of a Christian worldview. The test of acceptability is not their conformity to specific Bible texts or individual ideas but to the 'whole counsel of God' expressed in a such a worldview. The key question for such an approach is not, 'Does this idea from psychology receive support from Scripture?' but 'Does this fit with a Christian understanding of human nature/the mind/wholeness, etc?'

Fourthly, we have the *'Compatibility Model'.* This attempts to equate psychological and theological findings that seem to be saying the same thing but in different languages. Ideas from both are placed side by side to identify points of compatibility. Where these are discovered, a new synthesis is formed as the dual sets of ideas are integrated.

Finally, there is the model Farnsworth himself advocates – the *'Complementarity Model'.* Another name for this is 'Perspectivalism.'[16-19] Its basic contention is that any phenomenon can be described at different levels or from different perspectives according to the discipline that is asking the questions. Thus, anger might be described from a chemico-physical perspective as the release of certain substances into the bloodstream which induce reactions we call anger. Similarly, it might be described from a psychological point of view as the outcome of pent-up frustrations or the reaction against an oppressive childhood (or whatever). Or viewed from the social perspective, it might be explained as the means by which individuals force others to agree to their demands. Theologically, it might be viewed as an expression of sin or, alternatively, a sign of a lapse from grace.

The point is that if perspectivalism is correct, these descriptions need not contradict. If they are regarded as differing, yet equally legitimate, ways of understanding a phenomenon, they need not make conflicting claims. They are not competing but complementary descriptions. As Farnsworth says, 'The process of correlating the findings, then, is simply a matter of recognizing two equally valid but different views of the same phenomenon.'[20]

The analyses offered by these writers give some idea of the centre of recent debate. Kirwan, Carter and Narramore and Farnsworth all represent what Gary Collins has called the 'theoretician-researchers' of counselling, while Crabb represents the 'Christian professionals.'[21] But whether a researcher, or professional practitioner, the issues remain crucial to both.

Evaluation of Approaches to Counselling

It seems clear that in the models outlined above we have variations on a continuum of responses. (We have deliberately excluded the discipline of psychology of religion from the typologies discussed in this chapter since we are presently concerned not with religion but with theology.) These models range from outright hostility between theology and psychology through compartmentalized co-existence to complementarity and finally assimilation. This spectrum of positions is represented in both disciplines. There are theologians who reject psychology and psychologists who reject theology. There are theologians who are willing to reinterpret psychology in terms of theology and psychologists who wish to subsume theology under psychology. On both sides there are those who search for synthesis and yet others who accept perspectivalism.

So which should we choose? It seems to us that the positions which we must reject from the outset are those which reduce either psychology or theology to each other. Adopting Farnsworth's typology, this rules out the Credibility and Convertibility models. They simply cannot do justice to the totality of knowledge or truth and run the risk of imposing either a theological or a psychological imperialism. For the same reasons, the Conformability approach must be rejected. Although operating on a broader basis than the credibility model, it nevertheless suffers from the same defects. This leaves us with the Compatibility and Complementarity models. Both possess the virtue of taking complexity seriously and both recognize that phenomena require analyses from differing perspectives. The problem lies, however, in devising a method for choosing between perspectives when they appear to be incompatible.

If we take, for example, the concept of conscience how are we to match, say, the classical Freudian account with the Christian view? The former contends that conscience, or Super-Ego, is no more than the relic of parental authority carried forward into adulthood. Such an account also offers an analysis of the manner in which this stage of affairs comes about and a corresponding analysis of how it should and can be done away with.

Christian theology, on the other hand, has traditionally insisted that conscience should be seen as a reflection of God's image in us. It is a moral awareness planted within us by virtue of our createdness. It has a positive purpose and we should not try to dispense with it.

This encapsulates the essential difficulty of perspectivalism. For we are faced with two accounts which are not complementary but in fact are rivals. Certainly in terms of what the therapist should do, each perspective offers a competing prescription. So it seems in the end that we may be forced back to some form of conformability model. After all, if theology is, as it has historically claimed, the Queen of the Sciences, surely it must be granted an evaluative function?

We have deliberately painted the picture in its worst possible light because we suspect too many easy assumptions are made about the ability of perspectivalism to solve all our problems. In fact, the phenomenon of conscience can only be understood perspectivally, otherwise it cannot be understood adequately at all. The Freudian account of the Super-Ego certainly accounts for what Christian theologians and pastors call 'false guilt' but it cannot be allowed to go uncriticized. And this is where we are perhaps moving towards a kind of critical perspectivalism in which no discipline is allowed hegemony or totality of explanation but in which all disciplines subject themselves to *mutual* criticism. The purpose of such an approach would not be to play intellectual games, even less to arrive at a synthesis for the sake of agreement. What we have in mind is an approach where each perspective argues its case and stands back. It is then questioned by the others and if no genuine resolution of incompatibilities can be reached, this is accepted. The problem is 'bracketed' but not ignored. Each perspective continues to offer its insights but in the end we may have to admit that we are incapable of reconciling them. For operational purposes we may simply have to accept their partial truth but refuse to see them as the whole truth. Thus theology could accept the Freudian account of conscience as a useful analysis of *some* forms of moral awareness but not as an exhaustive account of all expressions of it. Psychology would be counted as disclosing partial truth but not the whole of it.

This approach is not easy. It requires acceptance of complexity and ambiguity as facts of practical and theoretical life. Moreover it requires humility in that questions of final truth may have to be put to one side pending further knowledge or the Second Coming! But we would argue that **critical perspectivalism** is the only approach which respects the integrity both of individual disciplines and of truth as a whole.[22] It bases itself on the belief that although our perspectives on truth may be limited, partial and provisional, all truth is nevertheless God's truth and that integration between theology and psychology is concerned with precisely that.

THE PHILOSOPHICAL/ THEOLOGICAL CONTEXT

Philosophy, Theology and Counselling

What have philosophy and theology to do with counselling? In the previous chapter we considered a number of attempts to establish how theology and psychology might interrelate; but these assumed the validity of the exercise in the first place. Suppose the value of theology and philosophy were not self-evident. What then would we say?

Our starting point must be to acknowledge that the theological and philosophical context in which counselling takes place is rarely made explicit. Few counsellors receive either theological or philosophical training and although some leading counselling theorists have recognised that mere therapeutic technique is not enough, at the day-to-day - clinical level, most counsellors operate without looking at their presuppositions at all. Counselling is perceived as dealing with real people in the real world with real problems. Philosophy and theology are perceived as dealing with high-flown abstractions which frequently appear baffling and meaningless. Much better (say some) to get on with the job and let the presuppositions take care of themselves.

We shall try to show that far from being irrelevant to counselling, philosophy and theology are essential. We shall show how this view has been advanced not by philosophers and theologians (who might be thought to have a vested interest) but by psychologists, psychiatrists and counsellors.

But what about the relationship between philosophy and theology? Although the two are not identical we believe they walk hand in hand. Throughout the history of ideas, theology and philosophy have been engaged in the same quest for truth. Indeed, theology has drawn heavily upon philosophical reasoning and has been expressed using philosophical concepts. Although theology is not reducible to philosophy it would be impossible without it, for behind every major Christian doctrine there stands a set of philosophical assumptions and arguments. As the philosopher Roger Scruton has pointed out, 'While theology alone is not philosophy, the question of the *possibility* of theology has been, and to some extent still is, the principal philosophical question.' [1] Likewise, the Oxford philosopher of religion Basil Mitchell has argued that 'to a large extent, theologians *are* philosophers.' [2] But while the two disciplines converge at many points, they do, nonetheless, offer distinct perspectives on counselling. These perspectives are related in four ways.

Perspectives

In the first place, we need to note that theology and philosophy are both concerned with ultimate questions: what does it mean to be human? Why do suffering and evil exist? What kind of meaning and purpose can we discover for ourselves and our world? Are we truly free or are we bound by external forces and internal drives? Does God exist and if so, what is His relationship to the world? These are just some of the profound questions with which philosophy and theology alike have traditionally sought to wrestle. The fact that they are the object of inquiry in both disciplines indicates how close theology and philosophy are in their common quest.

Such a quest is essentially about the discernment and exercise of practical wisdom. The answers to ultimate questions cannot be discovered by recourse to banalities and trivia. They require thought and reflection, the fruits of wisdom. In this, of course, Christian theology has a direct stake since the association of Wisdom with both God the Father and God the Son is strong and explicit in biblical writings. [3] But of equal importance is the fact that the literal meaning of the term philosophy is: 'the love of wisdom'. [4, 5] The seeker after the truth that embodies wisdom will therefore turn both to theology and to philosophy.

Secondly, the counsellor frequently finds that those who come for help are themselves seeking wise and truthful answers to perplexing questions which they cannot find elsewhere. In H. D. Lewis's words, 'Almost everyone asks philosophical questions – sooner or later.' [6] More often than not, counsellors find they are faced with philosophical-cum-theological questions demanding an answer they are ill-equipped to give. The suffering counsellee will often ask: 'Why me?' – a question which drives to the heart of philosophy and theology. Likewise those who find themselves enslaved to sexual drives beg to know whether they can find release and true freedom from forces over which they seem to have no control – a quest which raises the critical problem of the freedom of the will. And since all who seek counselling are vitally concerned with hope for the future, questions of purpose and meaning become central, once more exposing the crucial link between philosophy, theology and counselling. We could multiply the examples several times but the result would be the same: beneath all psychological problems lie fundamental philosophical and theological questions. It is the counsellor's duty to expose and confront these but can a councellor adequately do so without recourse to philosophy and theology?

Thirdly, the Christian counsellor needs to recognize that the kind of questions we have noted in the previous paragraph cry out for responses which can be supplied only by philosophy and theology speaking together. The counselling situation will throw up fundamental questions which philosophy can address, but if we believe that all truth is God's truth and that He stands over all human questioning, it will be the case that we look to theology in partnership with philosophy for ultimate responses. [7] This is not to say that we shall find simple answers or even that we shall find answers at all. Some issues are so deeply complex that we have to acknowledge the finitude of our knowledge and accept their essential mystery. We cannot hope to solve all philosophical problems by easy recourse to a Bible text or a theological slogan. The problem of suffering is an obvious case in point.

Fourthly, we need to acknowledge the role of presuppositions. All counsellors depend upon a basic number of these but they are often hidden. When we press them more closely we find that behind particular techniques lurk all kinds of presuppositions which are philosophical and theological in nature but which need to be tested and evaluated. We shall see how this is so in the next section but for the time being we simply need to note the power of implicit assumptions.

Why Counselling Needs Philosophy and Theology

History

To understand the link between counselling and philosophy we must understand something of the historical relationship between the two. For much of western history, psychology and philosophy have, in fact, been seen as equal partners in the study of human behaviour. Historically, modern psychology grew out of the discipline of philosophy. G. S. Brett in his *History of Psychology* [8, 9] traces the origin of psychology to the metaphysical speculations of Greek science in which there was no rigid distinction between philosophical questions of meaning and purpose and scientific study of matters of fact. The two were seen as part of the same investigative enterprise. Thus questions about human behaviour we would now think of as psychological were understood both as philosophical and as scientific.

This interrelation continued through the Christian period until the rise of modern science in the seventeenth and eighteenth centuries. At this point, a significant shift took place. Psychology began to move away from asking questions about meaning and purpose to asking questions about the mechanical operation of the mind. The question 'Why?' came to be replaced by the question 'how?' R. S. Thomson notes that from the 17th to early 19th centuries, 'psychology was principally a descriptive science and the main objective was to provide philosophers with an account of the workings of the mind which they could take into consideration when dealing with the theory of knowledge and ethics.'[10] It is easy to see how, under the impact of empirical science in the nineteenth century, principally stemming from J. S. Mill's empiricist philosophy, psychology sheared off from philosphy to become a quasi-science concerned with discovering how the mind worked and how this could be demonstrated.

The eighteenth and nineteenth centuries saw the triumph of Newtonian mathematics and physics in which the universe and its constituent parts (including human beings) came to be compared to complex and sophisticated machines. The mind therefore came to be understood as a kind of internal mechanism. From this it was but a short step to construe psychology as a form of mental mechanics. The task of psychology became the investigation of how this mental machine worked. Psychologists were to concern themselves with understanding the origins of mental disorders not by asking philosophical questions about meaning and purpose but by looking for the causes of mechanical breakdown.

In this way, psychology gradually split off from its roots in philosophy and became grafted onto the physical sciences whose methods and assumptions it increasingly sought to imitate. In this century there has been some strong reaction against this assimilation and it is now widely held that the future of psychology remains open. In the words of Elton McNeil, 'It is for the psychologists of the future to decide whether psychology will continue to pursue the aims of science or declare itself an art form or a philosophy.' [11-13]

From this brief survey we can see that there are good historical grounds for regarding philosophy and psychology (and therefore counselling) as related disciplines. Alongside this, however, we must set the historical relationship of philosophy to theology. Briefly, this can be characterized as a relationship of Siamese twins. From the birth of Christianity onwards, theologians found themselves drawing upon philosophy and engaging in critical dialogue with it. As Diogenes Allen has written, 'The two main sources of Christian theology are the Bible and Hellenic culture, especially Greek philosophy . . . Everyone needs to know some philosophy in order to understand the major doctrines of Christianity or to read a great theologian intelligently.'[14] It is impossible, for example, to make sense of either the early Fathers or modern theologians such as Barth, Bultmann, Pannenberg and Moltmann without realizing that their theology is grounded in the philosophy of their respective times and their reactions to it.

In the period preceding the growth of modern psychology, this process reached its peak with the publication in the thirteenth century of St Thomas Aquinas' *Summa Theologica*. This amounted to a thoroughgoing attempt to construct a philosophical theology based on among other things a theologisation of Aristotle. That it has survived the tempests of post-Enlightenment rationalism (though with varying degrees of success) witnesses to its persistence and durability. It also indicates how closely allied philosophy and theology have remained for the bulk of Western history since Christ.

But history alone is not enough. The association of the three disciplines in earlier times does not in itself demonstrate the case for connecting them in the present or the future. We shall therefore turn to a number of contempory justifications of the importance of philosophy put forward by practising counsellors and psychologists. In the light of the Siamese twin relationship we noted above, it is important that we see these as valid also for theology. In what follows, therefore, we should read 'theology' for 'philosophy' and *vice versa*

Preconceptions

All counsellors work according to a set of underlying philosophical conceptions whether they realize it or not. This is true both for Christians and for non-Christians. It is therefore better to make such assumptions explicit than to let them remain buried. By bringing them to the surface, the counsellor can expose them to critical insights and thereby evaluate and reshape them in the light of his or her wider set of beliefs and values. But as long as they remain hidden such evaluation cannot take place.

C. H. Patterson makes just such a point in his leading textbook on counselling theories: 'Every learning theorist is a philosopher though he may not know it . . . this applies even more forcefully to counselling theorists . . . It is therefore necessary to include in our discussions the philosophical bases that are implicit or explicit in the various counselling theories.' [15]

Another counsellor, Gerald Corey, has carried the argument one stage further. He contends that when counsellors ignore philosophy, they run the risk of an incomplete picture of the counselling reality in any given situation:

> Because they do not pay sufficient attention to their philosophical assumptions, many practitioners operate as though they had no set of assumptions regarding their clients . . . Our philosophical assumptions are important because they specify how much reality we are able to perceive. [16]

Corey thus warns us that there is a real danger that counsellors may fool themselves: they may believe they are operating without philosophical assumptions ('I look at each case on its merits') whereas in fact they have all sorts of hidden assumptions about human nature, behaviour, meaning and purpose. The task of the counsellor who is concerned with integrity is therefore to unmask those assumptions and subject them to critical scrutiny.

Moreover, as Corey goes on to point out, therapy is directly shaped by the counsellor's philosophy, whether acknowledged or unacknowledged:

> It is my conviction that our views of human nature and the basic assumptions that undergird our views of the therapeutic process have significant implications for the way we develop our therapeutic practices . . . Our views of human nature dictate our goals and our manner of working with clients. [16]

This is supported by the British counselling theorist and practitioner Windy Dryden:

> All approaches to psychotherapy are based on either explicit or implicit images of human beings. Such images do have a direct influence on the pattern of therapy. [17]

It is not only psychologists and counsellors who have recognized the vital connection between preconceptions and practice. Interestingly, a similar argument has been put forward by sociologists. According to Alan Dawe:

> All sociological work, like all work of thought and imagination, is founded upon and derives its meaning from views of human nature, whether they are stated explicitly or remain implicit (and often unrecognized even by those whose work rests upon them). [18]

In the same vein, Geoffrey Hawthorn has pointed out that:

> Even the most deliberately modest works rest upon such assumptions (of what human beings are and may be) and although they may remain unchallenged for generations, there is nothing . . . to suggest they will always continue to be. [19]

It seems, then, that the human sciences necessarily rest upon a foundation which is both philosophical and theological. The relationship between philosophy, theology and counselling is consequently very close. If Corey and others are right, what lie at the bottom of varying therapeutic strategies are not simply differences about which approach will yield the best results but philosophical views about what it means to be human. And what counts as therapeutic success will in turn depend upon what it means to restore a person to human wholeness - a question which is fundamentally philosophical and theological and which can only be resolved by philosophical and theological reflection.

This accounts for the often wide divergences between counsellors as to the relative value of competing strategies. Such divergence are determined not by pragmatic considerations alone but by the underlying philosophical assumptions of the therapists themselves:

> Concepts regarding human nature, the goals of therapy that are rooted in the view of human nature, and the techniques subscribed to tend to be different for each approach. Differences are especially noticeable among the philosophical assumptions underlying three very different models: the psychoanalytic approach, the behavioural approach and the existential-humanistic approach. [20]

The upshot of this analysis must be that counsellors should learn to develop rigorous ways of examining their basic assumptions from philosophical and theological perspectives. If Corey is right, this becomes a highly practical imperative since it will affect counselling practice at every level:

> In my opinion, a central task is to make our assumptions explicit and conscious, so that we can establish some consistency between our beliefs about human nature and the way we implement our procedures in counselling. [20]

It is not a matter, then, of seeing philosophy, theology and counselling simply as conceptually allied. They are partners in counselling practice also; and it is far better to make the nature of this partnership explicit than to ignore it. When the hidden assumptions in the relationship are brought into the open, the strength and credibility of the relationship can be tested.

So far we have drawn only upon the writings of secular thinkers to make the case for exposing hidden assumptions. We end this section therefore with two quotations from the Christian counsellor Gary Collins:

Psychologists are remarkably resistant to anything philosophical or theological and their students are easily enough
swayed by psychological analyses. To perform useful work in
this area one must be thoroughly familiar with both theology
and psychology. [21]

Our assumptions about the universe, human nature, right and
wrong, and what will and will not work all determine how
we think or act. This is certainly true in the area of
counselling.[22]

Evaluation

Recognizing one's underlying assumptions, however, is not the
same as becoming self-critical. It is one thing to acknowledge the
importance of philosophy or theology in helping to discover the
nature of one's presuppositions: it is another to use the tools of
philosophical and theological reasoning to evaluate them,
particularly if you hold them dear. It is not difficult to bolster one's
views by plundering philosophy and theology but that is not the
purpose of such disciplines. They function as God intended when
they enable us to put our beliefs under a critical spotlight so as
to produce a coherent picture of reality – a task from which we
should not shrink. This brings us to our next reason for giving a
high place to philosophy in counselling: the need to evaluate
counselling practice itself.

In this task critical self-awareness is absolutely vital to therapeutic
integrity. We may learn from the example of Freud who was
antagonistic to philosophy, regarding it, in the psychologist Harry
Guntrip's words, as 'intellectualized forms of fantasy life.' [23] But
Freud paid dearly for his cavalier dismissal of philosophy: 'one of
the penalties Freud paid was that he was not able to criticise the
philosophical assumptions underlying his own theorising'. As a
result, he became blind to his own philosophical shortcomings. This
left his system vulnerable to devastating criticisms once these
shortcomings were exposed. In particular, because Freud depended
upon a mechanistic model of the mind in which human beings were

driven by machine-like internal energies analogous to steam or electricity, once this model was overturned, the Freudian approach as a whole was thrown into question. [24] (Clinebell's comments on Freud was that his 'instinctive and biological reductionism . . . led him to a mechanistic model of human beings reflecting nineteenth-century Newtonian physics.')

Guntrip concludes from this that only by means of continuing philosophical reflection are scientists (including psychologists) able to assess the systems they espouse and equally importantly, judge between them. Most crucially of all, only through philosophy and theology can the most fundamental counselling questions be approached. Guntrip the psychologist declares himself sceptical about the assimilation of psychology into the natural sciences:

> Are the results of the psychological study of human beings as 'persons' capable of being adequately formulated in the impersonal terminology characteristic of the natural sciences . . . or by evolving a new terminology capable of representing personal phenomena? [25]

The upshot is that, in Guntrip's view, both psychology and philosophy must find their integrated focus in seeking to understand the nature of personhood. We are entitled to say, therefore, that this will require an alliance rather than competition between philosophy, theology and psychology.

Inadequacy

In touching upon Freud we noted a critical inadequacy in his view of psychology: namely that he saw psychology principally in terms of mental mechanics. This underlines once more why philosophy and theology are crucial. Rollo May argues that as long as psychologists and psychiatrists understand their role as machine repairers they will fail to ask the most serious questions dealing with meaning and purpose in human existence. For this reason, he contends, there exists now a 'growing awareness on the part of some psychiatrists and psychologists that serious gaps exist in our way of understanding human beings.' [26]

(Interestingly, Clinebell contrasts existential therapies favourably with Freud: [27] 'The basic philosophical orientation of the existential therapists is an invaluable resource in growth-oriented counselling, therapy and education. This orientation corrects any deterministic philosophy of being human.' This passage is also sufficient in showing the correction between therapies and philosophy.)

Of course, even a mechanistic view of human nature presupposes *some* meaning and purpose, just as the word processor we are using to write this book has a meaning and purpose. But the key point is surely that a machine can have no purpose of its own. It is meaningless left to itself. It can only have meaning and purpose in relation to its creator or operator. In short, a mechanistic view of human beings reduces them to a machine-like impersonality.

Counsellors and psychiatrists who see themselves simply as repairers of the mental machine, therefore, run the risk of reducing human behaviour to a series of machine-like actions and responses to internal biological instincts and drives (as in classical Freudianism) or reactions to external physical stimuli (as in behaviourism). In both cases, issues of meaning and purpose can be reduced to whether or not the machine is functioning properly. Thus we speak of a nervous breakdown in much the same way we speak of a machine breakdown.

Rollo May and other therapists who describe themselves as existentialists have reacted strongly against this. In their view, the goal of therapy should be to restore a patient to wholeness not by repairing the machine but by enabling her to 'analyse the structure of human existence - an enterprise which, if successful, should yield an understanding of the reality underlying all situations of human beings in crisis.[28]

Although May goes on to develop an approach to counselling which owes more to existentialism than theology, his basic contention is one with which Christians can agree: namely that the counsellor should aim to bring patients to a coherent set of personal meanings and values which enable them to make sense of the world and to develop healthy personal relationships which reflect a sense of self-worth and value.

The problem, as May sees it, is that to many psychologists this looks suspiciously like unscientific mumbo-jumbo. Basing their views on a mechanistic picture of the world, such psychologists are suspicious 'that existential analysis is an encroachment of philosophy into psychiatry and does not have much to do with science.'[29]

The view that May rightly criticizes so strongly is narrow in its understanding both of science and of philosophy. In seeing science solely in terms of that which can be quantified and measured, it restricts it to empirical explanations alone. We could fairly ask, on this line of reasoning, whether love should be viewed as other than a series of electrical brain impulses; or what room such a restrictive view leaves for fundamental questions of meaning and purpose? Presumably even such questions themselves are nothing but a collection of neurological reactions to stimuli. But if they are, then they possess no greater validity (there being no objective source or standard of truth) than any other set of statements which are similarly reactions to stimuli. The argument thus becomes self-defeating.

On a purely mechanistic view of the counsellor's function, therefore, we are left with an impoverished conception which fails to address the critical questions surrounding human nature. This, by itself, constitutes a decisive reason for seeing philosophy, theology and psychology as partners in the same enterprise. It is significant that the following words come from the pen of the humanist brain scientist Roger Sperry:

Science can see the brain as a complex communications network full of nerve-excitations, all governed by respectable laws of bio-physics, bio-chemistry, and physiology; but few investigators, and none that I know, have been ready to tolerate an injection into this causal machinery of any mental or conscious forces. This, then, in brief, is the general stance of modern science out of which has come today's prevailing

objective, mechanistic, materialistic, behaviouristic, reduct-
ionistic, fatalistic view of the nature of mind and psyche.'[30]

Questions

At this point in our discussion we come back to the argument we
advanced earlier concerning the place of ultimate questions. A
person who comes for counselling invariably raises deep questions
of truth, meaning and purpose:

What is happening to me? Why?
Is life an absurd joke?
If the cancer I have is going to bring a premature end, what will
      happen to me after death?
Can I ever find true freedom from the bonds of the past?
How can I be helped to behave differently?

These are just a few examples of how people in distress find
themselves asking very deep philosophical questions.

The crucial point occurs when the counsellor begins to supply
answers to such questions. One option is to say nothing and merely
to listen reflectively: to voice the counsellee's questions back
empathetically without giving a definitive answer. The strength of
this approach is that it takes seriously the client's feelings and
properly used may enable them to see the underlying problem. It
also avoids the counsellor imposing her own worldview upon the
counsellee.

But such advantages are bought at a cost. The counsellee may
never find the kind of deep answers his questions are crying out
for. At some point, unless the counsellor is willing to lead her client
into some philosophical and theological reasoning, he may well
simply be left with unanswered problems and superficial emotional
solutions.

Once, however, the counsellor moves beyond reflective listening,
she begins to enter the philosophical and theological undergrowth
which she may be poorly equipped to explore. Yet explore it she
must if she is to help her client to construct meaning and purpose
in his situation. So we are brought back to the centrality of

philosophy and theology; and the counsellor or psychologist who believes she is operating free of presuppositions drawn from these disciplines is blinding herself. As soon as she takes a position on any of the fundamental issues of life and death she is engaging in philosophy and theology. The 'encroachment' May suggests many psychologists fear is, in fact, inescapable. The best thing to do is to recognize it and engage with it.

Eclecticism

The final justification for a philosophical-cum-theological perspective is that the value of counselling approaches cannot be judged by apparent therapeutic success alone. Counsellors who are concerned with integrity in their methods will ask not simply whether a particular method seems to work but also whether it is true. For the Christian counsellor this concern for truth will be paramount.

Significantly, there is a philosophical term for those whose sole guiding star is therapeutic success: they are called pragmatists. Pragmatism originated with the late 19th and early 20th century American philosophers Charles Peirce, William James and John Dewey. According to pragmatism, truth can be defined as 'what works'. Consequently, to ask whether a belief (or in our case a counselling theory) is true we need only to ask whether it succeeds in its goals. On this basis, if a therapy restores a person to psychological equilibrium it can be regarded as true.

In practice, as Windy Dryden has noted, this view leads to therapeutic strategies which are dangerously eclectic.[31] Neither is this danger of selecting from a variety of ready-made methods confined to only a few. In recent surveys, between a third and a half of clinical counsellors described themselves as eclectic.[32] We are dealing with a very influential approach to counselling.

This carries important implications for the role of philosophical and theological reasoning. Before we examine these, however, we must note a crucial distinction between two different senses of the term eclectic. The first sense refers to choosing what is best from a range of therapeutic systems and techniques rather than following one system or therapy alone. In principle this is difficult to quarrel with provided that the choice is guided by some unifying criteria. But this is precisely where eclecticism in its second sense goes wrong. It bundles together in a random and arbitrary fashion bits from differing approaches which are often theoretically incompatible.

Thus a study of 154 eclectic counsellors in the United States in 1977 found that 145 of them used no fewer than 32 different combinations of systems and techniques blended in haphazard and idiosyncratic fashion. Counsellors Windy Dryden and Howard Clinebell respectively have described this in scathing terms as 'haphazard or hat rack' eclecticism and 'hash eclecticism'.[33, 34] In Clinebell's words, this kind of approach amounts to 'a theory from here, a technique from there with no integrating structure, no internally consistent core of assumptions about the nature, process and goals of therapeutic change.'[24]

Eclecticism without unifying criteria is consequently open to a number of major criticisms. Firstly, as both Dryden and Clinebell have pointed out, it can lead to an arbitrary approach to counselling which, because it has no solid base in theory, becomes vulnerable to precisely those criticisms levelled at each of the theories it has plundered.

Secondly, the counsellor who operates without some kind of underlying theoretical unity is in danger of adopting techniques which, although they may superficially appear to work on a piecemeal basis, can, at a deeper level, actually be in conflict. As Clinebell notes:

> Those who practise the growthing arts on such a shaky conceptual foundation run the risk of unwittingly using concepts and methods that work against one another and thus diminish the effectiveness of the process. Their approach lacks the power-for-growth that can come from using a consistent coherent conceptuality.[34]

It is significant that although Clinebell himself advocates a form of eclecticism, it has at its core a unifying therapeutic philosophy. Consequently, he argues that the issue that really faces counsellors is 'to develop an integrated electicism that utilises insights and methods from a variety of sources coherently.'[34]

Thirdly, if, as we have observed, a number of counsellors and psychologists now believe that effective therapy requires a coherent view of human nature and being, eclecticism by definition cannot supply such a view. At best it can hope to bring together a collection of views about what it means to be human but the problem is that when the counsellor begins to ask what image of human nature her therapy presupposes, she is in danger of finding that her range of eclectic therapies can offer no consistent view and may collapse in contradiction and confusion if pressed too hard. So the counsellor is left with a choice: either ignore the problem and carry on as before, thus running the risk of superficial success but underlying conflict, or try to find a unifying philosophy which will bring coherence to the range of eclectic methods and beliefs.

This brings us back once more to the importance of philosophical and theological reasoning. For what is being said by Dryden, Clinebell and other therapists we have noted is that a coherent picture of what it means to be human is not a theoretical luxury but a therapeutic essential. Only when this is achieved, or at least acknowledged, will idiosyncratic subjectivism on the part of individual counsellors be avoided.

If, as we have argued, counselling cannot be done without recourse to philosophy and theology, we are left with the stark realization that many practitioners will be underequipped to fulfil the task. There remains an urgent need to place counselling in its fullest possible context. This is where philosophy and theology have a vital part to play which amounts to more than the whim of theologians in search of a role.

THE SOCIAL CONTEXT I

The Social Significance of Counselling I

Counselling, by its very nature, possesses a social dimension. In this chapter we shall see how the counselling process is not simply significant for individuals but how it also has a much wider *social significance:* why it has assumed such importance and the role into which it has been cast by modern western society. In the next chapter we shall go one step further and investigate the *ideology of individualism* on which both the social significance of counselling and its practice have been built. Discussion of individualism in this way will prepare us for theological considerations in the second part of this book which, if taken seriously, would enable both the philosophy and practice of counselling to break out of the straitjacket imposed by secular post-Enlightenment individualism – a straitjacket that Christians have seemed at times almost too willing to take to themselves.

Why do western societies (and churches) attach so much importance to counselling? In the United States, the counselling profession and its ideas have become so great a part of social and institutional life that the sociologist Peter Berger has spoken of them as constituting 'a social phenomenon of truly astounding scope.'[1] But the phenomenon is not confined to America: throughout the industrialized world, counselling has become part and parcel of social reality. It has become synonymous with the professional task of caring. As A. W. Bolger has commented, 'increasingly, members of the helping professions . . . see counselling as an important component in their work and increasingly identify themselves as counsellors.'[2] Within the church, as we have already noted, there is enormous pressure to equate pastoral care with counselling.

So what lies behind all this? In what follows we shall consider a number of explanations put forward by various writers to account for the counselling phenomenon.

Peter Berger: Counselling and Modernity

In common with many sociologists, Peter Berger argues that the prevalence of counselling is intimately connected with the growth of modernity.[3] By the term modernity he means the impact of industrialization upon societies leading to the fragmentation of communities and families and the alienation of individuals.

Following the German sociologist Max Weber, Berger contends that industrialization has been the dominant force in modern societies since the eighteenth century. It has brought untold material benefits but at a considerable cost. This can be seen by reflecting upon how industrialization has actually worked.

In the first place we need to remember that industrialization overturned a way of life and social organization that had been relatively stable for centuries. The rise of the factory system divided families and communities and wrenched them from their historical roots. Mass migration to the cities resulted initially in rootless populations with few communal ties other than those centred on the factory. Moreover, the kind of work provided by factories was unlike anything which had gone before. Prior to the industrial revolution, individual families themselves could be viewed as economic units of production in which several generations, ranging from grandchildren to grandparents, worked together to provide income for the household. The workplace was not some distant (or even nearby) factory but was the home itself and its plot of land on which to grow food. In good times, surpluses could be sold for profit, though for most of the time subsistence ruled the day.

With the coming of the factory system all this changed. Families were no longer the primary units of production. People left home to find work in the growing cities. The family no longer provided the major focus for employment: individuals earned their living elsewhere. Moreover, work became individualized, with each worker fulfilling a narrowly defined role within the production system. Economic activity thus came to be built upon the cog-like individual within the industrial machine. Each worker became a world unto him or her self.

Out of this a second consequence arose which came to be pointed out by Karl Marx and Friedrich Engels.[4] According to their analysis, the individual worker became alienated or separated from the products of his or her labour. What came off the production line could no longer be counted as belonging to an individual worker, or even to a collection of them: they belonged to the employer. The worker was merely a component in a gigantic economic mechanism controlled and powered by the iron laws of supply and demand and geared to the interests of the capitalists. In times of recession, this alienation became even more pronounced as the individual worker found himself dispensable and without value.

Thirdly, at the heart of industrialism lay the crucial idea of the division of labour. This proved to be the single most important aspect of the industrial revolution since it enabled the economic machine to make the most efficient use of each worker. No longer did each individual have to learn a variety of skills: with the division of labour he or she had only to master one. But this development had another consequence: it ruthlessly split human life into distinct segments. These were often isolated from one another and so the individual found himself living a series of quite distinct lives. At the workplace he was a worker; at home a husband; at the pub a mate; and so on. Individuals thus came to play a number of *roles* according to whichever life-world they inhabited at any given moment.[5]

In the twentieth century this split between the public world of work and the private world of the home has become increasingly pronounced. The rapid growth of leisure since the second world war has further divided people's lives into two parts, work and leisure, each with its own internal assumptions, rules and goals. Moreover, it is assumed that the two constitute distinct and unmeeting worlds.

The net effect of this process, argues Berger, has been to generate a powerful sense of fragmentation and alienation in people's lives. Operating in several life-worlds at the same time has meant that a person's existence is no longer unified but fragmented. In short, the hallmark of industrial societies is a crisis of identity. Thus it is no accident that individuals find themselves in turmoil since the dynamic of industrialization will inevitably produce it. 'Consequently, it should not be a surprise that modern man is afflicted with a permanent identity crisis . . . modern man has suffered from a deepening condition of "homelessness" '[6] from which there can be no escape.

The upshot is that: 'the individual in modern society is typically acting and being acted upon in situations, the motor forces of which are incomprehensible to him.'[7] As a result, the individual is left mystified and puzzled about his role in society and his ultimate value:

> Society confronts the individual as a mysterious power, or in other words, the individual is unconscious of the fundamental forces that shape his life.[7]

It is not difficult to see how, on this argument, counselling has come to assume such an important social role. In particular it fulfills three crucial functions:

> Firstly, it provides a means by which individuals can discover and repair their personal identities. Psychodynamic counselling methods especially offer the counsellee the prospect of constructing meaning in an otherwise meaningless life by encouraging individuals to build up a coherent narrative of their lives and so developing a coherent identity. The individual can say, 'This is the real me! This is how I have become what I am! It's all of a piece!'
>
> Secondly, counselling acts as a kind of social safety valve. If the sociologists' picture of human reality is correct, the pent up anxieties and frustrations in industrialized societies

must be enormous. Moreover, the weakening of family and community bonds has left the individual with few ways of coping with these feelings. In this situation, counselling provides a socially acceptable way of venting destructive internal energies and of finding strategies for coping with them and the pressures which give rise to them. Hence what counselling offers is what Maurice North has called 'the myth of adjustment'.

Thirdly, theories of counselling offer credible explanations of the forces which shape our lives so that once demystified they no longer seem so menacing. If we can identify and explain what is happening to us we can deal with it. For the man who is worried about his irrational feelings towards his wife, it is a relief to be told that they have their origin in the disturbed relationship he had with his mother while still only a baby. And since such explanations are always clothed in the language and appearances of science, they both offer comfort to modern scientific societies (for whom science has replaced God as the ultimate explanation and salvation of the world)[8, 9] and also hold out the prospect that previously uncontrollable forces might now be manipulated and turned to good effect. Nothing better could suit industrial cultures that have already harnessed the powers of nature in pursuit of economic growth.

Counselling holds out the possibility of harnessing internal psychological energies and thereby enabling individuals to function more efficiently as economic producers and consumers. Counselling becomes an inevitable consequence of industrialization and at the same time supplies a means for salvation from it:

> The understanding of the self as an assemblage of psychological mechanisms allows the individual to deal with himself with the same technical, calculating and 'objective' attitude that is the attitude *par excellence* of industrial production.[10]

On this account, then, counselling and modernity go hand in hand. They cannot be disentangled since they are locked together like Siamese twins. Modern society needs counselling but counselling in turn is parasitic upon the ethos of modern industrial society.

Jacques Ellul: The Triumph of Technique

Ellul is a French lawyer and theologian who has spent a lifetime relating theology to social trends. In his books *The Technological Society* (1965) and *The New Demons* (1975) he expounds the theme that modern society is obsessed with what he calls 'technique'.

By technique Ellul does not merely mean what we mean when using everyday speech - in other words a particular way of completing a task. Taking up R. K. Merton's definition, he defines technique as 'any complex of standardized means for attaining a predetermined result.'[11]

But Ellul does not stop here. He goes on to distinguish between purely 'technical operations' which have existed throughout history and 'the technical phenomenon' which is distinctively modern. The difference between the two is vast. Technical operations refer to actions designed to accomplish specific tasks. These can range from making primitive flint arrowheads in prehistoric societies to programming computers in our own.

The technical phenomenon, on the other hand, is vastly different. It is a way of life, an ideology, a conviction that the whole of existence can be manipulated and controlled by devising systematic, rational methods at the behest of the human will. It is not simply a collection of particular means for solving particular problems but an all-embracing world-view. In Ellul's words, 'This phenomenon is the quest for the one best means in every field' and it is the 'aggregate of these means that produces technical civilization.'[12] As Maurice North has put it, 'All societies have possessed techniques but not all societies have been possessed by them.'

This is not the place to outline Ellul's theory of technique in detail but it is worth noting that like Berger he sees counselling as the outcome of industrialized modernity. This is true in two ways in particular.

In the first place, the drive to explain and control the natural and human world by means of rational technique has led to radical disharmony between humanity and its environment. In attempting to suspend and manipulate natural laws designed to establish boundaries for human behaviour, modern technological societies have succeeded in destroying the harmony of the natural order. Although writing before current ecological fears, Ellul foreshadowed the forebodings of the 1990s in which the ruthless exploitation of nature by means of technique now threatens the future of the planet. Nothing could better encapsulate the ethos and folly of reliance on technique than the destruction of the ozone layer or the greenhouse effect.

They are examples *par excellence* of the way in which modern society has been gripped by the 'new demons'. Ellul's exposure of the logic and operation of technique thus remains a startling indictment.

In the second place, the technical phenomenon has generated innately destructive forces within the human psyche itself, both individually and socially. As a result, argues Ellul, technique itself is forced to propose a technical solution to the nightmare it has created. This solution is psychoanalytical counselling. The problems thrown up by one area of technique are thus 'solved' by another. The all embracing ideology of technique simply moves from the manipulation and control of non-human natural forces to the manipulation and control of human psychological forces. But, from the point of view of technique, they are one and the same. Counselling is consequently an aspect of technique which reveals the features endemic to the technological mind-set. Just as counselling and industrialization go hand in hand, so do counselling and technology.

Kenneth Leech: Counselling as Social Control

Kenneth Leech represents a view of counselling which, from a Christian perspective, is in many ways the most radical. On the one hand he recognizes much of value in psychotherapy but on the other he rejects the view of counselling which sees social adjustment as the primary goal. Leech's argument is summed up in his criticism of Kathleen Heaseman's definition of counselling as 'a relationship in which one person endeavours to help another to understand and solve his difficulties of adjustment to society.' In reply, Leech contends that 'this seems to me to be a very dubious goal for the Christian.'[13]

Why does he argue in this way? At first sight it seems that Leech is trying to devalue counselling. But this is not the case. Elsewhere he says that 'the exploration of the frontiers of theology and the therapeutic disciplines has been of the greatest importance' and goes on in the same essay to speak of the 'positive aspects of this exploration.'[14] So radicals such as Leech are not out to rubbish counselling as such. Rather they are drawing attention to the dangers implicit within the conventional one-to-one counselling model.

The first danger is that if we see the aim of counselling as no more than personal problem-solving and adjustment we are likely to end up simply evading the *social* causes of the counsellee's distress. At best such counselling may enable the individual to come to terms with unjust conditions and structures so as to get on with the necessary tasks of daily living but this can be no substitute for dealing with the structures themselves. At the heart of the radical view is the belief that individual suffering cannot be divorced from social structures. Counselling which concentrates only on the inner world of the counsellee runs the risk of missing this point entirely.

Leech, however, goes further by challenging the Christian church to ask itself whether it has not colluded with this:

It seems that Christian theology needs to ask questions about the politics of therapy and counselling. What are therapy and counselling actually doing about the problems confronting human society? Are they in fact simply helping people to be well adjusted in a society whose fundamental values and interests remain unquestioned?[13]

In Leech's view, the critical capacity to challenge the political and social status quo must grow out of the theology which should underlie our counselling. Truly Christian counselling, he argues, will refuse to accept that social structures are irrelevant but instead will always strive to hold up a critical mirror to society and speak prophetically to it as required. The role of the counsellor will not be to seek inner equilibrium at the expense of outer struggle but rather to identify social structures which are oppressive and work for change:

> The real turning point in our dialogue will come when the search for inner wholeness and inner liberation comes into collision with the search for external wholeness and external liberation – when we see, in fact, that, in Roszak's words, 'the fate of the soul is the fate of the social order.'[13]

A further danger identified by radicals echoes the Marxist critique of religion. According to Marx, religion serves as a drug used by the ruling elite to bring temporary relief from the pain of injustice to those whom they are oppressing. Writing in 1844, Marx observed that 'Religion is the sigh of the afflicted creature . . . it is the opium of the people.'[15] By this, Marx meant that throughout history, rulers have used religion as a means of social control. The church has either acted as a conservative force to resist social change (as in pre-revolutionary France or pre-revolutionary Russia) or it has stood aside from criticizing the state for fear that the state would suppress religious liberties. In both instances, the church has perceived its pastoral work as no more than 'ambulance work' in which those who are damaged by unjust structures are patched up and sent back to cope. Hence Marx's equation of religion with a pain-relieving opiate.

Leech and other critics have argued that counselling and psychotherapy have been used in precisely the same way: as a spiritual narcotic to deaden the pain of oppression and divert attention from the real, material causes of human pain. Thus, Leech speaks of the 'growing danger of the misuse of therapy and counselling in order to dodge and evade fundamental social and political issues.'[13] Further, they can be used to reinforce and cover up the failures of the social *status quo*. Counselling carried out by institutions such as social work agencies and the NHS, he argues, inevitably tend to reduce political and social awareness by locating the source of distress within the inner world of the client rather than in objective external social structures.

This argument is made even more forcefully by Peter Selby. To view counsellees as abnormal people in need of adjustment to society's norms is fundamentally to misunderstand the nature of psychological distress. Distress, he contends (following R. D. Laing) is at least as much a socially defined fact as an individual experience and 'to deal with individual experience as though it were simply the private property of the individual who is having it is to reduce it to insignificance.'[16]

Furthermore, if we attempt pastoral care and counselling without taking the social dimension seriously, we avoid the real problem by taking refuge in a half truth:

> We neutralize the efficacy of our pastoral care by using it as a means of isolating people from the question of where they stand in the dramas of oppression and liberation, of peacemaking or warmongering in the world outside.[16]

Selby comments also that 'Pastoral practice has to be socially and politically aware . . . It means not less listening and attentiveness but a determination to lead relationships to the point where they are located politically . . . and that means their situation in the network of oppression, liberation, injustice and justice which are the features of our lives together.'[17]

The thrust of the radical social argument therefore seems clear: counselling has been used not as a means of true liberation from unjust political and social structures but as a means of covering up their deficiencies. The 'therapeutic state' (to use Szaz's phrase) has a vested interest in promoting counselling agencies since they detract from the struggle for change. In seeking to enable people to adjust to society, the counsellor may be colluding with injustice.

Hence a counsellor must be concerned not only with psychoanalysis but also with social analysis, and having analysed, must be ready to struggle for change not merely within the life of the individual but in social structures. Wholeness and justice cannot be separated. This amounts to a thoroughgoing critique indeed for it undercuts the entire basis of much counselling (certainly most of the Christian kind) today.[18]

Jurgen Habermas and Paul Ricoeur: Counselling as the Search for Meaning

Jurgen Habermas and Paul Ricoeur are two modern philosophers concerned with the discipline of hermeneutics. That is to say, they are concerned with the science of interpretation of human communication. Hermeneutics has classically addressed itself to the interpretation of written texts, seeking, by a variety of complex methods to discover the meaning of a text both to its author and to its readers. The task of hermeneutics has been to discover the meaning locked up in a text. According to Ricoeur, 'Hermeneutics . . . relates the technical problems of textual exegesis to the more general problems of meaning and language.'[19–21] Or in Norman Perrin's words, hermeneutics is 'the methodology for reaching an understanding of written texts held to be meaningful.'[22–24]

As might be expected, this comprises a complicated and highly technical field. However, of late, methods and insights derived from hermeneutics have been applied to other forms of expression, including film, politics and sociology. The question of what counts as a text has therefore broadened out considerably beyond the domain of the written word.

This broadening has important implications for counselling. The point of contact comes with the quest for meaning or meaningfulness. The notion of something being meaningful is common not only to written texts but to all realms of life. We speak of meaningful actions, a meaningful experience or a meaningful relationship as well as a meaningful story or work of art. From this basic recognition has sprung the idea that counselling can be considered a form of hermeneutics: that human action and experience constitute texts which the counsellee 'reads' with the help of an interpreter - the counsellor. On this argument, counselling has become important in modern society because it offers ways by which individuals may learn to read their own 'life texts' and thereby discover meaning and purpose. Hermeneutics helps them make sense of their identities.

The role of counsellor, therefore, becomes akin to the scholar seeking to understand and explain a book or an historical document, except that in the case of the counsellor, they are working not with a written text but with a 'life text' supplied by the counsellor. Thus Ricoeur writes:

> The analytic situation selects from a subject's experience what is capable of entering into a story or narrative. In this sense, 'case histories' as histories constitute the primary texts of psychoanalysis.[25]

It is significant that in saying this, Ricoeur directly follows Freud who patterned his use of dream interpretation in psychotherapy on the model of philological research into the science of language. In doing so, it is noteworthy that he compared the interpretative task of the therapist to the task of translating a foreign author (Livy was Freud's example).[26] For Freud the analogy with written texts was explicit.

But although similar in many important respects, the interpretative work of the counsellor or therapist differs from that of the philologist in one regard. It deals with *personal narrative* as the fundamental form of text. The counsellee recounts his life story as far as he can remember it and in doing so organizes collections of his experiences into a coherent flow. As Ricoeur puts it:

> But what is it to remember? It is not just to recall certain isolated events but to become capable of forming meaningful sequences and ordered connections. In short, it is to be able to constitute one's own existence in the form of a story where

a memory as such is only a fragment of the story. It is the narrative structure of such life stories that makes a case history.[25]

Both Ricoeur and Habermas (again following Freud) develop a detailed theory of psychoanalysis along hermeneutical lines. This need not detain us here. What is crucial to our considerations is the notion of recounting a meaningful life story. This is crucial because it is the act of recounting which invests a counsellee's account with coherent meaning:

> 'Who' I am is tied up with that narrative meaning which lies within my actions and binds them together into a single meaningful plot or personal story . . . Our personal stories are narrated in terms of a meaning-thread which holds them together.[27]

As the counsellee tells his story to the counsellor, then, her task is to provide interpretative clues to enable the counsellee to discover the meaning of that story, to reflect upon it and to find new meaning for the future. Thereby he can be liberated to change his attitudes and behaviour. This may involve a painful uncovering of feelings which had been buried or channelled elsewhere but in enabling interpretation and reflection to take place, the counsellor will be facilitating the healing process:

> [the counsellee] will see his past actions differently . . . and with a different thread of meaning connecting the narrative.[27]

But how is this in any sense a social act? How is the notion of social context relevant?

The hermeneutic approach is a social approach for five reasons:

Firstly, it requires the counsellee to move from the inner world of feeling and personal meaning to the outer world of sharing these with the counsellor. This is not, in itself, a very broad definition of a social act but, as we have noted above, it is nonetheless a move in this direction.

Secondly, in telling his story, the counsellee is forced to use publicly accessible language. The biography will not be told in some unintelligible gobbledegook but in the normal language of everyday speech. By doing so, the counsellee immediately passes from the world of uncommunicated private experience to that of publicly discussable experience. Language is always and everywhere social.

Thirdly, there is the question of how the individual comes by the symbols by which to express his experience. The answer is that he gained them from society. Whether he uses the symbolic language of dream or everyday prose he is still drawing upon means of expression handed to him by the society in which he lives. Symbols are not simply inborn: they are socially constructed and socially given.[28] (Some symbols seem to be buried deep in the collective unconscious of humanity.)

Fourthly, there is the question of interpretation. The counsellor's task is to give clues by which the meaning of the counsellee's experience may be unlocked. But just as the counsellee necessarily draws upon socially given symbols and language then so does the counsellor. The act of interpretation depends as much upon socially constructed concepts and language as does the act of remembering and articulation by the counsellee. The counsellor is a socially shaped creature too.

Fifthly, as the understanding of a language requires publicly agreed grammatical rules, so being able to understand and interpret analytic experience requires the same. Each school of counselling, whether it be Freudian, behaviourist, Gestalt, existential or whatever, relies upon an accepted frame of reference which governs that approach. In other words, each school has its own grammatical rules. This means that by definition the counsellor finds herself operating according to rules of interpretation which are socially agreed.

The hermeneutic approach to counselling is therefore undoubtedly a social approach. It is possible, moreover, to carry the argument one step further. Suppose we ask how the counsellee discovers personal identity and meaning. One part of the answer is through 'reading' the meaning of his past: interpreting his life text. But a second part of the answer must be that his willingness to accept the ideology of counselling itself furnishes meaning. In many respects, counselling, like medicine, provides meaning in contemporary society in the way that, say, religion did in pre-modern times. This in itself makes counselling a profoundly social phenomenon.

Halmos and North: The New Religion

For some writers, counselling has appeared as the new religion of the secularized, post-Freudian West. In their view it has taken over the role previously fulfilled by Christianity, now in a decline which could prove terminal. It is this collapse of religion which accounts for the popularity of counselling: it meets a need previously met by religion. Thus, Paul Halmos, writing in 1965, entitled his study *The Faith of the Counsellors;* while Maurice North, writing in 1972, entitled his similar study *The Secular Priests.*[29, 30]

It is not our purpose here to recycle the arguments of these books in great detail. However, it is worth asking what features of the counselling movement Halmos and North picked out as analogous to religion. In this way we can see how deeply embedded counselling has become within our social consciousness and how counselling, in turn, has itself been shaped by these features.

Firstly, there is the question of meaning. As we have noted earlier, contemporary industrialized societies require new ways of finding meaning and, by the same token, finding structures and institutions which can supply such meaning. Counselling is successful on both counts because it enables individuals to find meaning in their personal narratives. Moreover, it fuels a social expectation that identity crises can be solved by what Peter Berger has called 'agencies for identity maintenance and repair' i.e. counselling organizations.

Paul Halmos makes a further observation. He notes that the advent of counselling has gone hand-in-hand with the discrediting of political solutions for social and individual ills. Why has this occurred? Halmos argues that the scientific and technological mentality is essentially a rational, problem-solving mentality which sees problems as capable of technocratic solution without recourse to ideology. Politics is thus sidestepped because the problems it addresses can (on this thesis) be dealt with simply by looking for the most sensible, reasonable answer, irrespective of underlying beliefs. After all, we would not ask a surgeon his or her political views before we agreed to undergo an operation. Politics is therefore irrelevant:

> It would be too early to think that politics in the west has been supplanted by administration and technology. Yet the aspiration of the contemporary intellectual is that this state of affairs should at least be approximated. One might say that today's ideology demands that ideology be replaced by social science and that politics be made all but unnecessary by scientific and technological planning.[31]

This is an attractive explanation in which there is much to be affirmed. We should be wary, however, before accepting it without criticism. As a statement of the liberal intellectual credo of the nineteen-sixties and perhaps seventies, Halmos' summary is accurate. But in the much more politicized atmosphere of the late nineteen eighties and nineties, especially in Britain where socialized medicine and personal social services supply the majority of counselling, it is by no means so obvious that technocratic solutions can be divorced from politics.

The second analogy between counselling and religion lies in the area of mystique. Just as a professional priestly caste exists in religion to explicate the mysteries of transcendence to faithful believers, so the same is true in counselling. The counsellor initiates the counsellee into the mysteries of 'the truth'. By means of mysterious and magical formulae couched in specialist language, the innermost mysteries of the human self are opened up. But, as in religion, this can only happen with the aid of a trained mediator or quasi-priest - the counsellor.

> It can be said . . . that the mystique of counselling is based on the assumption of an inexplicable process that takes place during and in the relationship between counsellor and client and that leads to the uncovering of hitherto concealed and latent capacities in the latter.[32]

Peter Berger extends this argument to contend that the mystique of counselling actually answers a deeply felt need for a magical, numinous dimension to life. The process of scientific discovery has robbed life of transcendence so that we have now come to invest the scientific process itself with a kind of mysticism:

> Psychologism makes possible once more the ancient fascination with mystery and magic. Indeed, one is tempted to speak here of a form of neo-mysticism. Once more the true self is to be discovered through a descent into the presumed depths of one's own being, and, even if the ultimate discovery is not that of the divine, it still has the old flavour of the numinous.[33]

Space does not allow us to discuss Berger's argument. But, again, we must recognize its force. People (in the West at least) seek scientific explanation and control of natural forces in the ways we have noted. But at the same time they crave mystery and a sense of wonder. Hence the fascination with astrology, spiritualism, drug-induced states of transcendence and so on. As Marshall McLuhan has pointed out, 'The current interest of youth in astrology, clairvoyance and the occult is no coincidence . . . Mysticism is just tomorrow's science dreamed today.'[34] Counselling therefore occupies a paradoxical position. On one hand it promises to explain the mysterious forces of the psyche and offers control over them. To this extent it chimes exactly with the demands of technique for rational control. Yet on the other hand it wraps up its promises in a mystique bordering on the numinous. It masquerades as both a science and a religion and thereby exemplifies the dilemma of the modern West. Formal religion is going out by the front door but quasi-religious experience is creeping in by the back.

A third comparison between religion and counselling can be found in the use of language. In religion, specialist language is used to worship, to express a body of beliefs, to enable believers to communicate with others inside and outside the community of faith and to establish social status and power. With the exception of worship, these same uses of language apply equally to counselling. The jargon of counsellors and psychologists is used as a medium of professional discourse, but, more ominously also as a way of establishing priestly control. The counsellee faced with a barrage of technical explanations and labels to describe his condition is little able to question, let alone argue.

Yet there is another significant point to be made about the social impact of psycho-talk. Just as the terminology of Christianity came to permeate every stratum of society within Christendom, thereby binding together societies and cultures, so the language of the Freudian revolution has permeated everyday speech even among those who do not understand its technical references. We readily speak of unconscious desires, libido, psychosis, neurosis, repression and so on. Psycho-talk has become common currency and, arguably, the lingua franca of contemporary industrial societies. In Peter Berger's words, 'it belongs to those assertions about the nature of reality that every sane person in a society believes as a matter of course.'[35]

If this is indeed the case, we are faced not only with a 'social phenomenon of truly astounding scope'[36] but with a language system whose purpose is to provide a picture of reality which enables people to make sense of their experience. Psycho-talk thus takes on a determinative role in structuring the way in which a societye thinks about itself and its purpose. This is exactly analogous to religion.

If counselling possesses a professional elite and a religious language, then it also contains a third element common to religion (or at least the world's great religions) namely, moral authority. Paul Halmos traces two aspects of this: firstly, he argues that there is a paradox in the counselling profession's attitude to morality. On the one hand, it proclaims itself to be morally neutral; yet in reality it is packed with values which make clear that its goals are thoroughly moralistic: the goal of individual autonomy; the encouragement of social adjustment; the cultivation of openness and honesty in relationships – all these constitute fundamental moral values. Counselling offers itself overtly as non-judgmental in matters of values and morality. But in reality it operates on the basis of an implicit moral code every bit as dogmatic as the world's major religions.

Secondly, Halmos argues that the underlying *therapeutic* goal of all counselling theories (that people should be enabled to live in personal and social equilibrium) does, in fact, act as a *moral* goal. We are not isolated individuals but social beings; so the goal of a personal equilibrium has to do with equipping us to function socially. Once this is acknowledged, social morality follows. Counselling is thus inextricably driven by moral goals.

Although there is a superficial resemblance to religious morality here, one critical difference needs to be noted. Systems of religious morality are generally concerned with moral behaviour as a human response to God. Religious morality, therefore, may be described as both transcendent and theocentric. But when we turn to the morality of the counselling movement we find something vastly different: morality which is anthropocentric. The purpose of values is to provide a basis for reasonable personal and social behaviour into which God need not enter at all and frequently does not. Counselling thus provides a moral impetus and a moral tone but these are entirely human-centred. The moral authority implicit within counselling functions is in a manner similar to religious morality but its purpose is the good of humanity not obedience to God.

But it is a final comparison with religion which, in many ways, is the most important. We are speaking of the role of faith. In the kind of religious experiences proclaimed by the great monotheistic religions, faith serves to open a new world to the believer.

And so it is with counselling. To the client who has faith in the counsellor and her methods, a new world of understanding and liberation beckons. There may be no transcendent Being behind it all, but faith defined as trust and intellectual belief in the efficacy of the therapeutic ideology can propel the counsellee from despair to hope. Reinforced by therapeutic language and ritual, counselling takes the form of a religious way of life. Given the spiritual vacuum left by the march of technocracy, it is little surprise that counselling should have assumed the mantle of religion.

Conclusion

We began this chapter by asking how counselling has become a hugely powerful social phenomenon. We have looked at a number of explanations which attempt to place counselling in its social context. This has been crucial since any evaluation of counselling must depend upon understanding its roots within contemporary society. But the Christian reading this might be tempted to wonder what it all has to do with specifically Christian counselling. The answer is simple: the counselling we call Christian is to a very large extent dependent upon the counselling movement as a whole for its ideas and practices. This is true whether we are considering the adoption of psychotherapeutic models by Frank Lake in his development of clinical theology or whether we look at the nouthetic counselling of Jay Adams which (although he would deny it) is in many respects a form of behaviourism. The straightforward fact is that the Christian counselling movement represents a number of attempts (in various ways) to come to terms with psychology since Freud and in doing so it has borrowed and modified contemporary views and practices.

A second fact that must be borne in mind is that the social reasons which have brought counselling to prominence in society as a whole have operated no less within the Christian church. The explanations offered by Berger, Ellul, Leech, Ricoeur and Halmos are as relevant to the rise of Christian counselling as to any other kind. Christians have not been immune from the forces within society of which we have spoken. And in that the church itself constitutes a society of people who also are members of a wider society, it would be surprising if the values and beliefs of this wider society had not entered the church. Counselling, whether Christian or not, can only be understood properly if its social context is acknowledged and evaluated. The social context is thus crucial for an understanding of *all* types of counselling.

THE SOCIAL CONTEXT II

The Curse of Individualism

Although counselling is a social phenomenon, the significance of the individual within the process remains the central question both for theory and practice. The centrality of the one-to-one therapeutic model in modern counselling (despite the advent of group therapy and the notion of the therapeutic community) remains the dominant paradigm and has been adopted wholesale by Christians. Individualism, moreover, is reinforced by the supposed axiom that the goal of counselling must be to enable individuals to find personal mental equilibrium (or, as the Christian might prefer to say, to find a measure of inner healing).

However, merely to speak of the individual in this way requires us to ask what we mean by 'the individual'. The answer is nowhere near as obvious as it might seem. For lying behind the modern concept of the individual is a *philosophy of individualism*, or perhaps more accurately, several philosophies. Only when we see something of what these entail will we be in a position to offer a critical alternative.

Individualism runs deep within our society. It is the controlling ethos in Western politics, morality and Christianity. Some 50 years ago, Ralph Barton Perry in an essay entitled *The Individual as the Seat of Value* argued that 'the final values of life begin and end with individuals and with the states or acts of individuals.'[1] He went on to describe individualism as 'the most exquisite and fragile flower of that historic human enterprise which is called civilization.'[2]

Perry's essay must, of course, be understood in its historical context. Written in the midst of the second world war, its background was the struggle to defeat the totalitarian regimes of Germany and Japan which had deliberately sought to debase and control individuals. This accounts for Perry's florid language. Nevertheless, as the experience of the post-war period has shown, the cult of the individual remains supreme even half a century later.

Our purpose in this section is not to dissect the philosophy of individualism in all its shapes and sizes. Rather we need to pose the following questions: how has the individualistic model come to dominate the counselling movement? What significance does this have?

We shall argue that this state of affairs has not arisen by accident. It has come about because individualism as a *social* philosophy has become *the* paradigm for understanding the nature of human beings and therefore the paradigm for psychology. Out of this soil has the impact of individualism upon counselling grown. Our basic thesis, therefore, is that in order to understand how the individualistic approach to counselling has developed and to grasp its significance, we have to understand how philosophical individualism in turn has developed. The individualistic mind-set has become all-pervasive in Western society. And so it is to this we now turn.

The Concept of Individualism

Philosophers have customarily distinguished three types of individualism: ontological, methodological and social. We shall be concerned with the first and third but with the second only in passing. The reason for this is that ontological and social individualism are the most fundamental of the three and the most relevant for a consideration of counselling.

Ontology is the study of being (Greek *ontos* = being). Ontological individualism, therefore, is the view that the fundamental constituent of humanity is the individual human being rather than the human group. A counselling theory based on ontological individualism will thus take the individual as the locus of treatment and will seek to effect change primarily through dealing with his or her individual internal mental and emotional states. Insofar as the individual's inner world is affected by external relationships and conditions, the counselling process may have a social dimension but its basic goal will be to repair the individual's state of mind or to develop individual personal maturity.

Counselling can also be said to arise out of ontological individualism in a second sense: namely in its assumption that only as we encounter other people as individuals do we encounter the fundamental expression of what it means to be human. What's more, on this view each individual constitutes a separate being independent of all others and possesses an independent identity which cannot be subsumed within any other. If we were to suggest as an alternative that the world does not consist of lots of individual beings labelled Jim, Fred, Ann, Louise, etc. but instead that it is permeated by only one being of whom individuals are no more than particular expressions (as faces of a diamond are expressions of the same gem), we would be met first with blank incomprehension then with disbelief. It is self-evident to our culture that each human person is a distinct and discrete being in herself or himself. The notion of a cosmic being of whom we are but individual parts runs counter to the philosophical assumptions which undergird modern western society.

Yet it is crucial to realize that this is the result of particular historical developments in the West. In other cultures at other times (and even among some Western philosophers) alternatives to ontological individualism have dominated.

The Roots of Individualism

When we turn to the counselling movement, we find individualistic autonomy proclaimed as the central goal. The emphasis is upon enabling individuals to 'mature' into independent beings able to make self-determined decisions in the light of self-chosen goals in order to achieve self-fulfillment. Such goals are explicitly stated throughout counselling literature and are not wholly wrong, although the Christian will want to question carefully the notion of self implied by such aims as well as their adequacy without reference to the purposes of God for individual humans flourishing in fellowship with Himself and with other human beings.

Nonetheless, it is the case that the goal of individual autonomy lies at the heart of contemporary counselling. The question is: how has this come about and what needs to be said about it?

In modern times, the growth of individualism can be traced to three main philosophical schools:

(a) biological individualism;
(b) the psychological individualism of Descartes and a string of philosophers down to Freud;
(c) the social individualism of seventeenth and eighteenth century social contract theorists.

In their disparate ways, all have contributed decisively to the building up of individualistic pressures within Western societies.

Biological Individualism

From a biological point of view, it seems obvious that the building blocks of nature are individual organisms. Nature is not one single indivisible whole but a system of discrete organisms and entities, interlocking and to some extent interdependent, but nevertheless separable. This seems so self-evident that it can hardly be questioned. From the human standpoint, it seems equally obvious that the most natural unit of independence is the self-conscious individual. The fact that individual persons are capable of biological existence (i.e. they can survive as physically functioning entities) without others for a while (the Robinson Crusoe effect), strengthens the arguments for ontological individualism.[3] Furthermore, although there is such a thing as collective thought, knowledge and wisdom, it remains the fact that we encounter the world, ponder its meaning and discover truth first as individuals and only second as members of a group. Most significantly perhaps, in the end it is as individuals we are born and it is as individuals we die.

Psychological Individualism

The belief that each person constitutes a self-subsistent individual psychological entity did not begin with Freud. In the modern period, it has its roots in the philosophy of René Descartes, Thomas Hobbes and John Locke. In a number of important respects, Freud, for all his unique genius, was their inheritor and to understand contemporary psychological individualism we must enter into their thinking.

René Descartes (1596-1650)[4]

Descartes has been called the founder of modern philosophy best remembered for his famous dictum 'I think therefore I am.' In his view, the individual must be regarded as fundamental for one very good reason: only through individual self-consciousness can knowledge of the world and reality be attained. This is not to say that there is no such thing as collective knowledge but such knowledge is merely the sum total of knowledge gained by individuals. Individualism for Descartes, therefore, is foundational for any kind of knowledge at all.

To see how this works and how Cartesian assumptions have fed through into the modern worldview, we need to begin with Descartes' fundamental assumptions. In the first place, he argued that any serious investigation of reality must adopt a scientific analytical method: the whole must be broken down into its constituent parts so that it might become more intelligible, or in his words, 'clear and distinct'. This led him to ask what kind of knowledge might count under this heading. Could there be any such knowledge?

Descartes' reply to his own question was that there could be; but it cannot be knowledge derived from the senses. Our senses might (and do) deceive us: we suffer from mirages, illusions and fantasies which we frequently suppose to be true yet which delude us. Using a vivid metaphor he argued that our senses cannot guarantee true knowledge since they might even be misled by an evil demon so as to give us false knowledge:

> Suppose there exists an extremely powerful and, if I may so
> speak, malignant being, whose whole endeavours are directed
> towards deceiving me? Can I affirm that I possess any one
> of all those attributes of which I have lately spoken of as
> belonging to the nature of the body?[5]

Descartes' device of positing a deceptive demon should not be
taken for more than it was intended: a metaphorical means of
sharpening the question of how we can arrive at true knowledge.
But, even so, if we cannot trust our senses, how can we arrive at
any trustworthy knowledge at all? Descartes' answer was to affirm
the primacy of the human mind. The malignant demon might
deceive us about the nature of the world and the truthfulness of
our own bodily senses but he could not deceive us into thinking
we do not exist. The very act of thinking proves that we do:

> We cannot doubt our existence without existing while we
> doubt . . . For there is a contradiction in conceiving that what
> thinks does not at the same time as it thinks, exist. And hence
> this conclusion, *I think, therefore I am* is the first and most
> certain of all.[6]

By this route Descartes arrived at a theory of knowledge in which
the mind became all-important. What's more, he gave rise to three
further implications which have reinforced individualistic
psychology to the present day.

The first has to do with the significance attached to the mind
as an entity distinct from the body. By emphasizing the
untrustworthiness of the senses, Descartes effectively made the
mind supreme. If the bodily senses might be tricked so as to supply
false information, it follows that we must turn to the mind for true
knowledge. What Descartes understands this knowledge to
comprise is not the subject of our discussion here; but we need
to note that in advancing the view that only the mind can supply

trustworthy knowledge, Descartes supplied ammunition for the view that what really counts in psychology is to understand and maintain the individual mind above all else. It was but a short step to seeing counselling as a matter of maintaining and repairing the individual mind, for where else could truth be found?

The second implication for counselling arises out of Descartes' dualistic view of mind and body. In his view, mind and body are separate components within the human organism. The mind (which Descartes equates with the soul) constitutes the real person while the body serves as the mechanism in which it is housed. Hence Gilbert Ryle's taunt that for Descartes, the mind is no more than a 'ghost in a machine'.

Ryle regards Descartes' view as absurd since persons are self-evidently psychosomatic unities. Mind and body cannot be separated out like yolks and whites in eggs. They are bound up together and therefore psychology must address both body and mind. Indeed, Ryle is sceptical about a way of speaking which even suggests that body and mind are distinct entitles. Hence he describes 'the dogma of the Ghost in the Machine' with 'deliberate abusiveness' as 'one big mistake'.[7]

What Ryle points us to is the difficulty bequeathed by Descartes to Western philosophy and psychology alike: namely, that if human beings are to be regarded as made up of two distinct entities – body and mind – and if one of these (the mind) is somehow superior, then the task of psychology must be to deal with the mind independently of the body (which is impossible).

This leads us to the third, and in many ways, the most important implication for our theme. It can be expressed by asking the following question: who is it that exists as a thinking being? The answer, in Cartesian terms, is simple – the individual thinking 'I'. It is highly significant that throughout his writings (though not totally without exception) Descartes refers to the first person singular: *I* think therefore *I* am. This is quite deliberate. For Descartes, the fundamental human unit is the individual self-consciousness. It is the individual who is capable of self-awareness. It is the individual who reflects upon the nature of reality. It is the individual who, as a discrete biological organism, encounters the world. It is the individual body which houses the individual mind. It is the individual who may be deceived. And within this individual, it is the mind which is paramount.

Little wonder, then, that psychology came to be seen as concerned essentially with the repair of individual minds while the needs of the bodily machine were left to physiology.

These three implications add up to a powerful philosophy of individualism which has strongly influenced Western thinking since the seventeenth century. Insofar as psychology and counselling have been part of this flow, they have absorbed Cartesian philosophy often without realizing it. The impact of Descartes upon individualism has been immense and although heavy criticism earlier this century resulted in the eclipse of Cartesianism for a time it is not without significance that at present it is enjoying a degree of revival.

Thomas Hobbes (1588-1679) and **John Locke** (1632-1704)
Like Descartes, as seventeenth-century philosophers Hobbes and Locke lived in an age of emerging science. As a consequence, their paradigms for what it meant to be human were based on Newtonian mechanics which in turn was based on a theory of physics that regarded the universe as made up of individual atoms. Thus Hobbes saw complex phenomena in terms of assemblies of individual units. When faced with a phenomenon, the observer or investigator must seek to understand it by breaking it down using the analytical method: 'It is necessary that we should know the things that are to be compounded before we can know the whole compound.'[8]

Such an analytical approach carried with it two conclusions: in the first place, humanity, like any other phenomenon, could only be understood by analysing the human race into its smallest constituent parts (i.e. individuals). These were conceived of as relating to one another rather as components of a machine are related, namely not as members of a living organism but as different parts of an artificially assembled mechanism. In the second place, by applying this method of analysis to the internal workings of individuals, it could be deduced that each individual's mind operated in a similar machine-like fashion and similarly could be analysed into its component parts.

Thus Hobbes borrowed the language and concepts of the developing science of physics to explain human psychology. And since physics was concerned in the first place with discovering the characteristics of motion, Hobbes developed a model in which mental events were viewed as 'nothing but motion in the head' and life itself (including mental life) as 'but a motion of limbs'.[9] Moreover, there can be 'no such thing as tranquillity of mind, while we live here, because life itself is but motion and can never be without desire, nor without fear, no more than without sense'. We see here the predominance of seventeenth-century physics dominated by laws of motion. For Hobbes, hooked on the physicists' paradigm, all feelings and workings of the mind are consequently nothing but motions.

When we turn to Locke we find affinities with the individualism of both Hobbes and Descartes. Along with Hobbes, Locke assumed the atomistic physics of his day to explain psychology and so identified the mind with motion. The exercise of mind, he argued, was the 'power of exciting motion in body by will or thought.'[10] As with Descartes, moreover, Locke established a close connection between his theory of individualistic psychology and his theory of knowledge. It is self-evident, in Locke's view that all knowledge is mediated through individual consciousness; but, taking issue with many of his contemporaries, Locke argued that whatever knowledge the individual acquires he acquires it only through personal experience. There is no inbuilt moral or other 'natural' knowledge as Descartes and others had maintained. Departing radically from Descartes, Locke insists that individuals gain knowledge through the senses. Taking issue directly with the Cartesian view, he pictures the mind at birth as a *tabula rasa*, a blank sheet:

How then comes the mind to be furnished? . . . Whence has it all the materials of reason and knowledge? To this I answer in one word – from *experience*. In that all our knowledge is founded and from that it ultimately derives itself.[11]

Although this stands in stark contrast to Descartes, the significance of Locke's view is that in developing his theory of knowledge he, like Descartes and Hobbes, presupposed individuals to be the fundamental units of consciousness. But, unlike his French counterpart, Locke relied on the senses to give knowledge. It is the individual through his or her individual senses who acquires knowledge and truth. Collective understanding on the part of society as a whole is dependent upon the priority of the individual. Once again it is the individual in psychology who is paramount.

So we have two broad approaches which end at the same point. The rationalist school of philosophy deriving from Descartes mistrusted the senses but gave authority to individual reason instead. The empiricist school represented by Hobbes and Locke emphasized that knowledge of the external world outside the human mind is mediated through the senses. These are two opposing traditions but they nevertheless settle upon a common point: that the individual is supreme.

From this brief survey of three representative seventeenth-century philosophers we can see something of the strength of individualism in the western philosophy of mind. Moreover, as we shall note, these same philosophers moved easily from discussing mental and psychological individualism to expounding their respective versions of social individualism. Both were part and parcel of the same systems of thought. Hobbes and Locke were not merely philosophers of the mind but philosophers of society as well.

Social Individualism
Gordon Graham has offered a definition of social individualism as 'the belief that societies consist in nothing more than individual human beings.'[12] In other words, the notion of society is an artificial one. It refers to an association of people which would not have come about had it not been for a prior decision by those people *as individuals* to constitute such an association. What is

primary is not society but the individuals who voluntarily comprise it.

On this view, therefore, the essential nature of human beings is to be found in considering each person as a separate, self-governing unit. The individual is the locus of value: society is secondary. It may be a necessary historical development for individuals to come together for security and other purposes, but societies exist only because individuals choose:

> The fundamental principle of life in society . . . we may enunciate as follows: 'The collectivity exists for the sake of the individual, and not the individual for the sake of the collectivity . . . The group exists for the sake of its members.'[13]

This conception of society as an association of autonomous individuals has deep roots. It is worth noting at this point, however, that its ethos has extended beyond the political sphere to encompass all forms of association. Not only is political society ordered upon the principle of giving maximum autonomy to individuals but so is the church. For the majority of Christians in the West, belonging to a congregation is a matter of opting into membership of a religious association with the implication that opting out is equally a matter of personal choice. Again the individual reigns supreme; the autonomistic mind-set is all-pervasive.

But how has this social individualism come about? To some extent it has developed out of the individualistic theories of knowledge mentioned above. Significantly, however, it has wider roots in those early modern philosophers we call social contractualists and it is these to whom we now must turn.

John Locke and Jean-Jacques Rousseau The individualist tradition received a considerable impetus between the sixteenth and eighteenth centuries. The Reformation opened up conceptions of individual freedom of conscience and worship which were to lay the foundations for the 'triumph of individual reason' in the age of the Enlightenment. The belief that what counted in religion was the individual's relationship to God rather than corporate obedience to the Church meshed well with the Cartesian emphasis upon the priority of individual consciousness.

In the arena of political and social thought, individualism came to the fore through the writings of so-called contract theorists among whom John Locke and Jean-Jacques Rousseau were leading exponents. The fact that Locke and Rousseau's writings respectively formed the basis for the American and French revolutions and even now are used to provide a theoretical undergirding for liberal democracy testifies to the abiding impact of the contractualists. Our purpose, however, is not to discuss the breadth of their political ideas but to indicate how their radical individualism fed into the modern worldview.[14]

The common thread which unites contractualist writers is their belief that the relationship between the individual and society can best be expressed in terms of a *social contract*. On this view, society is formed by, and exists for, the will of its members. Society is not natural but artificial. It comes into existence because individuals band together deliberately for self-protection and common benefit. So when Locke and Rousseau spoke of a social contract they meant that the individual defines his identity in relation to others by contracting to associate with them for the good of himself and other individuals. Society possesses the right to exercise power over individual members only because the members themselves have consented to give society the right to do so. As Locke put it:

> Whosoever therefore out of a state of nature unite into a community, must be understood to give up all the power necessary to the ends for which they unite into society to the majority of the community . . . And thus that which begins and actually constitutes any political society is nothing but the consent of any number of freemen capable of a majority, to unite and incorporate into such a society.[15]

Locke was emphatic that only the free consent of individuals establishes legitimate government. The individual takes priority:

> Men being . . . by nature all free, equal and independent, no one can be put out of his estate and subjected to the political power of another without his own consent . . . For when any number of men have, *by the consent of every individual*, made a community, they have thereby made that community one body . . .[16]

Likewise, Rousseau argued that:

> Some form of association must be found as a result of which the whole strength of the community will be enlisted for the protection of the person and property of each constituent member in such a way that each, when united to his fellows, renders obedience to his own will and remains as free as he was before.[17]

He goes on to define the social pact in terms which underline the significance of the individual:

> Each of us contributes to the group his person and his powers which he wields as a person . . . and we receive into the body politic each individual as forming an indivisible part of the whole.[18]

At this point, two features of contract theory must be noted. Firstly, it is important to realise that when contractualists speak of a state of nature they do not mean that they believe in an historical situation: an actual Edenic pre-history when society did not exist. Rather, they use the idea of a state of nature as a device to throw into relief the present relationship between the individual and society. It would be a mistake to think that any of the contractualists actually believed that there had once existed a raw state of nature out of which individuals emerged to devise a agreement to form a society. That is not the point of contract language. Its purpose is to answer questions such as: What is the relationship between society and the individual? What gives society authority over the individual? From the answers of the contract theorists we can see that only the consent of individuals can be reckoned to give legitimacy to social order. Moreover, as Locke makes clear, this consent remains conditional: the government must act so as to preserve the liberty of its citizens.[19] Tyrannical governments cannot claim legitimacy: consent may be withdrawn and tyranny overthrown. The good of the individual stands above all else.

The second feature we need to note is the way in which contract theorists have contributed to forms of political individualism that have persisted in the Western tradition to the present day. Our democratic institutions and assumptions have been directly shaped by the belief that the state exists for the sake of the individual and not *vice versa*. So much is this a part of our social and political fabric that we simply take it for granted and notice only when it seems under threat.

This emphasis has not been confined to the political sphere but has permeated every area of life. The individualistic mind-set of pastoral counselling and church life has not evolved in isolation. It is but one aspect of a wider social ethos reinforced by deep political and social structures we would be naive to ignore. The individualistic tradition out of which modern counselling has grown has very strong roots indeed.

The Significance of Freud

'Few individuals, if any, have exerted more influence upon the twentieth century than Sigmund Freud.' This verdict by Frank Sulloway in his biography *Freud, Biologist of the Mind*[20] sums up the contribution of Freud to the counselling movement. Freud was the father of modern counselling whose children in some sense we all are. Moreover, he was the archetypal individualist in both his therapy and philosophy. His impact upon the individualist tradition has been enormous.

Freud's individualism can be seen in three areas. Firstly, in his determination to prove psychiatry a true science, Freud took as his model a combination of biology and physics. He thus neatly combined the thrusts of ontological and sociological individualism we have already noted. This approach, he contended, would 'put us in a position to establish psychology on foundations similar to those of any other science.[21] As a result, he found himself adopting methods which emphasized the importance of breaking down complex wholes into atomistic parts. And, as we have observed with Descartes, Hobbes and Locke, such an approach led directly to psychological individualism.

Within the model offered by the natural sciences, Freud took as his fundamental construct the idea of the human mind as an energy system. Human beings were to be understood as self-contained, living systems of psychic - essentially electrical - energy. Psychological disturbance represented a disruption or breakdown of the individual's psychic energy system. Psychotherapy could be regarded as an attempt to repair the system in such a way that the distribution and flow of energy might be restored - rather as an electical engineer might repair a generator or any other piece of electrical equipment.[22] Indeed, so committed was he to the natural science paradigm that at one point Freud thought that advances in the natural sciences might provide a physical solution to imbalances in psychic energy:

The future may teach us to exercise a direct influence, by means of particular chemical substances, on the amounts of energy and their distribution in the mental apparatus . . . But for the moment we have nothing better at our disposal than the technique of psychoanalysis.[23]

This comparison with physics led Freud to draw analogies between the operation of the mind and the functioning of scientific instruments. He regularly referred to the mind as 'apparatus':

I propose simply to follow the suggestion that we should

picture the instrument which carries out our mental functions as resembling a compound microscope or a photographic apparatus, or something of the kind . . . Analogies of this kind are only intended to assist us in our attempt to make the complications of mental functioning intelligible by dissecting the function and assigning its different constituents to different component parts of the apparatus.[24]

We can see, therefore, that although an innovator in many ways, Freud nevertheless accepted the assumptions and goals of the natural sciences of his time and in doing so accepted their atomistic individualism.

Freud's second contribution to the individualist tradition can be found in his detailed model of how human energy systems work. In his later writings, Freud constructed a picture of individual behaviour as determined by the interaction of three such systems within the human psyche.[25-27] The first of these he termed the Id. This he saw as the blind driving force of desire springing from the unconscious. It permanently demands gratification but cannot always be satisfied. It is the part of us which instinctually says 'I want!'. Needless to say, it constitutes a powerful force.

The second system Freud termed the Ego. We can think of this as the middleman between the unconscious Id and the real world. It is the Ego's task to say no to the Id at the same time as trying to satisfy its wishes. The Ego is thus pushed by the Id on one hand and constrained by reality on the other. This leads us to Freud's third system, the Super-Ego.

The Super-Ego operates in the same way as conscience. Indeed, Freud believed he had accounted for the phenomenon of conscience by positing this system. In his view, the Super-Ego acts as the voice of command telling us how we should behave at all times. According to Freud, it represents the voice of the human father carried over into the unconscious from childhood. Conscience is nothing but a relic of parental authority from which we need to be freed in order to become autonomous adults.

How, then, does tension arise? In Freud's theory, the individual is thrown into mental disequilibrium by the struggle between these three sub-systems. The Ego, which is the conscious day-to-day self, finds itself constantly pressured on one side by the Id screaming for gratification and on the other by the Super-Ego telling the Ego to conform to standards of right and wrong. The picture is one of powerful energies and forces surging around the human mind in conflict, desperately in need of discharge so as to restore equilibrium. The task of psychoanalysis is to help the patient find such equilibrium.

We are now in a position to understand more fully Freud's place in the individualist tradition. For his model of a three-part energy system is entirely based on the belief that such a system exists within each individual person. All of us are composites of these sub-systems, each of us containing within himself or herself this 'apparatus'. It follows therefore that, just as every human being is a self-contained physical entity, then so each is a self-contained psychological entity.

This leads us to the third aspect of Freud's individualism: the practice of therapy itself. Freud's approach was based on the one-to-one interview between client and counsellor. The aim of the counsellor must be to enable the client, through psychoanalysis, to reach equilibrium. But to achieve this some means must be found by which energy is discharged. It is here that the complex techniques of psychoanalysis come into play. The technicalities of these need not form part of our discussion here but it is worth noting that in the Freudian tradition, it is the individual's wellbeing defined as restoration of equilibrium between the Ego, Id and Super-Ego, which is the goal of therapy. The purpose of the therapeutic process on this basis is to restore the functioning of the total energy system we call the individual psyche. This is well expressed by Eric Berne:

> During analysis the image of the analyst tends gradually to
> become charged with all the piled-up energy of ungratified
> Id wishes which has collected since the patient's earliest

infancy. Once this energy has been coralled in one image, it can be studied and redistributed and the tensions partly relieved.[28]

In other words, the role of the therapist/analyst is to bring about the release of psychic energy within the client so as to achieve the restoration of the individual. Freudian theory from beginning to end, from presupposition to practice, is thus fully individualistic and it is this assumption which the Christian counselling movement has so wholeheartedly adopted.

Evaluation

We have seen so far in this chapter the extent to which the Western world-view has been influenced by various types of individualism. In the natural sciences, social and political philosophy, morality and psychology, individualist theories have triumphed. Although the title of the chapter speaks of individualism as a curse, in one major respect it must be regarded as a good thing. For the flourishing of intellectual and political freedom, of creativity and morality, depends upon upholding the dignity and independence of the individual. The alternative, as the history of this century alone has shown, is unquestionably worse.

Yet the discussion cannot be left there. We may recognize the value of individualism and acknowledge its dominance in counselling but that does not mean that it should go unchallenged. This must be our next task.

Taking Issue With Individualism

The effect of the individualist world-view upon both Christian and non-Christian counselling has been immeasurable. Almost without exception, it is assumed that the fundamental paradigm for counselling is the one-to-one interview modelled on Freud. A number of comments from leading Christian counsellors demonstrates this point well.

Jack Dominian writes that, 'Counselling is a process of helping people which is ultimately derived from psychoanalysis, and many of its features can be traced to the therapeutic technique which Freud initiated.'[29] Howard Clinebell speaks of 'the usual psychotherapeutic model' as 'a series of formal one-to-one interviews where persons are expected to talk at deeper and deeper levels about their feelings.'[30] Michael Jacobs emphasizes the individuality of '"the still small voice" of the counsellor appealing to the "still small voice" of the person to whom he listens.'[31] An Aston University course on counselling observes that 'the main tool of the counsellor is the one-to-one interview'[32] while Thomas Szasz describes psychotherapy as 'a particular kind of personal influence' whereby 'one person identified as the psychotherapist exerts an ostensibly therapeutic influence on another person identified as the patient.'[33] Gary Collins notes that 'Counselling is primarily a relationship in which one person, the helper, seeks to assist another human being with the problems of living.'[34] Finally, the British Association of Counsellors defines counselling as 'when a person, occupying . . . the role of counsellor, offers or agrees explicitly to offer time, attention and respect to another person or persons temporarily in the role of client.'[35]

The influence both of Freud and the individualistic ethos out of which he emerged could not be more obvious. Although some concession to the place of group therapy is made by Dominian, Jacobs and others, the underlying message is clear: Freud's model of the therapeutic relationship remains the bedrock on which current practice is founded. Christian counselling, often without realizing, has more or less adopted this uncritically.

How acceptable is the near monopoly of the one-to-one paradigm? We shall argue in the remainder of this chapter and in Part II of this book that as it is currently conceived, particularly in Christian circles, such a monopoly is mistaken both theologically and clinically. The hegemony of individualism needs to be challenged. As a conclusion to Part I we shall begin that task by introducing the notion of persons-in-community as the starting point for developing an alternative model.

First Thoughts on Persons

Our starting point in constructing a genuinely theological approach to counselling must be the concept of personhood. 'But nobody treats me as a person!' is the most basic of cries the counsellor regularly encounters. The psychological roots of such a cry frequently go deep into early life and can be identified by the skilled counsellor. But behind the pain lies an equally deep question: what is a person?[36-38]

This is a crucial issue because in the quest to bring help to the troubled person, the counsellor is concerned with restoring the true image of personhood. If, as we shall argue, we broaden our understanding of counselling to encompass corporate therapy and the ministry of the therapeutic community of faith, it becomes even more important to develop a conception of personhood which integrates the individual and social dimensions of human existence as the individual begins to find identity in a social rather than a purely individual context.

In this discussion we shall contend that true personhood is to be found only in community: that the individual becomes a person only in relation to other persons; and that authentically Christian counselling must recognize this truth and end (or at least modify) its flirtation with post-Enlightenment individualism. The modern Christian counselling movement will not find this easy. Indeed, it will find it as hard to give up its dependence on the individualistic worldview as the church at the time of Galileo found it hard to give up its belief that the earth lay at the centre of the universe. Nevertheless, in doing so, the Christian counselling movement will find considerable theological resources in its history which it will be surprised to discover give the lie to modern autonomous individualism.

What Is A Person?

We begin by reviewing four definitions of what it means to be a person. These may be labelled *a-theological*. We use this term rather than the term *non-theological* because although these definitions do not in themselves stand in opposition to theology, they require to be interpreted and filled out by it. In other words, they are neutral as far as theological conceptions of personhood are concerned but, theologically interpreted, can be used to form a composite view of what counts as a person.

Role

The first definition has to do with the *origin* of the word *person*. It is widely agreed that the term originated in the context of the classical theatre. The ancient Greek term *prosopon* and the Latin word *persona* both referred to an actor's mask worn on stage as a means of signifying the actor's role. Personhood thus related to the idea of playing a role.

John Zizioulas has argued for an even deeper meaning to *prosopon*. Greek thought, he contends, was unable to accommodate the notion of a free individual capable of standing over and against the world and nature, making independent decisions about his or her destiny. Such a conception ran counter to the Greek view of necessity. According to this, the cosmos exists in unity and harmony, bound by inescapable laws of inner logic and coherence. Hence the notion of Fate which controlled even the divinity: 'Not even God can escape from this . . . unity and harmony stand freely before the world . . . In such a world, it is impossible for the unforeseen to happen or for freedom to operate as an absolute and unrestricted claim to existence.'[39] Within this world-view, human personhood could never be defined by existential freedom.

But, despite the laws of necessity, the impulse for freedom did exist. And it was in the theatre that it could find expression. The theatre consequently became the place where this theme of freedom versus necessity could be worked out. Zizioulas points out that Greek tragedy, in particular, provided a vehicle for expressing such a conflict:

It is precisely in the theatre that man strives to become a 'person', to rise up against this harmonious unity which oppresses him as rational and moral necessity. It is there that he fights with the gods and with his fate . . . It is there, too, that he constantly learns - according to the stereotyped principle of ancient tragedy - that he can neither escape fate ultimately, nor show hubris [defiance] to the gods without punishment, nor sin without suffering the consequences.[40]

The result was that the theatre not only became the arena where these themes were played out but that the fatalist message, exemplified in tragedy, proclaimed freedom to be illusory and 'consequently the "person" nothing but a "mask"'. Personhood in the sense of individual freedom is nothing but a mirage.

Paradoxically, however, a second message came across: the Greek actor caught in tragic circumstances experienced something of what it means to be a person. Behind his mask he is able to exercise freedom - at least for a while - and he learns what it means to be a free individual: 'The mask is not unrelated to the person but their relationship is tragic.'[41] The mask enables the individual actor to pretend that personhood and freedom co-exist. The fates might win in the end but the taste for authentic personhood had been experienced. In the Greek theatrical concept of *prosopon*, therefore, we have the seeds of modern notions of individual personhood.

When we turn to the Roman understanding of *persona*, we find similar theatrical usages. But in addition, the Romans expanded this understanding by applying the concept of role in a political, sociological and legal sense. *Persona* came to mean the *social* role exercised by an individual through external relations with others. Such relationships, however, were defined by society rather than by the individual. Personal identity was consequently assigned by the state in virtue of the individual's social relations: it was not assigned by the individual to himself: 'This identity - that vital component of the concept of man, that which makes one man differ from another, which makes him who he is - is guaranteed and provided by the state or some organized whole.'[42] The idea of individual identity separable from social identity was thus unthinkable.

The implications of classical views are significant. In the first place, although in the Greek and Roman worlds the movement towards understanding persons as individuals was incomplete, it was nonetheless movement in that direction. Secondly, the struggle between necessity and freedom portrayed in Greek tragedy served to underline the connection between personhood and individual self-consciousness based on the struggle for existential freedom. In the face of iron laws of necessity nothing could be more tragic. Both these facts established within the Western tradition a bias towards associating personhood with the individual as distinct from the undifferentiated mass. A third fact, however, made a somewhat different point and thereby preserved classical and early Christian philosophy from individualism of the modern kind. This fact was the equating of *persona* with social role. As long as it was held that the individual could find identity only in community, the myth of the isolated, autonomous human atom remained largely in the future. The identification of *persona* with individuated self-consciousness awaited further philosophical and theological developments.

Reason

A second definition of personhood can be found in the sixth century theologian Boethius who defined a person as 'an individual substance of a rational nature.'[43] Here we see a much clearer movement towards the modern conception. Indeed, according to Wolfhart Pannenberg, Boethius displaced the Greco-Roman notion of person-as-role to supply instead a definition which has proved normative from the medieval scholastics through to the modern philosophical tradition. For this reason, Ray Anderson regards the adoption of the Boethian definition as disastrous since it resulted directly in 'an atomistic concept of person which led to a strongly individualistic as well as rational view of the human self.'[44] We have already seen this come to fruition in Descartes, Hobbes and Locke.

In defence of Boethius, it may be said that he was seeking to safeguard the link between personhood and the individual so that personhood could not simply be viewed in terms of humanity *en masse*. But even when this point has been made, the negative fallout from his redefinition has remained ever since. His equation of personhood with individual rational substance effectively made the concept of person captive to the combination of rationality and individualism.

It is this equation which underlies the primary goal in modern counselling: namely the recovery of mental equilibrium by the person in distress. Such equilibrium, moreover, is rationally defined. It is not simply a matter of enabling a person to find some sort of psychological balance so as to function adequately. Rather it is a question of restoring the capacity to act rationally. Hence 'the psychotherapist . . . is primarily concerned with the irrational, unconscious aspects of his client's or patient's difficulties.'[45] The modern counsellor would have no difficulty in describing her task as the restoration of the person to an individual substance of a rational nature. Such is the triumph of the Boethian tradition.

Story

There is, however, a third understanding of person which points in a different direction. Oliver O'Donovan, following Alasdair MacIntyre, has argued that if we take the classical meaning of *persona* as a mask in the theatrical sense, we are led immediately to the idea of story. The *personae dramatis* are the characters in a play whose identity is defined by the interaction between themselves and the play: they are 'not mere faces but characters who have their exits and their entrances, whose appearances and reappearances constitute the drama.'[46]

From this, three things follow. Firstly, the identity of the *persona* is constituted by his or her continuity as a character within the dramatic story. Each appearance of the individual, each appearance of the theatrical mask, has a history within the narrative. It exists over time. It has continuity. Its identity is intelligible only by understanding its history within the plot. By analogy, therefore, the identity of the human being in real life is tied to his or her narrative history. The individual person, like the *dramatis persona*, is defined not simply (or even) by the possession of certain qualities such as rationality but rather by his or her history within the human species. Thus Jane Williams is not a person by virtue of being an individual rational substance but by being a member of a family with a name and a history: 'To speak of a person, then, is to speak of "identity", that which constitutes sameness between one appearance and another, and so makes us beings with histories and names.'[47]

Secondly, as O'Donovan points out, although each individual *persona* finds his or her identity in relation to other *personae* within the drama, such identity is nevertheless differentiated from that of others. We can pick out one mask, one *persona*, from another both by understanding its relationship with other masks and by grasping its personal history. Jane Williams is who she is both because she can be identified in relation to her mother, father, brothers and sisters (not to mention other people) and because she has her own life history: she was born in such-and-such a town in such-and-such a year, went to such-and-such a school, and so on. 'Individual humanity does not lose its significance when it is part of a multitude; rather, the history of the multitude gains its significance from the fact that it is a multitude of persons, not ants, each of whom has a significant history in him- or herself.'[46]

But if we accept that personal identity is differentiated and individual, does that commit us to return to the individualistic paradigm from which we are trying to escape? The answer must be no. For on the analogy of *dramatis personae*, it has to be remembered that each individual has a history not *in isolation* from others but *in relation* to them. The totality of the drama is constituted not by observing the historical trajectory of every individual as if it had no connection with or were not affected by any other but by tracing the web of relations between individual histories. In short, just as in a play no single mask exists apart from other masks, so in life no single person exists apart from relations with others.

Relation

This brings us to a fourth dimension of personhood which we shall explore at length in Part II. This may be termed: 'Beings-in-Relation'. In summary, this view affirms both the individuality of *personae* while at the same time emphasizing that the individual *persona* is constituted only in community. John Macquarrie cites the early twentieth century English philosopher Bernard Bosanquet as saying that 'the true individual, the only reality which can be absolutely whole and undivided, is the human race in its solidarity, for we are bound together in this web of life.'[48] According to Kallistos Ware, 'As a person, I am what I am only in relation to other persons. My human being is a relational being. My personal unity is fulfilled in community.'[49] As John Macmurray puts it:

> The Self exists only in dynamic relation with the Other . . . The Self is constituted by its relation to the Other . . . It has its being in its relationship . . . Since mutuality is constitutive for the personal, it follows that 'I' need 'You' in order to be myself.[50]

We are thus faced in these four definitions of personhood with a radical choice. On the one hand we may opt for a model of the person which stresses the priority of individual substance possessing recognizable qualities such as rationality. Such a view essentially sees the person as a conceptual abstraction. On the other hand we may choose a model which stresses the formation of personal identity within a network of concrete relationships tied together in a shared history. It will become clear from Part II of this book that in our view, we must side unequivocally with the latter. But whichever model we eventually choose, we need to be clear that it will carry formidable repercussions for the theory and practice of counselling.

Conclusion

In Part I we have made out a case for regarding the notion of contexts as crucial for effective counselling. We have argued that there is no such thing as context-free ministry and that each person who presents himself or herself for help needs to be understood from a number of perspectives. The myth of the isolated individual is just that - a myth reinforced by the philosophical heritage of the modern Western world.

In Part II we shall go on to see how the Christian faith offers distinctive understandings of what it means to be human and how this is closely tied up with the character and purposes of God. In contrast to secular models which find no room for God, other than seeing Him as part of the problem rather than part of the solution, we shall put forward a model which owes as much to theology as to psychology. We shall do so in the conviction that counselling is too important to be left to counsellors alone but that Christian truth must inform whatever method a counsellor employs. Incorporating this insight, the counsellor will find that together with the client they are working in a liberating context in which the healing grace of God becomes increasingly known and the recipients increasingly shaped after the image of God's Son.

Part 2

A THEOLOGICAL
PERSPECTIVE

COUNSELLING IN A
CHRISTIAN CONTEXT

Our task in the second half of this book is to draw together some of the threads of our discussion in Part I, and to map out a Christian theological perspective on caring and counselling.

Although our primary concern will be theological, this is not to be understood as merely theoretical. Theology is a systematic way of expressing our knowledge of God and God's ways, and - as with all our human knowing - there is a constant conversation between experience and theory, between belief and practice. All theology in this sense is practical theology: a conversation between what we come to know of God through revelation in Christ, and what we come to know of God through our knowledge of the world and of ourselves within it. It is from practice that we refine our beliefs; from doctrine that we reform our practice. Each puts questions to the other. Much of what we say in this section will be doctrinal, for it seems to us that one of the areas most needing attention in the field of Christian caring and counselling is the doctrinal basis of our work, and the guiding assumptions about God (metaphors such as Father, Lover, Saviour, Guide, Judge and so on) which shape our understanding of the moral and pastoral dimensions of Christian ministry. But although we will be working at the level of doctrine and systematic theology, we will always try to have in mind; for example:

- the pastor at the church door, looking for a gap in his diary to agree to meet the distressed parishioner who has just asked to see him;
- the neighbour pausing at the gate to listen to the elderly lady whose memory is failing, and who needs help filling in her forms;

- the trained therapist in her consulting room, faced with a couple whose marriage is in difficulties, and whose teenage daughter is pregnant.

How does our doctrine engage with their practice? What questions do their experiences put to our theology?

In Part I we discussed some of the contexts of Christian caring. We referred to the assumptions which underlie any approach to caring and counselling, secular or religious. Our task is now to set out some of the theological markers which can help us evaluate contexts, and to clarify the Christian assumptions on which pastoral ministry is based.

Before we go further, some explanation is needed of the phrase 'caring and counselling' which we have been using. The word 'counselling' has a long religious pedigree. In the Old Testament, we sometimes find 'counsellors'. At times these were counsellors of the king, speaking divine wisdom, engaging in political issues as parts of the Book of Proverbs make clear. The 'wise' are a class of religious sages from whom the wisdom literature (for example, the books of Ecclesiastes, Proverbs and Job) derives. Much of this teaching was geared towards helping people make sense of their lives, and cope with the uncertainties, frustrations, and pains of living in this world.[1] Now requiring discipline, now offering consolation,[2] the various wise guides of the Old Testament kingdoms brought the divine perspective to bear on life, showed the ways towards establishing justice in society and promoting goodness in personal life. Isaiah's vision of the Messiah includes the name 'Wonderful Counsellor' (Isaiah 9:6).

In the New Testament, as we shall see in more detail later, the Holy Spirit is called another 'counsellor' (John 14:16, 26; 15:26) (as well as Jesus himself), and the word 'paraklete' used of the Holy Spirit indicates a ministry which ranges from 'coming alongside' and 'just being there', to 'confrontation' and 'warning'. In the New Testament, paraklesis includes empathy, listening, exhorting, encouraging and guiding.

In Christian tradition, therefore, the word 'counselling' has included a wide range of ministries, many of which we would now more usually call 'caring'. It has covered discipline as well as consolation; it has been used for ongoing spiritual direction as well as episodic crisis intervention; it is a concept which covers directiveness as well as empathy; social needs as well as individual ones; well-being at all levels of life, not simply emotional health.

In recent years, as Part I illustrates, the word 'counselling' has come to have a more restricted meaning. 'Christian counselling' as now commonly understood is but one aspect of a broad concept of Christian caring ministry. Partly through the rise of clinical psychologies in the innovative work of Freud and Jung, and then through the development of pastoral psychology movements in the UK and the USA, partly through the processes of secularisation which have made some clergy and church counsellors feel deskilled and unsure of their calling, and partly through the development of the secular 'caring professions', the word 'counselling' has tended to move out of the church and into the secular professional world. The British Association for Counselling Ethics and Standards Committee described the process as one in which:

A person, occupying regularly or temporarily the role of 'counsellor' offers or agrees explicitly to give time, attention and respect, to another person temporarily in the role of 'client'. The task of counselling is to give the client an opportunity to explore, define and discover ways of living more satisfyingly and resourcefully within the social grouping with which he identifies.

The point we wish to stress is that this modern usage includes part of what the Christian tradition has meant by 'counselling', but there is much more to the Christian caring ministry than this. In these chapters, we will try to address this broader perspective. It is hoped that the professional counsellor who is a Christian will be able to recognize what he or she does in these pages. It is hoped that Christian pastors engaged in wider caring ministries will find themselves addressed here also. 'Caring and counselling' is thus used to indicate the breadth of these concerns, although for convenience this has sometimes been abbreviated to 'counselling'.

We begin our theology of caring and counselling by returning to the discussion in Part I concerning contexts and assumptions.

Contexts and Assumptions

In the first part of this book, we explored some of the contexts: professional, psychological, philosophical, social, in which caring and counselling ministry takes place. We will need to bear in mind in our theological map-making, such issues as professionalism, and individualism which were raised there. We will also explore further the relationship of theology to psychology. We must confront the fact that a great deal of 'caring' and 'counselling' in the secular world is problem-centered, whereas the history of Christian ministry of care is much more broadly based, concerned with the ongoing lives of people in health as well as sickness, in ordinary day-to-day living for Christ as well as coping with problems and crises. Part of our purpose in Part II is to look back at these questions through the framework of Christian faith. In other words, to explore what it means to speak of counselling in a Christian context. We begin with the basic assumptions which inevitably undergird all work which is directed towards human change.

As was made clear in Part I, every system of counselling, every approach to caring, makes certain assumptions. Whether we are Christian or secular, Freudian or behaviourist, paid or voluntary, on a church staff or an employee of the Health Service, we make assumptions in our work. At this point we will concentrate particularly on three:

assumptions about human nature;
assumptions about values;
assumptions about the processes of change.

Assumptions about Human Nature
Every approach to counselling and caring operates with a certain view of human nature. Some concentrate on particular aspects of the human person: behaviour, feelings, thoughts, relationships, the

capacity for personal growth and so on. Some take a more optimistic and others a more pessimistic view of our human capacities to deal with life.

When we write or read about human persons, as we are doing now, we are expressing something of the ambiguity of what being a 'person' means. For we are both treating human persons as objects of study and investigation, distancing ourselves from 'the human person' in order to think about what being a person means. And yet it is as persons, subjective centres of consciousness, that we are doing so. There is much about us which tells us that it is possible for human persons to be the objects of study; we share a nature with the rest of creation. Like all creatures, we are 'of the dust of the ground'. And yet we also know that we are more than that: we can think about ourselves, read and write about ourselves, stand back from ourselves and ask ourselves who we are. There is in us a 'self-transcending' capacity, and this, it seems, is something unique in creation - it sets us humans apart from other created beings.

In his characteristically extravagant way, the French thinker Blaise Pascal expressed the ambiguity like this:

> What sort of freak, then, is man! How novel, how monstrous, how chaotic, how paradoxical, how prodigious! Judge of all things, feeble earthworm, repository of truth, sink of doubt and error, glory and refuse of the universe![3]

The psalmist was somewhat more polite:

> When I look at Thy heavens, the work of Thy fingers, the moon and the stars which Thou hast established, what is man that Thou art mindful of him? Yet Thou hast made him little less than God, and dost crown him with glory and honour (Psalm 8: 3-5).

A small, finite creature, and yet little less than God! Contemporary thinking about the human person seems unable to decide on which aspect of our humanity to concentrate. Stephen Evans characterises the situation[4] in terms of a struggle between reductionism and self-deification: do we concentrate our attention of the physical, biological basis of human life, understanding human beings primarily in terms of our physical make-up, or do we focus on the mental and spiritual aspects of our humanity, and the ways in which we transcend our material limitations? Stanley Jaki wrote a book called *Angels, Apes and Men*[5] refuting the ideas of those who see human beings as merely naked apes, or only as disembodied minds. Among the former there are those who want to describe and analyse the human person only in terms of the lower levels of life. Scientists such as Richard Dawkins assure us that 'we are survival machines, robot vehicles, blindly programmed to preserve the selfish molecules known as genes'.[6] The behaviourist B. F. Skinner produced an elaborate reductionist programme, asserting that 'to man *qua* man we readily say good riddance'.[7] Yet others discuss humanness only in terms of body chemistry or sociobiology. Human beings are 'seen as products, mere objects of nature, not as subjects, responsible beings with an interior life and the power to make choices.[8]

On the other hand, and at the other extreme, there are thinkers who see human persons almost as gods. Human beings have the power to create value and create meaning. The title of Erich Fromm's book *You shall be as Gods*[9] captures the theme. In a culture which has largely abandoned belief in God, human beings themselves have to take over His functions. This is the age of Nietzsche's superman. Human beings, some people argue, hold the only key to meaning, purpose and value.

As we shall go on to argue, neither reductionism nor self-deification are consistent with a Christian view of the human person, but neither are they consistent with our experiences of what it is to be human. Our experience is one of ambiguity. We know that there is that in our makeup which is 'of the dust'. We are clearly physical, embodied beings who get ill, become frail, will die. We get hurt. 'If you prick us, do we not bleed? If you tickle us, do we not laugh? If you poison us, do we not die?[10] We also know that there are in our lives what Peter Berger called 'signals of transcendence'.[11] There is, for example, a sense of moral obligation which confronts us from beyond ourselves, requiring us to do our duty, loading our conscience with guilt when we are in the wrong. We also believe that falling in love or experiencing deep grief are more than physiological mental processes. It is not enough for Boris, having made love to Lola (in Sartre's *Age of Reason*) to dismiss the process with disgust: 'Its physiological'. There is also in us, as Becker reminds us forcefully in *The Denial of Death*,[12] a defiant refusal to accept death, even - for many of us - a death-defying hope that death is not the end. We are 'of the dust' and yet share in transcendence; we need a way of holding both these aspects together.[13]

To quote Pascal again:

> It is dangerous to explain too clearly to man how like he is to the animals without pointing out his greatness. It is also dangerous to make too much of his greatness without his vileness. It is still more dangerous to leave him in ignorance of both, but it is most valuable to represent both to him. Man must not be allowed to believe that he is equal either to animals or to angels, not to be unaware of either, but he must know both.[14]

A similar ambiguity arises when we look at our human moral capacities. We all know ourselves in experience to be both good and bad, morally strong at some points, morally weak at others; partly able to exercise self-control and responsibility, partly driven by forces which do not seem to be the real 'us' that we would like to be. We aspire high, and fall low. St Paul put it this way:

> I do not understand my own actions. For I do not do what I want, but I do the very thing I hate . . . I delight in the law of God in my inmost self, but I see in my members another law at war with the law of my mind and making me captive to the law of sin (Romans 7:15, 22f).

Any pastor or counsellor recognizes this 'divided self'. Some thinkers try for example to understand such ambiguities from what we might call an 'optimism of nature'. Jean Jacques Rousseau, for example, believed that 'man is naturally good, and only by institutions is he made bad'. 'To undo evil in man, all that is necessary is to abandon civilisation, for man is naturally good, and savage man - when he has had his dinner - is at peace with all nature and the friend of all his fellow creatures'. There is comparable optimism in some contemporary humanistic psychologists. To refer again to Erich Fromm:

> The position taken by humanistic ethics, that man is able to know what is good and act accordingly on the strength of his natural potentialities and of his reason, would be untenable if the dogma of man's innate evilness were true.[15]

Carl Rogers believes that the innermost core of our nature is basically socialised, positive, forward-moving, constructive and trustworthy.[16] Abraham Maslow likewise believes that our inborn nature is essentially good and never evil.[17] When we are sinful, unhappy or neurotic, it is our environment that makes us that way, so it is claimed. On the other hand, there are thinkers who operate with quite the opposite view. This we might call a 'pessimism of nature'. The philosopher Thomas Hobbes, for example, an empiricist who was a thorough-going materialist, wrote:

> Life is nothing but a motion of the limbs . . . In a state of nature, before there is any government, every man desires to preserve his own liberty, and also to acquire dominion over others. Both these desires are dictated by the impulse to self-preservation. From their conflict arises a war of all against all - which makes life nasty, brutish and short.[18]

Though different in many ways, Freud shares a materialistic and deterministic view of human nature, which is basically pessimistic. Life is essentially the struggle of the ego to mediate in a conflict between the pressures of the super-ego (that part of the ego which is a sort of internalized critical parent voice) against the demands of the id (a largely unconscious repository of aggressive and sexual impulses). The result is either destructiveness or neurotic frustration.

For yet others, like some of the existentialist nihilists, life is a bad joke, or ultimately absurd.

But perhaps we are neither good nor bad. Perhaps, with John Locke, we believe that at birth we are simply a blank page on which our culture and life experience writes its script. Some contemporary psychologists seem to take this view, suggesting that we are the products of stimulus-response bonds, with no power of choice, and little ability to control our environment. Words like 'freedom' and 'human dignity' cease to have meaning, as B. F. Skinner's *Beyond Freedom and Dignity*, from another perspective, eloquently argues.[19]

None of these approaches are fully consistent with a Christian theology of the human person. As we shall see, it is preferable to talk not about an optimism of nature, nor a pessimism of nature, but rather about an 'optimism of grace'.

At this point, however, we simply note again that every secular system of caring and counselling makes assumptions about human nature. None are free of a particular faith concerning what makes humans tick. It is exactly the same with the Christian faith, and with Christian carers and counsellors. There is a distinctive Christian view of what it is to be human which we shall explore more fully in the next chapter. We shall need to clarify what Christian faith says about human nature, and about what counts as 'normal' human life. We shall need to develop a Christian theology of the personal, and try to understand personal relationships, particularly counselling relationships, in that perspective. That is one way in which Christian approaches to care and counselling are set apart. That is one dimension to counselling in a Christian context.

Assumptions about Values

A second dimension to caring and counselling concerns the goals, aims and purposes of our work. If each of the various approaches to counselling is in its own way 'that activity which seeks to help people towards constructive change and growth in any or every aspect of their lives through a caring relationship and within agreed relational boundaries (taken from the Association of Christian Counsellors Policy Document), each gives its own sense to the phrase 'constructive change'. What counts as 'constructive'? What are our goals, our aims? What counts as 'the good life' we are seeking to help one another to discover?

As with our assumptions concerning human nature, so here, we find ourselves faced with a range of possibilities. If we were to ask Freud the purpose of healthy human life, he would reply 'to love and to work'. The goal of therapy for the Freudian, is by the processes of psychoanalysis to provide sufficient insight for the client into his or her neurotic needs, for him or her to be able to function well in his or her social world.

For Jung, on the other hand, the task was the integration of the opposites within a person's life, the bringing into play of the shadow sides of the personality; the recovery of harmony in personal functions.[20] This is the process of individuation, whereby a person becomes an integrated whole.

For the humanistic psychologists such as Rogers and Maslow, the goal is sometimes described as 'self-actualization'. Maslow indicates that all human beings have what he describes as a hierarchy of basic needs (food, drink, sleep, shelter, etc. belonging, friendship, personal fulfilment). 'Self-actualisation: is the ongoing actualisation of potentials, capacities and talents, as fulfilment of mission (call, fate, destiny, or vocation), as a fuller knowledge of, and acceptance of, the person's own intrinsic nature, as an unceasing trend towards unity, integration or synergy within the person.[21]

For others, who believe that behaviour is determined by inner thoughts and outer environments, the task of therapy is to help a person to change by adopting more constructive patterns of thought and adapting more constructively to their environment. Clearly what is thought to be constructive is related to fundamental assumptions about human good - usually the desire to live more creatively and with less pain.

Don Browning refers to what he calls 'metaphors of ultimacy' in the modern psychologies, the fundamental assumptions about the world which dictate the way we understand human life and behaviour.[22] For Freud, he suggests, the 'metaphor of ultimacy' is 'mechanism': the human person is a mechanism of biological instincts. For Jung, the metaphor is of 'opposites': God becomes a symbol of the Deep Self where conscious and unconscious meet. For Maslow and Erikson, the metaphor of ultimacy concerns the 'satisfaction of the self', whereas for Skinner, the focus is on social controls. As Christians we need to formulate our 'metaphor of ultimacy' in relation to our understanding of God - although we have to notice straightaway that there has been a tendency to divide Christian approaches in accordance with the way different Christians sometimes selectively describe God. If we think of God primarily as Creator and heavenly Father, our understanding of human life may be primarily one of dependence and response. If our guiding metaphor for God is lawgiver and judge, we may focus our understanding of what it is to be human more in terms of duty, obedience and conformity. If we start with God as Saviour and Redeemer, our approach to life may be mostly in terms of the restoration of relationship. Furthermore, to begin with the Holy Spirit and the harvest of the fruits of love, joy, peace, may lead us to think of human life mostly in terms of the processes of human development and growth towards the character of God. Later on we shall try to show how these different features of Christian understanding all have their part to play within the primary Trinitarian metaphor for God as Father, Son and Holy Spirit: Creator, Saviour, Redeemer; Law-giver and Lover; Persons in a Community of Love.

Clearly some of the secular approaches begin with past causes, genetic, or environmental conditioning and the client's life history.

The goals of such therapies are to enable a person to come to terms with, or respond appropriately to the past. Other approaches are more future directed, concerned with asking questions about future goals, hope and aims. Both are important, as Anthony Storr expresses well:

> It is clear that it is as legitimate to ask towards what end a process is directed, as to inquire from what cause it originated, and I believe that any psychological description of human beings must attempt to answer both questions. The highly complicated facts of human behaviour can be related to both enquiries; and whilst some facts are better explained in terms of what has happened in the individual's past, others are more easily comprehended in terms of the goals towards which the individual appears to be striving. Neither description is complete without the others.[23]

Clearly the Christian faith has a particular understanding of what is good. In Old Testament terms 'the good life' was described by H. H. Rowley in these terms:

> The good life ... as it is presented to us in the Old Testament is the life that is lived in harmony with God's will and that expresses itself in daily life in the reflection of the character of God translated into the terms of human experience, that draws its inspiration and its strength from communion with God in the fellowship of His people and in private experience, and that knows how to worship and praise Him both in public and in the solitude of the heart.[24]

One Old Testament word which encapsulates much that is said about human well-being and the goals of human life is the word *shalom*. Often translated 'peace' shalom means much more than the absence of conflict. *Shalom* is the presence of order and wellbeing at all levels of life and relationship. Gideon's altar was built to proclaim that 'the Lord is Peace' (Judges 6:24) and where the Lord gives *shalom*, there are good relationships between people and between communities, there is health and well-being in all aspects of life; there is contentedness, conciliation and prosperity.

The kingdom of *shalom* is established and upheld 'with righteousness and justice' (Isaiah 9:7) and so *shalom* is never fully present until righteousness and justice are present also. In this world we are only ever on the way to *shalom*. The day will come when 'righteousness and peace will embrace' in humanity's response to God's covenanted 'steadfast love and faithfulness', (Psalm 85:10). And that day will centre on God's Messiah, the Prince of Peace (Isaiah 9:5ff).

There are many times in the Old Testament when *shalom* is bracketed together with a Hebrew word translated 'health' or 'healing'. Jeremiah writes 'We hoped for peace, but no good has come, for a time of healing, but there was only terror', (Jeremiah 8:15. See also Isaiah 2: 1-5; 42: 1-4; 53:5).

The New Testament opens up to us the insight that Jesus is God's Messiah, and 'Christ is our Peace' (Ephesians 2:14). His healing ministry, His self-understanding as the One who came to preach good news to the poor, to proclaim release to captives, recovering of sight to the blind, to set at liberty the oppressed (Luke 4:18ft), His coming to save (Matthew 1:21) and to serve (Mark 10:45) all indicate that Jesus Christ is presented as the bringer of health and healing, *shalom*.

In the New Testament the good life for human persons is understood in relation to the life of Jesus Christ, and the calling of Christ to 'Follow Me'. In Christ, God's kingdom comes, God's justice is seen, God's peace is available. Christian assumptions about the good life, are inescapably bound up with the person and teaching, life, death and resurrection of God's Messiah. In the Jewish context into which Jesus was born, the hope of the Messiah was bound up with God's deliverance of Israel, and through Israel, the whole of the human race. Jesus' message was that the time of deliverance had dawned: the long awaited kingdom of God was at hand. He embodied in Himself the values of the kingdom which He taught His disciples to 'seek first, and everything else you need will be yours as well' (Matthew 6:33).

Christian pastoral caring and counselling will, therefore, need to find a way of expressing these Christian assumptions about values, aims and goals in terms of these biblical perspectives on the good life. Our assumptions will be coloured by our Christian under-standing of the character of God's love and justice, righteousness and peace, and his purpose, expressed cryptically for the people of God in the Old Testament in Deuteronomy 5:33 'that it may go well with you'. That character is expressed personally in Jesus Christ. So as a goal for pastoral ministry, perhaps we can best take our direction from St Paul's word in Colossians 1:28: 'Him [Christ] we proclaim, warning every man and teaching every man in all wisdom, that we may present every man *mature in Christ*'.

What 'mature in Christ' means, we will need to explore further. But as with our discussion of human nature, so also in this discussion of goals and values, we realise that here is another perspective which gives Christian approaches to caring and counselling a distinctive direction, another dimension to counselling in the Christian context.

Assumptions about Change

Every approach to caring and counselling makes certain assumptions about the processes by which people's attitudes, responses, thoughts, feelings or behaviours may change.

In a very general and somewhat oversimplified sense, we may divide up the approaches to counselling in the secular world (and there are Christian counterparts to each of these) into three broad models, which we may call 'relational', 'cognitive' and 'moral'.

The **relational models** of therapy, which include psychoanalysis, psychodynamic object-relations approaches, Junigan psychotherapy and some of the humanistic and transpersonal approaches, place a very high value on the quality of the relationship established between the counsellor and the client. These models focus on aspects of that relationship which give insight into the client's general patterns of making relationships, and the feelings and thoughts associated with them. This relationship is itself the primary therapeutic resource. We will explore further in due course why, from a Christian perspective, this claim is made, and seek to evaluate it.

The **cognitive models** focus more on the inadequate or irrational patterns of thought which the client has developed, and the consequent destructive feelings and patterns of behaviour which may derive from such thoughts. Approaches such as Ratio-Emotive therapy, some aspects of Gestalt, Transactional Analysis, and so on, indicate that change comes through changing thought patterns. Feelings and behaviour follow thoughts. Once again, we will need to look more closely at some of these models from a Christian vantage point.

A third set of approaches, which we may loosely call **moral models** focus primarily on the responsibility of the client to make appropriate choices in his or her life. There is a moral account-ability which needs to be acknowledged, and the consequent feelings of guilt when wrong has been done need to be addressed. Some of these approaches concentrate on behavioural changes. Some focus more on the will of the client to choose. In William Glasser's *Reality Therapy*, for example, the human needs to love and be loved, and to feel that we are worthwhile to ourselves and to others, are bound up with maintaining a certain standard of behaviour. Morals, standards, values, are all intimately related to the fulfilment of our need for self-worth. The complicated business of acquiring responsibility thus becomes, for Reality Therapy, an essential ingredient, and this can be achieved through the development of an emotional relationship between the client and a responsible therapist. The relational and moral models here begin to come together.

Of course, may therapists and counsellors work with more than one model, but even in such cases, assumptions about change are inevitable.

Does change come though relationships, through insight, through choices, through adapting behaviour patterns, through a complex mix of different factors? For a Christian with a holistic view of the human person, it may seem that none of these is sufficient, though aspects of all of them may on occasion be appropriate. But, recalling what we said about an optimism not of nature but of grace, the Christian will also wish to bring the understanding of sin, failure, grace, redemption, progress, and the work of the Holy Spirit into the picture. Is there a way of drawing a Christian map of the processes of personal change, which can do justice to the various insights of the human sciences, and which also adequately recognises the therapeutic significance of the Gospel of grace? To do so we will also need to recognise the Christian understanding of the church as a community of faith. It is 'with all the saints' (Ephesians 3:18) that we come to know the love of God. The Church as the Body of Christ, the Household of God, is depicted in the New Testament as a community of character-building, a community of reconciliation, a community of healing. Personal change takes place within a network of personal relationships; often it is in the setting of a ministry team of persons within different gifts (and different needs) that 'the whole body, joined and knit together by every joint with which it is supplied, when each part is working properly, makes bodily growth and upbuilds itself in love' (Ephesians 4:16).

Our Task

Our task in the rest of Part II of this book is therefore to spell out in some detail the implications of these Christian assumptions about human nature, values and the processes of change for the ministry of Christian caring and counselling.

Christian ministry derives from the ministry of Christ to and with God the Father in the power of the Holy Spirit for the sake of the world. God the Father, we read, sent His Son, because He 'so loved the world' (John 3:16). From and in that love, the Son of God 'loved me and gave Himself for me' (Galatians 2:20). The love of God is now 'shed abroad in our hearts' by the Holy Spirit (Romans 5:5). All of our Christian ministry derives from and is a sharing in the ministry of Christ. Jesus said to His disciples 'As the Father has sent me, so I send you' (John 20:21). Our caring, our counselling – as well as our serving, teaching, preaching, quest for social justice, healing and evangelism, and so on – is part of Christ's ministry, through His Body, the Church. In other words, our caring and our counselling, as with all other aspects of Christian ministry, derive from the Gospel of Christ. They must have a Gospel rationale, and must take on a Gospel shape and find expression within a Gospel community.

In the light of this, our method will therefore be to work with what we would like to call a 'Gospel-shaped hermeneutic'. In other words, we will endeavour to let the Gospel of Jesus Christ shape the way we set up our questions and seek to work at them. Rather than working from the basis of various secular therapies and – so to speak – 'baptizing' for Christian use the parts that we find useful, we want to work from the basis of the Christian Gospel itself, and bend the insights of the secular world to that perspective. We will not close our minds to secular insights. All truth is the truth of God, and what true insights are available to us about human nature and human needs, we must evaluate for use within the Christian pastoral ministry.

The Christian assumptions concerning human nature, values and the processes of change all derive from the Christian Gospel that God loved the world, and loves us; that God was in Christ reconciling the world to himself; that in Christ we discover what it is to be true human beings, how to love our neighbours, and how to be just in all human affairs; that in Christ, the future kingdom of God's glory, of justice, righteousness and peace has been inaugurated. That kingdom is being brought into being, and its future reality stretches back towards us in time to transform our life in the present in the light of God's future. Through Christ we are offered the grace and power of the Holy Spirit for personal and social life and by his help God's kingdom may come and God's will be done on earth as it is in heaven. This is the fundamental Gospel context for our work.

We will now discuss further some of these theological themes and relate them to the day-to-day ministries of Christian caring for and counselling of people. We will look first at the theological model of covenant as a framework within which to understand the relationships which form the heart of pastoral ministry. We will spend some time exploring further the Christian understanding of what it is to be a person, and all the varieties of personality with which persons are endowed. Then we will move to a discussion of the Christian ministry of caring and counselling, dividing this discussion up under the Trinitarian headings of 'The Grace of our Lord, Jesus Christ', 'The Love of God'; and 'The Fellowship of the Holy Spirit'.

COUNSELLING PERSONS

Counselling is a word which describes a process between persons in a particular sort of relationship with each other. We need to clarify how best to understand that process, if our counselling is truly to be 'in a Christian context'. We need also to think some more about what it means to be a person. We begin with the doctrine of God as a Holy Trinity of persons in relationship.

God: Persons in Relation

If we are to try to make sense of what is going on when someone knocks on the pastor's door and says 'May I come and talk to you?' or a parishioner makes an appointment after the service to come and see the vicar 'about a personal problem', and the two sit down to talk together; or a minister prepares with her healing prayer group to meet someone she has been counselling – we need, as we have argued earlier, to place this process in a theological context. The question is not only what do we think is happening between the people concerned, but what if anything do we think God is doing in the process? Here are two people, or perhaps a small group, engaged in a very particular sort of relationship together, with certain assumptions and a certain goal. How are we to understand this theologically?

To begin to understand the meaning of persons we begin with the understanding of God as a Holy Trinity of Persons in relationship.

There has been a renewed interest in the doctrine of the Trinity among theologians who wish to develop a theological anthropology.

Karl Barth's doctrine of humanity is rooted in his doctrine of the Trinity. Torrance,[1] Zizioulas,[2] Moltmann,[3] Gunton[4] and others[5], in their different ways, have been emphasizing the importance of this doctrine. Colin Gunton has recently commented on the way Western culture tends either to subsume the individual into the mass, or so focuses on the individual that in the resulting individualism, the value of the other person is discounted. By contrast, the orthodox understanding of the Trinity especially as developed in the Eastern church,[6] and in writers such as Richard of St Victor,[7] open up ways of thinking about God relationally, and so give a relational meaning to human persons made in the divine image (see the discussions in Ramsey[8]; Hughes[9] gives a different view).

In *The Call to Personhood*, Alistair McFadyen proposes a model of the Trinity 'as a unique community of Persons in which Person and relation are interdependent moments in a process of mutuality. Each Person is a social unity with specific characteristics unique to Him or Her but whose uniqueness is not an asocial principle of being. The terms of personal identity within the Trinity identify not just unique individuals but the form of relation peculiar to Them. The Father, Son and Spirit are neither simply modes of relation nor absolutely discrete and independent individuals, but Persons in relation and Persons only through relation. Persons exists only as they exist for others... Persons are what they are only through their relations with the others.[5]

This seems fully consistent with what some theologians have called the 'social doctrine of the Trinity'.[3,10] It gives further theological weight to the relational concept of person explored earlier with reference to John Macmurray.[11]

Human Persons in Relation

If God is essentially Persons in relation, then this opens up a way of conceiving human persons as 'persons in relation', for it is in His light that we must understand the nature of human persons. Personal identity must and can only arise out of a person's relations and community with others.[12]

This approach to human persons holds together both the importance of the individual and the fact that we are necessarily - and are intended to be - persons in relation.

Christians often use the Genesis language of being 'in the image of God' to describe their particular view of humanness. But we need to be clear that there is considerable debate about the proper meaning of 'the image'. Some people have understood the image of God to refer mostly to some sort of capacity we have, which perhaps other animals do not have, for example our ability to think, or communicate verbally, or to fall in love, or to know God. No doubt all of these, and other capacities, are part of what human beings need if they are to give full, mature, adult, healthy expression to their humanness. But there is another approach to the 'image' which is less to do with capacities and abilities, and more to do with relationship. The analogy of the angled mirror is a help here. When a mirror is set at a particular angle - or as we might say, in a particular relationship - to its object, it reflects its object. We see an image of the object in the mirror. This is in fact the sort of picture St Paul had in mind when he described Jesus Christ as 'the image of the invisible God' (Colossians 1:15 and 2 Corinthians 4:6). Jesus was in such a relationship to God the Father, that by looking at him, we see God. Jesus is God for us within the terms of this physical world's space and time. He is a unique reflection of God because the images arises from the unique relation Jesus bears to the Father.

To describe other human beings as being in God's image can only within this present world be to describe something which is very far from perfect. The Christian doctrine of sin means that the mirror is cracked, and the angle is wrong. When we look at erring, sinful human beings, we do not see God in his perfection. The story of Genesis 2 and 3 illustrates a view of humanity which rings true to the ambiguity of our nature as we experience it. In these chapters of Genesis, we find obedience and rebellion, openness and shame, responsibility and guilt, freedom and bondage, blessing and curse, sexual complementarity and subordination, creativity and drudgery, fellowship and banishment, life and death. The picture is of humanity in the ambiguity of a fallen world in the context of Genesis 1 to 11.[13] The image is still there, but is distorted and broken.

Persons on the Way

Persons are therefore unfinished this side of heaven; communities of persons are unfinished. If the fundamental thing to understand about persons from a theological perspective is that human beings are essentially persons in relation, then personhood is a process of becoming. The process is one of restoring the image, of growing into wholeness; we could say, of growing into full humanity. 'We are persons on the way', to quote Macquarrie.[14]

The reflection of the image of God in us, then, is not only a gift but also a task. God has set us in the world in a certain sort of relationship with Himself which is intended to reflect into the world something of His being, His light, His nature. We are to represent God to the rest of the created order. By looking at human beings, we are intended to see the divine being, the divine activity and creativity, the divine love, the divine justice. But if the God whom we reflect is himself 'Persons in relation', a 'social' God,[15] then the way we human beings most closely reflect His nature is through our interpersonal relationships with one another. When our relationships between persons are marked by the sorts of qualities which mark God's character, (love, justice, patience, sacrifice, blessing, the fruits of God's spirit), then these display something of God in the world. And if that is how human beings are *intended* to be, that is what makes for the best for human life in this world. Personal communion is what the image of God is about, it is what human life is about. The realities of sinful humanity are that these aspects of God's life and character are never in this life unmixed with failure, shame, guilt, alienation and decay.

From this perspective, we can see that Christian caring, ministry, counselling, can be understood as helping to remove the blocks that get in the way of truly human functioning, the blocks that spoil human personal communion, that distort the image of God.

Christian caring ministry is about enabling one another to grow as persons nearer to what God intends humanity to be.

Persons in Integrity

The concept of integrity is used not to suggest that human beings are complete or perfect. We have just said that we are ambiguous and flawed. It indicates rather that we need to understand the human person at many different levels, and that we cannot speak of 'person' without speaking of an integrated picture of many levels together.

At one (chemical) level, we are 'of the dust of the ground', beings whose body chemistry can be described. At another (biological) level, we are living organisms, in whom many different organs and processes function together. We can think of ourselves in terms of our psychological processes of emotion, attitude, thought, behaviour patterns. We can focus on the central relational dimension, as we have just been doing. We must include a moral dimension, in which awareness of moral categories is significant, and the exercise of the will is recognised. And we must set this whole picture in a particular physical and social environment within which personal relationships are made, and develop, and which is open to God through the fellowship of his Spirit.

There are many reductionist approaches to the person which concentrate only for example on the biochemical or the psychological levels. From a theological perspective these can only lead to stunted and distorted views of human persons.

If Jesus Christ is the one true image of God, if he is the normal Human Being, it is not surprising to see in him an integrated person, aware of his body and the bodily needs of others, open in relations to women and men, able to manage his emotions appropriately,[16] morally clear that His will was to do the will of Him who sent Him (John 6:38; Hebrews 10:5-10) and open to God in an intimacy of fellowship.

Note that many of the healing miracles in the Gospels concern bodily well-being: Jesus touches the leper, heals the blind, opens the ears of the deaf, helps the woman with the discharge of blood, heals the man with the withered hand. It is His body that is broken on the Cross, and which is presented resurrected to Thomas in the narrative of John 20. Note, too, the nature of His relationships with the disciples, especially Peter, James and John – the fourth Gospel refers to 'the disciple whom Jesus loved' – and His particular friendships with Mary, Martha and Lazarus. (Matthew 11:25-27; John 17).

Christian ministry will need to operate with a holistic and integrated approach to human persons in which body, emotions, mind, spirit, will, relations and environment are all considered.

Christian Ministry

What is a person doing when they offer ministry? How do caring and counselling fit in to our understanding of Christian ministry?

All Christian ministry derives from the ministry of Christ to and with God the Father in the power of the Spirit. In the earthly ministry of Jesus Christ we see a fulfilment of the Messianic hopes of the Old Testament that a coming King, Servant and Conqueror would embody in Himself the purposes of God for Israel (Isaiah 33:17; 42:1; 61:1ff). Israel was God's chosen means of bringing about His purposes for all humanity. So in Jesus we see the focus of all God's purposes for all people. He is the True Human Being. And He offers Himself in ministry as One 'sent by God'. In Him, the Messianic promise of good news for the poor, release for captives, recovery of sight to the blind and liberty for the oppressed, and the announcement of the inauguration of the Messianic age, all find their fulfilment (Luke 4:18-21).

The Letter to the Ephesians explores the way in which the Gospel of Christ unveils the mystery of God's purposes for his whole world (1:10). And the vehicle for that disclosure is Christ's body, the Church (3:10). In the gift of the risen Christ, the Church as His body is caught up into His ministry. As the Gospel of John has it: 'As the Father has sent Me, so I send you'. All Christian people, therefore, as part of that body, are part of His ministry. Because it is part of the identity of the people of God, ministry is an inescapable task of the people of God. According to Ephesians, grace was given to each of us according to the measure of the ascended Christ's gift, and His gifts were for the work of ministry to build up the body of Christ (Ephesians 4:1-16).

The picture of the ministry of the Body of Christ to the Father in the power of the Spirit, developed in Ephesians 4, has these dimensions:

(i)   it is a mutual ministry - we are persons in relation;
(ii) it is ministry to one another within this world - we are persons in the world;
(iii) it is ministry with a goal - we are persons on the way (until we all attain to the unity of the faith and the knowledge of the Son of God).

This ministry is set in the context of the purposes of God for His world, to sum up all things in heaven and in earth in Christ (1:10). It is a ministry of the Church, through whose proclamation the wisdom of God is now made known (3:10). It is a ministry in the love of Christ (3:19) and the power of the Spirit (3:20). It is a ministry geared towards the development of character (4:22-5:20), towards the development of structures in family and society which reflect the Gospel (5:21-6:9), and towards confrontation with the powers of evil in this world (6:10f). Ministry is therefore to do with individuals, with relationships, with growth, with structures, with deliverance, with proclamation. It derives from God the Holy Trinity, and is offered through Christ in the power of the Spirit to the Father. Our ministry belongs within, and is caught up in, the ministry of the Cosmic Christ - the image of the invisible God, in whom and for whom all things were created: it is 'Him we proclaim, warning every man - teaching every man in all wisdom that we may present every man mature in Christ' (Colossians 1:15, 16, 28).

All Christian caring and counselling finds its rationale as one way in which Christian ministry is exercised. The vicar in the study helping prepare a couple for marriage; the caring neighbour delivering food to the shut-in elderly person next door; the trained Christian therapist in a counselling session; the Christian social worker trying to make a case for social justice for a client: all are part of the ministry of Christ.

Counselling as a Covenant

The quality of the relationships developed between vicar and parishioner, neighbour and neighbour, therapist or social worker and client, members of a house group with each other, are important in Christian ministry. How can such relationships be described?

Some therapists talk in terms of **contract**, and of course there are contractual dimensions to professional counselling, and indeed in a less explicit and often tacit way in many caring relationships. Whether or not there is a decision to offer limited time, to meet at a particular place, to undertake to work at a particular set of problems or questions, to charge a fee for services rendered, there is - or should be - some sort of contract. It does not need to be written down, and in pastoral ministry rarely is. But there needs to be some recognition that you are coming to me with certain expectations, and I am agreeing to offer certain gifts. Without such a contract, pastoral caring and counselling lacks the sort of shape and the sort of boundaries which are very often precisely what a distressed person needs provided for them. A loose, open-ended, unstructured willingness to be available at all times, for all needs - what some call the door-mat syndrome - *seems* to model God's inexhaustible grace, whereas it often simply models laziness of purpose and actual exhaustion in the carers. For the carer's sake as well as the needy person's, some boundaries are required.

Having said that, however, the notion of *contract* is not enough. If our caring is intended to model the caring of God, and if our purpose is to help one another reflect something of the nature and character of God, we need to ask how God makes relationships. One of the key biblical words which describes God's pattern of relating to his people Israel, is the word **covenant**. This is more than a contractual word, though it can include the notion of contract. It is essentially a personal word, describing persons in a particular sort of relationship with each other. It is a word used very early in the biblical story of God's personal relationship with every living creature in the story of the Flood, in Genesis 6-9. It expresses God's law, and justice, God's mercy and grace, God's provision for sinful human beings to live in God's world in relationship to Him. It begins with God's gracious initiative ('Noah found grace' Genesis 6:18) on the basis of which a context of care is established.

The covenant story becomes more specifically focused in the narrative concerning Abraham (Genesis 17:7ff). God calls Abraham by name, and makes him a promise. On the basis of that promise given and received, the covenant command is established: I will be your God, and you shall be My people. There is a basis of personal communication in the promise and the command. In the later story of Moses, the covenant is renewed in the initiative of divine grace at the Exodus, and was focused in the law, the Torah, the fatherly instruction of God to his people which described a pattern of life appropriate for living in line with God's character. The covenant begins when God makes a certain promise 'I will be your God', to which are attached certain obligations 'You shall be My people'.

There is a publicly known contractual dimension to the covenant making: undertakings are given and accepted. And on the basis of these undertakings given and received, a personal relationship begins, and over time is intended to grow, and provide healing and sustenance for the covenant partners. The covenant is thus a reciprocal relationship of personal communication, acceptance and trust. It takes place in a moral context, and has a particular moral shape. It is rooted in the covenant words: steadfast love and faithfulness, though it includes the self-giving of sacrifice, the gift of patience when the relationship is strained, and the gift of forgiveness to restore the relationship when it is fractured. The covenant of God with Israel was renewed through the sacrificial system, which kept on reminding the people of God's establishment of them as His own people through the Exodus from Egypt and the judgment of Passover night. The covenant was renewed at the time of Joshua (Joshua 24) was reaffirmed before King David (Psalm 89:28) and was constantly in mind in the prophets (Hosea 11:1, Amos 3:1-2; Micah 7:15-20).

Throughout the story of God's covenant, we are given glimpses of God's way of making relationships. Sometimes the emphasis is on law and obedience, more often on grace, patience and forgiveness. The key words which books like Hosea illustrate so poignantly are steadfast love, faithfulness and forgiveness (Hosea 3:1), whereas Amos reminds us of the divine justice (Amos 5:24), and Micah tells us of the journey of hope (Micah 7:7).

In the New Testament, the covenant theme returns as Jesus is presented as the Mediator of the renewed Covenant, a covenant in His blood. And, especially in the writings of St Paul, He is seen as the One in whom the promises to Abraham come to their fulfilment, the One in whom the covenant with David is completed, and the One in whom all Israel is summed up, embodying the new humanity which comes to birth in the resurrection of Jesus from the dead.

So much for a brief outline of God's covenant. One of the features of this biblical covenant is that it has implications for the way God's people are related not only to him but to each other. The relationships that people establish with each other are intended to reflect something of the divine covenant with them.

The Holiness Code (of Leviticus 19), for example, gave specific instructions as to how the people were to live in many different aspects of their lives, (family, work, religion, agriculture, economics), in order to express the fact that Yahweh is the Lord (Leviticus 19:4-37). In the Old Testament, the relationships of masters to servants, husbands to wives, parents to children, Israelites to strangers and aliens, the divine covenant was meant to be reflected in these covenants which people make with one another. This way of thinking is picked up in the New Testament in the way Christian discipleship is described as following Christ, imitating Christ, obeying Christ, growing in the knowledge and love of God in Christ.

Covenant, in other words, is a relationship of personal communion, based on certain contractual undertakings given and received, but which grows and develops in time within a certain moral context and according to certain moral and spiritual values and goals, so that each can be to the other, as appropriate, a source of healing, growth, sustenance, delight. No wonder the divine covenant is often used in the Bible as a pattern for what a marriage is intended to be. But there are other human covenants than marriage. And in each of these, teacher to pupil, parent to child, doctor to patient, friend to friend, employer to employee – and especially for our present concerns: counsellor or carer to client, pastor to church member – our human covenant is intended to reflect something of God's covenanted ways of relating to us.

The task of Christian ministry, then, could be understood in terms of helping one another find ways of expressing in our human covenants, something of the character of divine faithfulness and love, mercy and justice, righteousness, steadfastness and grace. Recently there has been a renewed emphasis in some Christian writing on a theme which has been obscured, certainly within Protestant Christianity, namely of the vision of God, and the importance of seeing discipleship in terms of growth in Christian character. The covenant model reminds us of this theme. There is obviously an imbalance in the pattern: God is perfect and we are sinful; God is eternal and we are limited by time; God is the source of life and love and we are dependent on Him for life and breath and all things. But it still nevertheless makes sense for us to seek, as far as we are able this side of heaven, and with the aid of the Holy Spirit, to renew our minds in accordance with the mind of Christ (Romans 12:2), to tune our wills to the will of the Father (John 7:1) and to seek first the kingdom of God and His righteousness (Matthew 6:33).

Returning now to the counselling relationship, or the relationship of carer to one who is being cared for: it seems most appropriate to understand this relationship as a covenant. Clearly there is a contractual element: certain goals, terms and limits are decided on, but the relationship is more than a contract. The counsellor models grace by saying 'I am for you; I am with you; I am on your side'. The relationship needs to recognise the moral boundaries within which human flourishing can be aided. The cognitive and other features of personal communication are central to the development of a satisfactory counselling relationship. There is the hope of progress, change and development. Above all, within the counselling or caring relationship, there is mutuality. If we see the Christian's caring and counselling task as a covenant responsibility, that will enable us to keep in mind as we proceed that the appropriate goals, resources, boundaries and limits, are to be determined by reference to the character of God, and our desire in Christian ministry to help one another grow towards Him.

There are two particular features of the processes of Christian caring for and counselling persons which will be our concern for the remainder of this chapter, before we develop in more detail our theology of Christian counselling. The first is the importance of personal variety; the second is the importance of personal development.

Personal Variety

It is worth reminding ourselves of the varieties of human personality. In Christian carers, pastors and counsellors, there is a wide range of approaches, abilities, techniques, and very often our style will depend on not only our training, but our personality - what works for us. There is also a wide variety of personality differences among those we are seeking to help. There are, indeed, many different ways of being religious, and expressing our faith in religious forms. In William James's classic study of religious experience he says that 'the final consciousness which each type reaches of union with the divine has the same practical significance for the individual; and individuals may be allowed to get to it by the channels which lie most open to their several temperaments'.[17]

Not all psychologists these days are comfortable with the concept of 'temperament', but, whatever system of analysis they use, all recognise a rich variety in human personality. From a Christian theological perspective, this opens up discussion of the variety of spiritual gifts used in ministry, and the variety of models of Christian discipleship.

There may be a social-historical dimension to this variety, as an example from Andrew Walls illustrates. He asks us to imagine a long-living scholarly space visitor who makes periodic visits to earth to study Christian behaviour. In AD 37 he visits Jerusalem to find that the Christians were Jews, met in a temple, offered animal sacrifices, used old law books as a sacred text, kept the seventh day holy and appeared to be a sect within Judaism. They identified Jesus of Nazareth as their Messiah. When the space visitor came back in AD 325, however, to Nicea, he saw Christian leaders with hardly a Jew amongst them, who were horrified at the idea of animal sacrifices, kept the first day of the week as their holy day, used the law books used by the Christians in Jerusalem but had others with them, and used titles like 'Lord' to refer to the same Jesus of Nazareth. Three hundred years later on the coast of Ireland, the space visitor found a group of men in a common habit, standing ice-cold up to their necks in cold water reciting psalms. They were deeply concerned about personal holiness. Holiness was also a major preoccupation of the Christians some centuries later in the nineteenth century at Exeter Hall in London, where a large crowd were listening to speeches about Africa. They proposed to send missionaries with Bibles and cotton seed to Africa, and were much concerned about holiness, but had no interest at all in standing in cold water. Their concerns were much more political, the abolition of slavery and other social issues, which they related to their understanding of their Bibles. When in 1980 in Nigeria, the space visitor asks to see the Christians, he finds a group of excited worshippers in white robes dancing their way to church, proclaiming the healing power of God. They carried the same Bibles as the people in Exeter Hall, but were not at all politically active.

Why, we may ask with Andrew Walls, are there such varieties?

Some are due to cultural changes, some to upbringing and life experience, some to the current ideological and metaphysical thought forms, some due to town size and contemporary political concerns. But other variations may be due also to what many people call 'personality', which is affected by these social issues, but also reflects the individual genetic inheritance, learning experiences and social context of the individual concerned.

To illustrate this, it might be instructive to reflect on the differences between the four Gospels in the New Testament, especially in relation to the pictures they paint of discipleship. Clearly it is difficult to get behind any ancient text to a clear view of the personality of the author, but the pages of the New Testament suggest four very different styles, which are not altogether explained by the different social settings of the writers nor their different readerships:

In Matthew, for example, there is a concentration on the teaching of Jesus, with an emphasis on His authority. There is an interest in law, in order, in judgment, in the fulfilment of OT prophecy. Jesus is presented as fulfilling a prophetic role. If we were to ask the author of Matthew what Christian discipleship means, it would not be unexpected to have an answer in terms of *obedient service, conformity to God's will, duty.*

In Mark, the pace and style is different. There is much activity. The word 'immediately' links paragraphs over 40 times. There is much concentration on the humanity of Jesus, His example, His simplicity, His immediacy, presence, touch. Perhaps for Mark, discipleship would be described in terms of *sensitive and consecrated activity.*

Luke is different yet again. For him there are many more references to compassion, to joy, to expectation. There is a sense not so much of the activity of Jesus as His presence. There are many journeys (from Jerusalem to Jericho, to Emmaus, for example) which do not feature in the other Gospels, and faith is much more often thought of in terms of seeking and searching - for lost coins, lost sheep, a prodigal son. Discipleship for Luke is more of a *quest, a travelling with Jesus.*

In many ways the Fourth Gospel of John is set apart from the Synoptics. While we meet Jesus in His humanity, He is also presented more strongly in His divinity. The images of love, life, light, grace, truth, glory and freedom fill its pages. There is an intimacy (the great prayer of John 17); much more of a self-consciousness ('I am . . .'). Discipleship is about *love in spirit and in truth, a capturing of the spiritual imagination.*

The above list illustrates something of what the First Letter of Peter calls 'God's many-coloured grace' (1 Peter 4:10). He urges his readers that, as each has received a gift, to employ it for one another 'as good stewards of God's varied grace'. St Paul makes the same point by frequently setting his discussion of the varieties of Christian gifts within his exposition of the Christian church as one body of many different members.

We may assume that God intends to use the rich varieties of different personalities in His world and His church - and indeed in the caring and counselling professions - as he does his other gifts of grace. It is therefore essential for carers and counsellors to recognize their own distinctive personality characteristics and those of the people they are seeking to serve.

To give an example, two members of a church were asking for help with a difference which had emerged between them. The vicar was getting annoyed with the caretaker of the church premises (the church building itself and a nearby hall and community centre) for her failure to finish jobs when she started them, for her lack of a sense of duty to her work, her tendency to spend time chatting to people who came by, a lack of loyalty to him as vicar. He did not like the caretaker's familiarity and joviality, and described it in terms of lack of respect for the vicar's authority, and a refusal to do what was asked of her when it was needed. The vicar came with the caretaker for counselling help, wanting the caretaker to recognize her sinful failure, to come to repentance and to mend her ways. The caretaker could not understand this stance at all. She enjoyed having a whole range of tasks on the go at once, so that when she got bored with one she could enjoy another. She did not accept this was a failure in duty, but she did like to order her own timetable to get her work done, and not have every minute dictated by the vicar. She did spend time chatting with people, but she saw that as part of her ministry of warmth, welcome, and providing a human environment in the church premises. She had begun to resent the vicar's 'standing on his dignity' and laying down the law. Were we not members together in Christ's family – why all this 'us and them'? The caretaker refused to see the difficulties in terms of sin on her part. She rather urged the vicar to accept her as a fellow Christian and stop criticising the way she did things. Was there in fact any example of her failing to finish her work when needed?

Clearly the personal dimensions to this relationship had got frayed, and it was being set up in terms of spiritual issues: priestly authority, sin, repentance, obedience. When the counsellor explored some of the personality characteristics of these two, however, on nearly every measure they were polar opposites. One was highly extrovert and people-centred, the other more introvert and task-centered. One liked things finished with a heavy sense of closure, the other was more relaxed and open-ended. One focused on duty and authority, the other on relationships and personal warmth. One liked to decide things by what made sense according to his structured forward planning, the other by what felt good at the time. Clearly for a good working relationship these differences needed to be explored, but when the personality factors were exposed, each was more able to see the strengths of the other, and decided to be less inclined to dress up their differences in 'spiritual' terms.

There have been a number of attempts to classify personality and temperament differences over recent years, though many psychologists as we said, are unhappy about the concept of 'temperament', and there is little consensus on how best to classify 'personality'.

From Jung's initial work in the 1920's,[18] there has grown the Myers-Briggs Type Indicator,[19] now widely used in many different professional fields from career counselling and vocational guidance, to spiritual direction in various religious communities. This is based on the declared preferences of individuals, accessed through questionnaire techniques:

for 'extraversion or introversion' in relation to the source of personal energy;

for 'sensing' or 'intuition' in relation to information-gathering processes;

for 'thinking' or 'feeling' functions in relation to decision-making processes;

for 'judging' or 'perceiving' depending on the person's preference for closure and decidedness, or for openness and spontaneity in relation to the external world.

This leads to sixteen possible combinations, and some further mixed combinations, of preferences, which - it is held - give an indication as to personality preferences with regard to behaviour patterns, work and relationship skills, capacities to work with groups and so on.

The value of such an inventory is that it provides a way of posing a person with the question 'Is this me?' It can be a most useful tool in self-discovery, in recognising strengths and weaknesses, and in showing areas of life a person may wish to work at and develop. Its danger is that it can be used as a sort of deterministic astrology: 'This is me', which feeds into a fatalism, and a refusal to change when that is both appropriate and possible.

There are other ways of classifying personality. Eysenck[20] used four dimensions expressed on two axes: Unstable to Stable and Introverted to Extroverted, and suggested various descriptions of personality characteristics on these four axes:[20]

Unstable and Extroverted might be touchy, restless, aggressive, excitable, changeable, impulsive, optimistic, active;

Extroverted and Stable leads to sociable, outgoing, talkative, responsive, easygoing, lively, carefree, leadership;

Stable and Introverted covers calm, even-tempered, reliable, controlled, peaceful, thoughtful, careful, passive;

Introverted and Unstable includes quiet, unsociable, reserved, pessimistic, sober, rigid, anxious, moody.

More recently, some psychologists[21] have put together what some call 'The Big Five' factors in personality:

Factor	Description
Emotional stability	calm versus anxious secure versus insecure self-satisfied versus self-pitying
Extraversion	sociable versus retiring fun-loving versus sober affectionate versus reserved
Openness	imaginative versus practical preference for variety versus preference for routine independent versus conforming
Agreeableness	soft-hearted versus ruthless trusting versus suspicious helpful versus uncooperative
Conscientiousness (the will to achieve)	well-organized versus disorganized careful versus careless self-disciplined versus weak-willed

Whether or not such analysis can be shown to be based on physiological or other differences at the genetic or hormonal level of human being, they illustrate something of the rich variety of human diversity, which all carers and counsellors need to acknowledge. Part of the story of any person's request for help, or need for care, will be their own personality. This may include their own genetic inheritance, their own early learning experiences and responses to external environments, their own system of values and learned or chosen goals in life; their own pattern of attitudes and cognitive and behavioural responses to certain situations. In sum, we could say that our genetic inheritance, plus our early environment, plus our assumed values, hopes and goals, contribute to what we might call our 'personality'. When our personality interacts with, acts in, or responds to a particular social environment, it leads to the attitudes, behaviour patterns, anxieties, stresses, needs, fears and joys that we observe in one another.

There is thus in each of us something uniquely 'us', which cannot be adequately expressed through psychotherapeutic labels, nor adequately responded to through a routine counselling technique. Alongside all that must rightly be said about the inescapable importance of community and indeed, must be much more emphasised in our culture which has become so over-individualized - we must not lose sight of the precious, unrepeatable, rich and God-given variety of individual human persons, whose individuality is a function of and contributes to the network of relationships in which they are set.

Personal Development

If we are 'persons on the way', then part of the task of Christian ministry is to enable each other to grow up as people and grow up into maturity in Christ. In the belief that all truth is God's truth, we take seriously the insights from developmental psychologists into the ways human beings change, grow and mature.

In broad outline, the major psychological approaches to human development operate with stage models, for example, for cognitive, social and moral development. We can benefit from the ways in which psychologists such as James Fowler open up insights into human development.

The best known model of cognitive development is that of the Swiss psychologist Jean Piaget,[22] who defined four stages in which young children's cognitive capacities develop, and in which rational operations of different sorts become possible. His work has been subjected to radical critique,[23] and most psychologists today have moved beyond Piaget's tidily defined chronological model, but its value in opening up exploration of the processes of cognitive development was very significant.

Erik Erikson[24] proposed a model of psychosocial development, related to the growth of a sense of personal identity, a model which has been widely appreciated and used. Following, but moving much further than Freud, and focusing not on biological instincts but critical psychosocial phases, Erikson identified eight stages which cover the entire life span, organized around the concerns that different social pressure place upon an individual at different times of life. Again, Erikson is not without critics, but his eight stages have proved remarkably persistent as a basis for discussing the development of personal identity.

Erikson's psychosocial stages cover the balances achieved between:

trust and mistrust (early months);
autonomy and shame (subsequent early months);
initiative and guilt (first few years);
industry and inferiority (latency period);
identity and role confusion (adolescence);
intimacy and isolation (young adulthood);
generativity and stagnation (mid-life);
integrity and despair (older ages).

The psychology of moral development has received a major contribution from the work of Lawrence Kohlberg.[25] Based to some extent on Piaget's research, Kohlberg identified six stages to describe human capacity for judging in terms of moral principles. Broadly, human beings move from a prudential through an authoritarian to a personal approach to morality. Kohlberg's work has been called in question both from feminist perspectives[26, 27] for working mostly with male candidates, and for a masculine understanding of morality in terms of rule-keeping, and also been criticised by Christian theologians.[28] It does, though, serve to remind us that development of moral capacity is a process.

Such research as that referred to above, together with other recent work in the field of developmental theory, has suggested that faith itself is subject to the wider processes of human growth and development identified by psychologists. The American James

Fowler has brought together an impressive amount of evidence to show that faith is so much woven into the human make-up that we may talk in terms of 'stages of faith' as we mature as human beings.[29] Put another way, faith cannot be isolated from the total psychological and physical developmental processes which are common to us all.[29-34]

Fowler's claim has been disputed by some Christians on the ground that such a view seems to reduce faith to a purely human experience. This would be a valid objection if faith development theory argued that faith were *nothing but* the product of wider processes. But neither Fowler nor those who accept his argument favour this kind of 'nothing-buttery'. They contend, rather, that all humans have some kind of faith by virtue of having been created by God and retaining something of His image, however marred or weakened by sin.

This does not mean to say that they possess saving faith. For such faith is the work of the Holy Spirit in regeneration (to use terminology drawn from Reformed theology). However, all human beings possess some sort of faith, whether directed towards a religious figure or towards an ideology or person. It is this which must be understood in relation to human developmental stages.[31]

Michael Jacobs has discussed fully a number of developmental models for understanding Christian faith maturing.[35] What is important for our purposes is the underlying insight that in order to counsel a person in distress it is helpful, even essential, to know where they have reached within the developmental process.[36] It is here that the insights of faith development theory become central.

The Fowler Model

Fowler's model is explicitly scientific in orientation and method, owing fundamentally to the work of Jean Piaget, Lawrence Kohlberg, Erik Erikson and latterly also to Robert Selman and Robert Kegan.[33] Based on considerable empirical research,

Fowler has constructed a model comprising seven stages. He regards these as hierarchical, sequential and invariant. That is to say, each stage follows on from previous stages in an incontrovertible order leading from lower to higher. Individuals cannot skip stages and thereby have to progress through the hierarchy. Each stage must be experienced in turn. Moreover, successive stages are increasingly complex: 'Each new stage builds on and incorporates into its more elaborate structures the operations of previous stages'.[37]

These are not merely vague phases of development but are well-defined, integrated units incorporating observable empirical characteristics which mark out one stage from another. Each is a 'structural whole . . . a dynamic unity constituted by internal connections among its differentiated aspects'.[38] Movement from stage to stage is triggered by crises and challenges which threaten the equilibrium of a person's current stage of development. Life crises such as bereavement or divorce would typically bring about transition between stages.

Fowler's seven stages are not rigidly tied to chronological age but nonetheless can be related to human growth and development through the life cycle:

Stage 0: Primal faith Faith is experienced as simple pre-linguistic trust. It is the faith of babyhood engendered by an infant's trust in its mother.

Stage 1: Intuitive-projective faith This is the stage of unordered yet powerful images. The child constructs meaning by using these images to interpret experience but no concepts are yet available to order them intellectually.

Stage 2: Mythic-literal faith The child between 6 or 7 and 11 develops thinking skills based on a literal interpretation of the world. Story telling is crucial to development but abstract thinking is not yet a feature.

Stage 3: Synthetic-conventional faith The adolescent develops abstract thinking abilities and so is able to create meaning beyond the literal. This is also the stage of conformity to peer group beliefs and may continue well into adulthood.

Stage 4: Individuative-reflective faith The young adult develops critical judgment and begins to choose faith for his- or herself: a 'critical distancing from one's previous value system'.

Stage 5: Conjunctive faith The dissolution of previous certainties sets in. The adult (typically in mid-life) must rework the faith meaning created in previous stages, often under the impact of a life crisis. The hallmark of this stage is critical openness.

Stage 6: Universalizing faith A very rare stage attained by few usually later in life. Its central characteristic is the abandonment of self. Fowler cites Mother Teresa of Calcutta, Dag Hammarskold and Martin Luther King as examples.

From this it can be seen that the counsellor's task would be greatly facilitated by identifying and understanding which stage underlies the counsellee's situation and response. For this reason, Fowler's work has been welcomed by psychologists of religion, educators and pastoral carers alike. It offers some analytical tools for both counsellor and counsellee. While it would be true to say that Fowler's theories have not gone without criticism and that they should not be erected into a rigid ideology, nonetheless the insight that faith moves through identifiable developmental stages is a valuable one.

As one recent evaluator has put it: 'It is possible to view the work of Fowler and others as a useful tool . . . while more careful amplified work is always needed, and theoretical criticism is always essential, some of the central themes of faith development are too important . . . to be cavalierly ignored.[39] For a much less positive view of cognitive development see Margaret Donaldson.[40, 41]

We conclude this chapter by reminding ourselves of the essentially relational nature of human personhood. We are not isolated individuals, despite the rich variety of our individuality. We are not simply part of the mass of humanity, despite the common processes of development we may all share. Our calling, gift and task is to share in and reflect something of the nature of God as persons in relation to other persons, persons in communion, persons in fellowship. Christian counselling is part of the wider task of Christian ministry in helping one another to grow into our true humanity in Christ. It is to the fuller exploration of the shape, task and resources for that ministry that we now turn.

THE GRACE OF OUR LORD, JESUS CHRIST

Christian ministry is a process of being caught up into the ongoing activity of God the Holy Trinity. In some senses it becomes difficult, if not rather artificial, to separate out the Persons of the Trinity as a basis for our further exploration. However, it might help our discussion to focus attention separately on different aspects of our caring and counselling ministries to use the headings of the Christian benediction: 'The grace of our Lord Jesus Christ and the Love of God and the Fellowship of (or 'in', or 'created by') the Holy Spirit, be with you all' (2 Corinthians 13:14).

In this chapter, with its focus on the grace of Christ, we will concentrate on the *shape* of our ministry as Christian people, united with Christ, for whom his teaching, example, life, death, and resurrection are our life and our guide. In the following chapter, focussing on the love of God, we will explore more fully the *task* of the Christian counsellor to be a channel for the love which liberates and heals. Then we shall focus on the Holy Spirit and the fellowship the Holy Spirit creates as our *resource* in the counselling and caring opportunities and responsibilities of ministry.

Any biblically rooted theology of ministry needs to say much about grace. We spoke earlier of an optimism of grace. We have already looked at the covenant of grace, and noticed how the pastoral relationships of caring and counselling can be understood as covenants which - in their own appropriate ways - can reflect and participate in God's covenant of grace with his people.

One of the key themes of the New Testament, particularly clearly expressed in the Epistle to the Galatians, is that Jesus Christ is the focus, climax, and consummation of the covenant which God made with Abraham. Paul described Jesus as the true child of Abraham, and all those who 'walk by the Spirit' in union with Jesus Christ as sons of Abraham. Through Israel, God's promise to Abraham means that Israel becomes a light which shines out to all the nations around, so in Jesus, the embodiment of Israel, we see the new humanity summed up. Jesus is the true human being. In Him all God's purposes for Israel, and therefore for the whole human race, are to be achieved. To be a true human being is to be united to Jesus Christ.

Jesus is also depicted in the New Testament as the fulfilment of the Jewish expectations for a Messiah. The people of God were hoping for a deliverer to come, to confront oppressive powers and set the people of God free. This expectation was expressed by the prophet Isaiah in terms of giving good tidings to the afflicted, binding up the broken hearted, bringing liberty to captives, opening the prison for those who are bound, and proclaiming God's mercy and judgement. Jesus takes this prophecy onto His own lips in Nazareth: 'Today this scripture has been fulfilled' (Luke 4:18).

Jesus Christ himself, in other words, embodies both the covenanted promises of God, as His Word spoken to His people, and also the authentic human response of willing obedience. Jesus is the True Human Being, in whose light, we can see ourselves to be - as John Macquarrie once put it, - Human Becomings. Or to use T. F. Torrance's rather more opaque expression: He is the Personalising Person, we are Personalised Persons. He is God's Messiah, God's liberator, the One through whom humanity is set free from its hurts and bonds to become more truly human.

A crucial perspective on the tasks of Christian ministry - including those on which we are concentrating, namely caring and counselling - will be to understand the mode of Christ's ministry in grace, and see what implications that has for our ministries.

In the following paragraphs we will pick out several different aspects of the ways in which the grace of God comes to us in the life and ministry of Jesus, His incarnation, handling of people, death and resurrection, and explore their relevance for Christian ministry today.

His Incarnation

One of the key components of successful counselling, everyone agrees, is empathy. By this is meant a willingness on the part of the counsellor to stand with another in their pain, and so to communicate an understanding of the painful situation without becoming submerged by it, that the hurting person feels understood.

The incarnation of Christ, His taking human form and coming among us as a servant, gives us a model of empathetic involvement. Some years ago Thomas Oden wrote a ground-breaking study called *Kerygma and Counselling.* He built on Karl Barth's doctrine of the analogy of faith beginning with God's action as it is received in faith, and then seeking to understand our human relationships from that vantage point. Part of that analogy is the incarnation of Jesus Christ. 'Incarnation means that God assumes our frame of reference, entering into our human situation of finitude and estrangement, sharing our human condition, even unto death.[1] This, Oden argued, gives a meaning to human empathy, which is itself 'the precondition of all therapeutic effectiveness'. Empathy involves the descent of the therapist into the depths of the hell, and internal conflict and alienation of the client. This is directly analogous to the incarnate love of 'God with us'. God, in Christ, has Himself 'taken up our cause.'[2]

The incarnation speaks of God dwelling for a time in our midst; as the Fourth Gospel puts it, He 'tabernacled with us'.

The kenotic hymn of Philippians 2.5-7 draws the analogy directly: 'Have this mind among yourselves which you have in Christ Jesus who . . . emptied Himself, taking the form of a servant.' Further, 'even as God participates in our estrangement without being estranged from Himself, likewise the therapist participates in the estrangement of the client without losing his self-identity.'[3] The effective counsellor continues to be himself, to feel his own feelings, and is not submerged in the feelings of the client. Here is the crucial and well-known distinction between a proper empathy (which communicates 'That must make you feel . . .') and an unhelpful sympathy (which says 'I know exactly how you feel, I feel the same myself . . .') Oden develops the theme by discussing the congruence between God the Father and God the Son: in the incarnation God does not lose his identity; it is the very congruence of His being that gives hope to those whose frame of reference He assumes.

Clearly there are places where the analogy between the incarnation of Christ and our own ministry breaks down. We do not have divine knowledge. Our involvement with others is constrained by many limits – in ourselves and in our world. And we do not have divine power. But even so, the therapist, whether Christian or not, is displaying something of the grace of God incarnate in Christ, when sitting alongside another person, to understand, interpret and help them live with less pain. 'The counsellor may be totally unaware of the Christian *kerygma* concerning the divine Word of which his work is an analogue. When effective, however, he himself is nevertheless existentially involved in a process which embodies that Word.'[4]

We do well to see Christian caring and counselling ministries as ways of 'embodying the Word'. There is a place, of course, in Christian ministry for the 'proclamation of the Word' (and some of the 'moral' approaches to counselling adopt a proclamation model). There is a place for 'teaching the Word' (and some of the cognitive approaches may be understood in such terms). But there is a powerful and effective ministry understood as an 'embodiment of the Word', which is what the relational models of counselling, sometimes unknowingly, exercise.

When a social worker comes alongside a family in distress – the husband has left the wife with three teenage children, the oldest is on drugs, the younger two continually at war with each other – part of the ministry is to 'be there'. When a young person is suffering with a post-viral fatigue following an illness immediately after 'doing God's work' on an exhausting summer beach camp, and her faith in God's goodness and purpose is going through some trials, the pastor's first task is to 'be there'.

In *The Go-Between God*, John Taylor movingly describes such ministry to a bereaved West Indian woman whose husband had been killed in a street accident. The woman was numbed, in a state of shock. 'For a long time her terrible tranced look continued to embarrass the family, friends and officials who came and went. Then the schoolteacher of one of her children, an Englishwoman, called, and seeing how things were, went and sat beside her. Without a word she threw an arm around the tight shoulders, clasping them with her full strength. The white cheek was thrust hard against the brown. Then as the unrelenting pain seeped through to her the newcomer's tears began to flow, falling on their two hands linked in the woman's lap. For a long time that was all that was happening. And then at last the West Indian woman started to sob. Still not a word was spoken and after a little while the visitor got up and went, leaving her contribution to help the family meet its immediate needs.'

'That' says Bishop Taylor, 'is the embrace of God, His kiss of life. That is the embrace of His mission and of our intercession. And the Holy Spirit is the force in the straining muscles of an arm, the film of sweat between pressed cheeks, the mingled wetness on the backs of clasped hands. He is as close and unobtrusive as that, and as irresistibly strong.'[5]

The grace of God is incarnate in Jesus Christ. This is part of what Stanley Hauerwas calls 'Suffering presence.'[6] Christian ministry is 'incarnational'.

The Emotional Life of Christ

Ministry is also inevitably engaged with our emotional life - a part of life which many Christians find disturbing or even frightening. Sometimes we have developed such a cognitive, even rationalistic, approach to faith, as heirs of that Christian tradition which sees the rational mind as the control over our wayward bodily instincts, that we are scared of our feelings, and are we not sure how to get them 'under control'.

B. B. Warfield wrote an illuminating paper entitled *On the*

Emotional Life of Our Lord,[7] discussing the humanity of Jesus. He begins by saying that 'It belongs to the truth of our Lord's humanity that He was subject to all sinless human emotions.' He then goes on to survey all the Gospel references to Jesus' emotion, beginning with compassion and love; moving on to the moral sense which reacts to evil in terms of indignation and anger, then the afflictions of the Man of Sorrows leading to the joy that was set before Him. Jesus' soul is troubled; there is a repugnance to all that death meant. He is distressed and despondent (Matthew 26:37), or as Mark has it, appalled and despondent (Mark 14:33); sorrowful unto death; the agony of Gethsemane; the anguish of dereliction of the Cross. Sometimes Jesus experiences wonder (Matthew 8:10; Luke 7:9); once desire is attributed to him (Luke 22:15). He had set his heart on eating with his disciples; and once he speaks of himself as conceivably the subject of shame (Mark 8:38). Warfield goes on:

> Our Lord's emotions fulfilled themselves as ours do in physical reactions. He who hungered (Matthew 4:2), thirsted (John 19:20), was weary (John 4:6), who knew both physical pain and pleasure, expressed also in bodily affections the emotions that stirred his soul . . . Not only do we read that he wept (John 11:35), and wailed (Luke 19:41), sighed (Mark 7:34) and groaned (Mark 8:12), but we read also of his angry glare (Mark 3:5), his annoyed speech (Mark 10:14), his chiding words (Mark 3:12), the outbreaking ebullition of his rage (John 11:33,38); of the agitation of his bearing when under strong feeling (John 11:35), the open exultation of his joy (Luke 10:21), the unrest of his movement in the face of anticipated evils (Matthew 26:37), and the loud cry which was wrung from him in his moment of desolation (Matthew 27:46). Nothing is lacking to make the impression strong that we have before us in Jesus a human being like ourselves.'[8]

There is thus a full range of emotions, yet in the expression of them Jesus is, as Warfield put it, 'master of himself'. There are those, Christian people among them, who will not allow themselves to feel anger, or do not have the freedom to exult with abandoned joy. There are those who believe it would be a sign of weakness to shed a tear at a triumphant Christian funeral. Others are so caught up in the anxieties and stresses of life, that their emotional hatches have to be kept firmly battened down in order, it seems, to survive. One of the riches of the New Testament picture of Jesus is that He is emotionally free.

The importance of this for Christian carers is to reassure us that it is possible within a human life to find ways of expressing emotions appropriately and in a way that is pleasing to God. It also encourages us that it is safe to try to learn how to release and use our emotions appropriately, because He has been there too. As the writer to the Hebrews put it 'He is not untouched with the *feeling* of our infirmities'. (Hebrews 4:15). This, too, is an expression of grace.

Intimacy and Openness

One of the key Gospel passages for understanding the ministry of Christ, and therefore our ministry within the Body of Christ, is Matthew 11:25-30. 'All things have been delivered to me by my Father; and no one knows the Son except the Father, and no one knows the Father except the Son and anyone to whom the Son chooses to reveal Him.'

The revelation of God to the world through His Son, Jesus Christ, derives from the intimacy of relationship within the Godhead. Jesus refers to God as 'Father, Lord of heaven and earth' (v.25).

Elsewhere, he prays to the Father using the intimacy of the family word 'Abba' (Mark 14:36). It is from that intimacy that the Son knows His own identity. He knows His status and He knows His task. It is not surprising, therefore, that the paragraph immediately moves into pastoral care: 'Come to Me, all who labour and are heavy laden, and I will give you rest.' The offer of support, refreshment and rest for our souls comes from the lips of One who knows His Father, and knows why He has been sent.

The pattern is very close to that developed by Dr Frank Lake from his studies in the Gospel of John and which he called 'The Dynamic Cycle'.[9] Drawing on the life of Christ depicted in the Fourth Gospel, the Dynamic Cycle in the Life of Christ begins with **acceptance**. Christ is accepted as the Son by the Father: 'This is My beloved Son'. He knew the intimacy of going up the mountain to pray. He knew the closeness of constant access to God: 'I know that Thou hearest Me always' (John 11:42). The second phase of the Cycle is **sustenance**. Jesus draws emotional strength from 'abiding' in the Father: 'I am in the Father and the Father in Me' (John 14:11); He has the gifts of the Holy Spirit without measure (John 3:34). Phase 3 is described by Frank Lake as **status**. Jesus knows who He is: 'I am from above' (8:23); 'I am' the light, the bread, the vine, the Good Shepherd, the door, the way the truth the life, the resurrection. And that sense of status leads to phase 4, **achievement**. His work, to 'do the works of Him who send Me' (9:4), is depicted in the images of giving light to the world, providing the bread from heaven, giving life, being the truth that sets us free. This cycle of acceptance leading to sustenance, in relation to Christ's intimacy with the Father, leads to status, and to achievement in Christ's openness to the world in obedience to the Father. Lake then uses this model as a hypothesis for the analysis of the origin of normal, healthy human development and personal interactions.

Although Lake's theological undergirding of the model has not been without criticism, the model itself (closely linked as it is with various other theoretical models in Object Relations theory, for example), has proved very useful for Christian carers and counsellors. It not only provides an insight into clients' personal journeys and needs, but provides a check on the counsellor's own life story and needs also.

Furthermore, this pattern of Christ's ministry gives an example to all who would minister in His name. The closeness of our relationships of intimacy with God, is inescapably linked with our own sense of spiritual sustenance and status, which again affects our ability to serve others. As with Jesus, so with us, there needs to be a rhythm of engagement and withdrawal, of healing the crowds on the beach, and a retreat to the hills to pray, of six days creative activity and a sabbath rest of creative renewal. Without such a rhythm, we either (Type A personalities) live on our adrenalin with too much stress, and end up with heart disease, or (Type B personalities), find ourselves experiencing burn-out, related to unreal expectations, unfulfilled demands and consequent depressed disappointment.

The grace of our Lord Jesus Christ comes to us from the relationship of intimacy with God his father, and an openness to others. Our ministry of grace to others needs the same rhythm.

Jesus at Work

There is one particularly instructive incident in the Gospel narrative from which we may draw some implications for pastoral care. The last healing miracle recorded in Mark is the story of the healing of Bartimaeus, (Mark 10:46–52). It feels as though it is the record of eyewitnesses. Was Bartimaeus known in the Church to which Mark was writing? Jesus is on his way to Jerusalem (10:32), with all that that implied for Jesus' mission (cf. Luke 9:51, when the days drew near for him to be received up, he set his face to go to Jerusalem). And yet he has time for the blind beggar who is calling out 'Jesus, Son of David, have mercy on me!' We read first that 'Jesus stopped' (10:49). And in that stopping there is grace. Here is the gift of time and attention to one who is in need. Jesus is listening to the cry of someone's heart and making space in his own pre-planned schedule to give this person attention. All pastoral ministry begins with stopping, listening and giving space.

Secondly, Jesus' next move is to offer hope. He tells His followers to 'Call him', and they interpret this optimistically: 'Take heart, rise, He is calling you.' Implicit in this exchange is the gift of hope that things can change. Jesus' words also helped the man to make a decision for change: 'He sprang up and came to Jesus'. Pastoral ministry must always be ministry in hope. Clearly there are unhelpful ways in which expectancies can be inappropriately raised, impossible cures promised, easy answers offered to complicated tangles of emotional questions. It is also the case that, this side of heaven, some of us seem to have to live with handicap, disability, sickness or pain. But despite the ambiguity of the human condition, there can be substantial change in life here on earth. And the Christian has every reason for confidence that the road closer to Christ is the road closer to wholeness of body and mind. Pastoral ministry lives and works in encouragement and hope – not that all sicknesses will be cured, but that for all who ask, there is grace to help in time of need. (Cf. Hebrews 4:16). We clearly cannot promise an answer to all questions, a panacea for all ills. We are part of a creation which is groaning (Romans 8:10), waiting for its redemption. But we can promise grace. The grace of which St Paul learned when three times he had cried to God in his distress. God's reply was 'My grace is sufficient for you'. Grace which brings to birth in us the faith, not that we have all the answers, but that it is safe to live with the uncertainties, for we are loved with an everlasting love, and God does not let go of our hand.

Thirdly, Jesus leaves the responsibility for choosing to ask for help with the person in need. The question 'What do you want Me to do for you?' was hardly necessary if it were simply a request for information. It was obvious to everyone what the man wanted and needed. But by asking it, and requiring Bartimaeus to put his request into words, would not only have strengthened Bartimaeus' faith, but also left him with the dignity of carrying a measure of responsibility for himself. One of the primary purposes of Carl Roger's client-centred approach to counselling, and indeed of many of the 'moral' models which tend to criticize Rogers, is to give back to the client their own responsibility. Pastoral ministry needs to beware of the syndrome of co-dependency, in which the carer's need to be needed, overrides the good of those they are seeking to help. Some of us offer services of healing, counselling, care, more for our own affirmation than for the needs of the clients. There is great wisdom in the pattern of James 5, when those who are sick are encouraged to 'call for the elders of the church'. It is not for the elders to say 'we are coming to help you now', but for them to make clear that their willingness to help is on offer, whenever they are called. This seems to be the pattern of Jesus with Bartimaeus.

The Prince of Peace

We noted earlier that the Messianic mission of Christ is closely linked with the OT sense that God's Messiah will bring *shalom*. Often translated 'peace', shalom as we have said, means much more than the absence of conflict. When the Lord brings *shalom* there is contentedness and a sense of well-being at all levels of life and in all human relationships. It is not surprising that frequently the biblical writers use the concepts of *shalom* and *healing* very closely together. Health is part of the meaning of *shalom*, and in several places in the Old Testament, *shalom* is bracketed together with the Hebrew word translated 'health'. The vision of peace in Isaiah 2:1-5 is set in contrast to the sickness of the nation (1:5-6), its idolatry (2:6-22), and social injustice (3:13-15). These ills bring the judgement that the Lord will not be a healer (3:7b). The Suffering Servant brings justice to the nations (42:1-4), and suffers for the healing and atonement of the people: upon Him was the chastisement that made us whole (*shalom*), and with His stripes we are healed (53:5).

And in several places in the NT, *shalom* and health are linked together (Luke 10:5-9; Acts 10:36-38; Mark 5:24-34; Hebrews 12:13-14; I Peter 2:13 - 3:12). God's purposes for humanity are that we should know and live in the light of His kingdom of righteousness, justice and peace. In the synoptic Gospels, the coming of the Kingdom of Christ is depicted as a conflict with the prince of this world, and the exorcisms and healings demonstrate that Jesus is the Messiah. Jesus Christ is the bringer of peace, *shalom*, wholeness and health and Christian ministers are likewise to be ministers of reconciliation.

When a Christian couple open their home to a young wife who cannot make her marriage work, and give time and attention to her, and then to her husband; when they together as a foursome work at ways of deepening the communication between the aggrieved couple, helping them to recognize that conflict does not necessarily mean breakdown but can be an opportunity for creative renegotiation of the relationship; when as a result of that the couple decide to explore ways of living more creatively together, there is the Prince of Peace.

He is there too whenever a person is helped towards greater health, physically, emotionally, spiritually; whenever some disorder or injustice is confronted and put right; whenever a person harbouring resentments is given the courage to forgive.

Justice and the Honour of God

One of the most dramatic incidents in the Gospel stories is the cleansing of the temple. In St John's account, it is placed at the start of Jesus' ministry (John 2:13-17) as his first great public action. In the synoptic accounts, it is his last public act, placed at the climax of his ministry. For their different reasons, and in their different ways, the Gospel writers use the story to demonstrate the Messianic ministry of Christ. It is not only His zeal for the honour of God in that the house of prayer had been turned into a den of robbers, it is His clear distinction between the religion of law and the gift of grace. The action of Christ brings a purge. It demonstrates His own authority right in the centre of Judaism. It shows that Jesus fulfils the faith of Israel. Underneath this action, we can catch echoes of the call for justice in Amos, where once again religious institutions had become taken over for other ends. Perhaps under the rage of Amos, and the yearning for God's honour, we can also hear the quest for reconciliation which is depicted so tenderly in Hosea. Perhaps there is here a fulfilment of the high point of eighth-century prophecy in the Old Testament. 'He has showed you, O man, what is good, and what does the Lord require of you, but to do justly, to love kindness and to walk humbly with your God' (Micah 6:8).

The ministry of Jesus, the bringer of *shalom*, is a ministry of justice, and righteousness, which sometimes has to sweep away money changers and their tables of trade.

Calvin sees evidence of what he calls the 'common grace' of God in those social institutions which curb evil and promote a context for good. The quest for social justice in the work of Wilberforce and Shaftesbury and the many they have inspired, can be understood as part of the working of God's common grace through the establishment of more just social structures.

In the Report of the 1988 Lambeth Conference of Anglican Bishops, their discussion of mission includes a summary of the signs of the presence of God's kingdom. They refer not only to men and women becoming new creatures in Christ, to their healing at spiritual, physical and emotional levels, to their formation into the likeness of Christ through the Holy Spirit. They refer also to the time when 'the poor are no longer hungry and are treated justly as God's beloved', and to the time when 'unjust structures of society are changed into structures of grace.'[10]

All Christian caring and counselling is set within a social context in which questions of social justice and the healthiness or otherwise of social structures are necessarily part of the story. The Christian task is to further as far as possible 'the structures of grace'.

Miriam is a mother just going through the trauma of a very nasty divorce. She has two children. The older one is 18, quiet and hoping to get married soon. Miriam wants her daughter's marriage to work better than her own has done. The mother worries about her. But then she worries about everything. So much so that the GP is tired of her worryings and regards her as a nuisance. The younger daughter is 14, up until now a good girl, but recently uncontrollable. She has been refusing to go to school for some weeks. The educational social workers have tried to speak to her; the school seems to have lost any authority. It has recently been said that she is spending a lot of time with young men, some older teenagers and some in their twenties. They stay out for the whole night in the house of a friend. The rumour is of drugs and group sex. Miriam, the mother, becomes frantic. Her neighbour thinks the daughter is at risk, and that the mother's health is fragile. She rings the social services for help. Their staff member is not available, but says she will pass the information on to the adolescent unit. The neighbour rings the GP to ask him to contact the social services urgently but is told that he knows the family well and that she should not interfere. The neighbour rings the police who do send someone round, but say it is really the job of the social services. Meanwhile, the educational social worker sends a letter to Miriam to say that if the daughter does not go back to school, they will take legal proceedings against her.

In desperation, the neighbour asks the local clergyman, a neighbour of hers for help. How does he fit into this picture of professional care?

- What is his role in relation to hard-pressed social services, which appear to be doing their best with insufficient resources, but in which one department does not seem to know what another does?
- Should he contact the doctor and put another point of view, or would he, too, be regarded as another interfering do-gooder?
- Is it his role simply to give Miriam time and attention to work through her feelings, or does his care extend to the daughters, and the now exhausted neighbour?
- Does caring mean confronting the social structures and seeking to bring some humanity and justice into what comes over to Miriam as threatening and unfair?
- How should he go about doing that?

It is instructive at this point to recall Robert Lambourne's discussion of the healing ministry of Jesus. Lambourne saw Jesus' healings essentially as community events. 'The healing works of Jesus are visible signs of the breaking through of the power of God . . . and therefore they are moments both of salvation and judgement for the community in which the healing work is done.'[11]

Pastoral ministry is a ministry of grace. And that sometimes means a ministry of moral demand, social justice and religious discipline. The clergyman cannot help Miriam at all in her needs without opening himself up to the social setting of her need.

Grace in the Cross and Resurrection of Christ

One of the most powerful themes in the New Testament is that Christ has suffered for us. In the passion and death of Jesus, God is showing His love to us and the extent of His willingness to be identified with human suffering, alienation and despair. In the God-forsaken cry of Jesus on the cross, not only is God suffering in the suffering of Jesus, but Jesus is identifying with all of us who, at any time and for many reasons, have cried out 'My God, why?'

Part of the power of this theme is Christ's empathetic involvement with us. As Roger Hurding has written:

> Sometimes the counsellor is readily empathetic because he too has suffered and has learnt through his suffering. Such an attribute can be seen in Paul's second letter to the Corinthians where he wrote: 'Blessed be the God and Father of our Lord Jesus Christ, the Father of mercies and God of all comfort, who comforts us in all our affliction, so that we may be able to comfort those who are in any affliction, with the comfort with which we ourselves are comforted by God' (2 Corinthians 1:3-4).[12]

St Paul roots this ministry of comfort directly in Christ's sufferings. Because Christ has suffered, He can comfort us, and we in turn not only can see our sufferings as a share in His sufferings, but can also through Him comfort one another.

The centre of the New Testament story of the suffering of Christ is, of course, His death on the Cross. And though the Cross is frequently linked to the forgiveness of our sins, and this is the centre of its meaning, there is even more to the healing which is ours through the Cross. The doctrine of the atonement needs to be expressed more broadly than a focus on individual people finding forgiveness for individual sins. In the Book of Common Prayer service for Holy Communion, there is a prayer thanking God for 'The forgiveness of our sins and all other benefits of his passion.' What are all these 'other benefits'?

Throughout church history, different theologians have tried to find ways of expressing the meaning of the death of Christ for contemporary experience. Some of the early church fathers used the imagery of the slave market – a ransom price paid for our freedom. Anselm wrote about the afront of sin to God's honour, in the language appropriate to a feudal lord. Calvin brought his skills as a lawyer to give an account of atonement in terms of penal substitution, and the removal of guilt. Luther – and more recently Aulen – have concentrated on the metaphor of victory: in the Cross, the principalities and powers are defeated.

A century ago, optimistic liberalism depicted the Cross primarily as an example of loving, sacrificial self-offering, which inspires and motivates love in us. In our post-World War II world, there has been a ready acceptance of the approach eloquently expressed by Jurgen Moltmann in *The Crucified God:* that God suffers with humanity in the suffering of Jesus Christ. All of these metaphors and models can find roots in the New Testament. One of the tasks of contemporary theology is to find ways of expressing the mystery of the atonement in a language which engages with our thought forms and our needs.

Some of the insights of contemporary psychology and sociology can be harnessed to give us a language in which to express the doctrine of the atonement for our day. When Erikson[13] speaks of the processes of maturing involving psycho-social stages related to problems of mistrust, shame, guilt, inferiority and confusion, he is using language most of us understand. When Melanie Klein[14] talks about a 'split ego', and Ronald Laing[15] writes of 'the divided self', they are referring to a sense of personal dislocation which we recognize. In social terms, the language of alienation describes what many in our society experience. And these are all aspects of what the Scriptures mean by sin. To speak of the Cross as 'healing', or 'peace-making', therefore, would seem to engage with the contemporary world more straightforwardly than the language of ransom, redemption, sacrifice, substitution, or even victory. Healing through the crisis and resurrection of Christ can mean:

- the rebuilding of trust in relationships;
- the development of self-esteem in place of shame;
- moral courage and forgiveness in place of guilt;
- a capacity to work and to play, to love and to create, in place of fear;
- the recovery of the sense of belonging and significance in place of alienation.

There was a small group in one church which met as needed to talk and pray with people after services about personal matters. One person, Garry, who had received several weeks of counselling help on a one-to-one basis, decided that he wished to bring himself to God in prayer, and offer to Him some of the things that had come to light through the counselling process. He saw prayer as a way of 'casting our care onto God, for He cares for us' (1 Peter 5:7) of asking for 'grace to help in time of need' (Hebrews 4:16). So Garry and his counsellor joined the prayer group for a special meeting. Very little was said; very little of the detail which had emerged about his traumatic childhood was rehearsed again; some of the painful memories were just too much to say in any case. The group simply prayed together in silence, each person quietly offering this person's pain and need to God, and asking for grace.

Eventually one person asked Garry 'what are you thinking, now?' Garry said that when the prayer started, all he could think of was one particularly painful and cruel incident when he was a child. But as the prayer had continued – for about 5 minutes in silence – he had gradually become aware of a picture in his mind of Jesus and the Cross. As the moments went by, this picture, which began just as a small hint in the corner of his mind, grew and expanded – his arms outstretched in love – until it filled Garry's whole mind. It was a picture of acceptance, of welcome, of peace, of healing. He cried, and was able to thank God for hearing the group's prayers.

It was a very moving moment for all those present. Since then, although if some other event triggers the painful memory, he can still remember the painful moments, when he does, this other picture of Jesus's love now also comes to mind. This was one of the 'other benefits of his passion'. It was a further step into wholeness. It was a gift of grace.

Prophet, Priest and King

We can summarize the ministry of Christ's grace through adopting and modifying the traditional Reformation metaphors of the Offices of Christ: Prophet, Priest and King. These titles of Christ match closely Seward Hiltner's approach to pastoral care in terms of guiding (the Prophet), healing (the Priest) and sustaining (the King). The Ministry of Christ's church, His body, needs to find ways of expressing these dimensions of ministry also. Indeed, the four headings used by Clebsch and Jaekel, which we referred to in Part I also pick up some of these same themes.

In Christ the Prophet there is a proclamation ministry of making clear the Word and will of God. This reminds us that all our ministry, as Don Browning has argued cogently[16, 17], is set in a particular moral context. Moral theology is part of pastoral theology: ethics and pastoral care belong together. In the ministry of Christian caring and counselling, we will recognize the given moral framework of the character of God, and his covenant requirement that his people should live in the light of his character. This is the good life which God wills for us and is in fact for our best good. Without moralizing, without turning counselling into moral directives or giving moral advice (neither of which usually help to develop personal responsibility or maturity), the Christian carer and counsellor will be clear about the moral foundations of their work.

In Christ the Priest, there is a mediatorial and reconciling ministry, bringing people into touch with God, and therefore into touch with each other. Christian ministry must have this reconciling dimension, and part of the work of spiritual direction, and of pastoral counselling is to facilitate the ministry of reconciliation. When the Christian carer and counsellor can help a family live together more harmoniously, can help an employee find more constructive ways of coping with a difficult boss, can sit with the children of a broken home and enable them to relate as well as possible to their foster parents, there is the ministry of Christ the priest.

Part of the function of the King was to establish the kingdom of *shalom*. Isaiah's vision of the coming king (Isaiah 9:2-7), was of a saviour who supports the needy and crushes the oppressor, who establishes justice and so brings peace. The Godly king provides for the needs of his people, sustaining them in what is needed for their welfare. When we speak of sharing in the ministry of Christ the King, the focus is on the material conditions and environments in which people live their lives, the social structures which make for well-being or get in the way of healthy living, and the environments required for meeting the universal human needs of food, friendship, sexuality, shelter, as well as the conditions needed for affirmation, love and the freedom to be creative. Christian caring includes a concern for these dimensions of human *shalom*.

Christian reflection of the Kingly aspects of Jesus' ministry brings before us a reminder that 'healing' should be understood not only in terms of individual disease, illness or sickness, but in the broader social context of public health and environmental restoration. A great deal of Christian writing on health and healing focuses almost exclusively on individual well-being. However, 'health' includes all aspects of personal and social health. We must, in other words, take note of nourishment, clothing, hygiene, housing, recreation, sports, sleep, the social structures which facilitate or impede health, clean drinking water, avoidance of toxic gases, enforcement of speed limits, the priorities in the allocation of scarce health care resources, and the use of epidemiological studies for the preventative aspects to public and community health. These are all of concern to Christ the King.

There is another aspect to his Kingship: Jesus is the Servant King: 'your king comes humble, and riding upon an ass' (Zechariah

8:9-10). His model of ministry is described in Mark 10: 'You know that those who are supposed to rule over the Gentiles lord it over them, and their great ones exercise authority over them. But it shall not be so among you; but whoever would be great among you must be your servant, and whoever would be first among you must be slave of all. For the Son of man also came not to be served but to serve, and to give His life as a ransom for many.'

John's Gospel speaks of Jesus as the 'Lord and Teacher', but this is in the context of his role as the servant, taking the towel to wash his friends' dusty feet (John 13). Christian ministry is never a ministry of lordly domination or authoritarian control. Even the New Testament language of 'headship' is not the language of authority, so much as the language of facilitating the life of the body of which Christ is the head. Christian ministry, and therefore caring and counselling, is always the ministry of service. It is a ministry of making available to one another within Christ's Body, His resources of healing, sustaining and reconciling grace.

THE LOVE OF GOD

Gospel ministry, in Christ and in Christians, begins in and lives in the love of God.

God is love, St John tells us (John 4:8). In His love He freely creates, sustains and redeems His world. His love is expressed in His free creativity, freely giving others their freedom to be. But His freedom is not an arbitrary display of power; His freedom is constrained by His love.

These twin themes of love and freedom seem to reach to the heart of the meaning of ministry. When in the Fourth Gospel, we read that Jesus loved His disciples 'to the end' (John 13:1), immediately, as we noted at the end of the previous chapter, we are given the picture of the Teacher and the Lord taking the servant role and washing the feet of the disciples. Through his loving service, others are given their freedom: 'you are clean'. And we who are 'sent in his name' are not greater than he who did the sending (John 13:16f). We, too, are called to the service of love, that others may find their freedom in Christ.

In the Gospel portraits of Jesus' own life and ministry, we see a person of freedom:

- free from the demands of others' expectancies;
- free from the legalism of religious duty;
- free to make friends with social outcasts;
- free of fear in His speaking of the truth.

It is the freedom of living in the truth. He embodies in His own life the message that he passes on to others: 'If you continue in My word, you are truly My disciples, and you will know the truth, and the truth will make you free . . . and if the Son makes you free, you will be free indeed (John 8:31ff).

In Jesus' life and ministry, we also see 'the love of God made manifest' (I John 4:9). By love is meant the willingness to give oneself, to extend oneself, for the sake of others' growth and health.[1]

This chapter takes further these twin themes of freedom and love in relation to the Christian ministry of caring and counselling. And these themes belong together - as they do in the Being of God Himself. A freedom that is not 'constrained by love' becomes a freedom associated with fear. As Erich Fromm illustrated in *The Fear of Freedom*, there are freedoms that we do not want, and cannot bear; freedoms that are isolating, where relationships are impersonal and insecure; freedoms that drive us towards totalitarian systems in which, vainly, we might hope to belong. But Christian freedom is a freedom suffused by and constrained by love. It is precisely the freedom that comes from belonging in loving relationships with others. It is the freedom of reality celebrated by the Velveteen Rabbit, who, along with other toys in the nursery, became real by being loved:

> The Velveteen Rabbit turned to the old wise experienced Skin Horse in the nursery and asked 'What is real? Does it mean having things that buzz inside you and a stick-out handle? The Skin Horse replied 'Real isn't how you are made. It's a thing that happens to you. When a child loves you for a long, long time, not just to play with, but REALLY loves you, then you become Real.' 'Does it hurt?' asked the Rabbit. 'Sometimes,' said the Skin Horse, for he was always truthful. 'Does it happen all at once, or bit by bit?' 'It doesn't happen all at once,' said the Skin Horse, 'you become. It takes a long time . . . Generally by the time you are Real most of your hair has been loved off, and your eyes drop out, and you get very shabby . . . but once you are Real, you can't become unreal again. It lasts for always.[2]

Here, in wonderful, child-level language, Margery Williams is giving the best possible answer to the individualism which was criticized in Part I of this book. In contrast to Descartes' individualized cogito ('I think, therefore I am'), the Velveteen Rabbit would learn through relationship, gradually over time, with pain and struggle no doubt, to say 'I am loved, therefore I am'. Or perhaps, even, 'we are loved, therefore we are.'

There is, however, a form of 'love' which, rather than creatively setting us free to be and to become real, enslaves us. There is a form of love which does not extend itself for the sake of the others' good and well-being, but is rather a love which smothers. R. D. Laing in *The Divided Self*[3] even talks about a love which 'terrorises'. A love which does not set free, is instead a 'love' which creates dependency, fear and enslavement.

The New Testament paints a picture of human need, and human possibilities, which avoids both the dangers which Fromm and Laing illustrate. We will elaborate this picture further under the two headings 'the love which casts out fear' and 'the truth which sets us free', and draw implications for Christian ministries of caring and counselling.

The Love which Casts out Fear

It seems to be a well-established feature of counselling theory, that far more important than the psychological models which are used, far more important than the therapeutic techniques employed, is the quality of the relationship established between the client and the counsellor. According to the researches of Truax and Carkhuff in 1967[4], the three essential qualities for effective counselling are genuineness, non-possessive warmth, and accurate empathy. When these are present, progress may be possible; when these are absent, progress is much less likely. One fairly extreme example may illustrate why this may be so.

Liz had a difficult home background, a fairly confused adolescence, with bouts of depression. She married at 23, and her first child was born two years later, followed by the second two years after that. The post-natal depression following the first child was contained by antidepressant drugs, but after the second, a girl, Liz had a major breakdown. She was put into hospital, fed with far too much valium, given Lithium Carbonate to try to stablise mood swings and had lengthy electro-convulsive therapy. She saw the psychiatrist for five minutes every week, and most of her therapy was provided by nurses and occupational therapists. She did not make much progress, and it is fair to say that the medical staff got very irritated that she did not seem to improve. No one could get to the bottom of her muddle, and she was accused of giving everyone a different strand to follow up. Liz simply did not fit into any neat psychiatric compartment.

Eventually she was discharged from hospital (too early, some people thought) and was offered a home by a Christian couple who cared for her. Through the supportive love and care of that couple and others in the church, she made considerable progress. Later, she received some Christian counselling of a highly directive and confrontational sort from a qualified therapist, but this, by contrast, did not seem to help. God seemed to stand over her as a threat, making demands.

It was several years later on that Liz, now living more steadily with the help of some antidepressants, but still finding her moods sometimes becoming very bleak and suicidal, started therapy with a psychologist in the health service. He did not offer drugs or ECT; he did not confront her with the text of Scripture. He offered space, warmth and understanding. As the therapy progressed, she felt safe enough to face some of her fears. Her dreams became more explicit and apparently significant. What gradually over time came to the surface from her suppressed memories, was a series of strands which really make sense together only if the truth was that Liz suffered some severe abuse in her very early years. All the circumstantial evidence fits that. Coming to terms with this was painful and difficult, but has been very positive and healing.

In the light of this discovery about herself, it is clear how very far off track the earlier attempts at help had been. The picture of the demanding God had fed the deep seated fears. What had helped (and had been glimpsed a little by the love from the church earlier on), was the provision of a safe enough, warm, caring, unconditional empathetic relationship, which allowed the truth to be looked at without catastrophe. This was an illustration of love extending itself for the sake of another's growth. It was through the loving environment provided by the therapist, and through his understanding and willingness to sit beside Liz and work with her through her struggles, that fears were gradually recognized and named, and 'cast out'.

Part of the reason why many of the relational approaches to therapy work effectively, is not because Kleinian theory can be scientifically supported (it can't), not because Jungian archetypes can be demonstrated (at best, they are useful models), not because Rogerian optimism about human nature is true (human nature itself is much more ambiguous), but because these relational approaches model something of the love of God. Using the title of Winnicott's book, [5] they are providing a 'facilitating environment' in which the 'maturational processes' can take place. That is the work of love: to enable others to find the freedom to be. That is the love which can cast out fear.

Despair

There are many fears which afflict human beings. In *Sickness unto Death* [6] the nineteenth-century Danish thinker, Søren Kierkegaard, suggested that one way of understanding emotional and mental disorder in people, is to interpret their lives as being out of balance. Despair, or fear, results from a loss of the self, perhaps due to imbalances in at least three of the major polarities of our human existence. We could describe this in terms of three axes: the first between 'finitude' and 'infinitude'. By 'finitude' is meant the sense of the mundane, the ordinary in life, the regular routine of being part of this finite created order. Of course, that is part of what life is about, but if our whole perception of life concentrates on this end of the axis; if all we perceive is the mundane and the routine, then we lose ourselves in total conformity, we become just one atom in the human mass, one link in the human chain. We cease to matter any more. And that is the road to despair. However, if we move to the other extreme of this same axis, to 'infinitude', we are talking about the sense of being able to transcend life and its limitations. And if we have an exaggerated view of our abilities here, we may give way to perfectionism, and so to the sort of self-judgement which has disappointment built into it. We will always fail. We will always make mistakes. But if our view of the world is that we should never fail, that also can lead to frustration and fear.

Kierkegaard's second axis runs between the sense of 'necessity' and the sense of 'possibility'. When exaggerated, the sense of necessity, where everything is given and decided and fixed, required and unchanging, leads to the sort of fatalism in which we are robbed of all hope. Once again, nothing I do matters. So I despair. But at the opposite pole of 'possibility', when this becomes unbalanced, the despair of possibility comes from the loss of awareness of the very real constraints that are 'givens' in this world, and we float off into a world of wishful dreaming or malevolent fantasy; of unrealistic hopes or unrealistic dreads.

The third axis joins 'consciousness' to 'unconsciousness'. If we become obsessively fixed at the 'consciousness' pole, we shall end up in the despair of over-explored self-examination, constantly gazing at our navels in a destructive way. But an exaggerated swing to 'unconsciousness' can, by contrast, lead to a lack of appropriate self-reflection, and a failure to recognize the true self within. Such a person becomes essentially spiritless.

For Kierkegaard, then, our health and well-being consists essentially in being able to resolve or live with contradictions. When appropriately balanced, these three polarities are the source of emotional and spiritual health, using the strengths of both ends of each axis. As David Augsburger has commented on Kierkegaard's analysis:

A person finds the means of being authentically grounded in the life-situation, yet capable of transcending it; of actively dealing with the daily necessities of existence yet envisioning possibilities; of living with the free, joyous naivety of childhood, yet with a deep consciousness of self, of others, of life. [7]

We all know people whose emotional lives get out of balance. The 'doormat' people, whose low self - esteem never allows them to lift their heads up high; they are hidden in the human mass, and never find their rich and joyous individuality:

The perfectionists, who are never satisfied, and whose standards are always unattainable: they are always disappointed and frustrated.

The fatalists who have got beyond caring and who 'eat and drink, for tomorrow we die', the fatalists who care very much and live in apprehension.

The dreamers who live in their own world of wish-fulfilment or nightmare, because the real world is too difficult to face.

The navel-gazers who are so self-absorbed with their own needs, their own failures, their own stories, that they never appreciate how their story inevitably impinges on the stories of others.

Those who are totally lacking in self-awareness, and wonder why others find them so abrasive, boring and difficult to live with.

For Kierkegaard, the balance is found and the contradictions handled, through a commitment of faith in the Creator. At each point the possibility of falling off balance, and of despair and fear, stares at us because we are faced with ambiguity. There is always a choice. To make the choices which align ourselves with the will and purposes of the Creator, in whose love the balance is found and the contradictions held together, is the road to stability. Partly through our own wilful wrong choices, and partly through the pressures of the environment around us - through the flesh, the world and the devil, in other words - we may fail to make the creative choices, and live instead with despair and fear.

A Facilitating Environment

So how does love cast out fear? Fear can at least begin to be cast out through the sort of 'facilitating environment' in which trust can grow, choices can be made, ambiguity can be lived with. In Winnicott's writings about the relationship of baby with mother in the early months of life, he talks about what he calls the 'good enough' mother. [8] To aspire to 'good' motherhood may be a perfectionist dream. But it is possible for parenting to be 'good enough'. To grasp the principle of 'good enough' is to be set free from both perfectionism and fatalistic laziness. It is a principle of living with ambiguity. It recognizes that this side of heaven, we are not angels, but nor are we apes. We can, even in this sinful and fallen world, find ways of being 'good enough'. And those ways are helped by the sort of loving environment which is facilitating, not demanding, which is supportive and empathetic, not inappropriately confrontational and judgemental.

That is why many of the 'relational' models of therapy are effective. Because they provide an environment in which love can cast out fear.

What we have written so far can apply to many therapeutic settings, not only specifically Christian ones. They are working in an area which we have called 'God's common grace'. God's grace is active in the world not only in the Church, but in every experience of evil being held back, and goodness being furthered, in every step forward into maturity, health, justice and righteousness. Whenever someone is helped to overcome fear in their own soul, or in their relationships with others, whenever someone is helped to live with less pain and more constructively and freely, whenever there is a move towards greater health of body, mind, emotions, these are moves towards the life of God's kingdom. These are moves towards *shalom*. These are evidences, whether acknowledged or not, of the common grace of God.

In a Christian context, however, more can be said. For though the love of God can be experienced through the care of a therapist incognito, so to speak, the love of God experienced and expressed through the shared fellowship of the Holy Spirit, who sheds the love of God abroad in our hearts, opens up an acknowledgement of spiritual resources of grace which are themselves therapeutic. In all our contexts of interpersonal relationship: family, community, church, we can either help one another to grow by holding each other emotionally in a facilitating environment in which we can develop the trust to make choices and to live with ambiguities, or we can effectively push each other to one of the extremities of Kierkegaard's axes - to the points of despair. A love which extends itself for the sake of the other is a love which can cast out fear.

It is one of the central themes of the New Testament that the Christian church is a community of love. We will pick this up further in the next chapter, but note at this point how, for example, the discussion of the Body of Christ in Ephesians Chapter 4 recognizes mutual need and a variety of gifts, and moves towards a picture of the Body in which, when every part is working properly, is built up in love. The 'working properly' no doubt includes the one - to - one pastoral ministry, but it also includes teams, groups, fellowships, households, in which the varieties of God's gifts of grace can be given and received in love, so that the whole body can grow.

The Truth which Sets us Free

We have spent time discussing love in relation to fear. We move now to a discussion of truth in relation to freedom.

The Jesus depicted in the Fourth Gospel says 'I am the Truth' (John 14:6), a statement at once affirming that there is a difference between truth and error, and that ultimately truth is not a set of propositions but a person. When He then goes on to say 'the Truth shall make you free' (John 8:32), He is not only meaning that a recognition of the truth of certain propositions about the world set us free from living in error, but that human freedom is bound up with the personal freedom which a relationship with Himself can give.

Part of that relationship, however, is to recognize that there is a difference between what is true and what is false, in our thinking, in our perceptions of the world, in our beliefs about ourselves and others. Part of the ministry of Christ, that same chapter in John's Gospel indicates, is to confront the work of the 'father of lies' who holds people in slavery to falsehood and error. Part of the task of Christian ministry is for us to enable one another to confront what is false, and to live in the freedom of the truth.

If, as we have been suggesting, one of the possible contributors to emotional instability and mental pain is an imbalance leading to fear and despair, another might be the flight from truth. Winnicott developed the concept of the False Self in his therapeutic writings, [9] by which he meant the capacity of people to build a defensive emotional wall around themselves in order to protect their very fragile True Self. A False Self may develop through lack of adequate parenting for the young baby, who builds up a false set of relationships with the outside world. It may continue as a pattern of emotional and cognitive responses into later life. The False Self is a defence to guard against the perceived exploitation or the anihilation of the True Self.

Perhaps this is a way of saying that reality is, for whatever reason, too painful to face. As T. S. Eliot put it, humankind cannot bear very much reality. [10] Or perhaps it refers to distorted psychological processes which prevent a person living in the Truth. Either way, to live in untruth is unhealthy and may be painful and destructive. Furthermore, some mental disorder may be a flight into a world of unreality precisely in order to escape from the pain of the real world, even the pain of love.

Laing's work on schizo-affective disorders three decades ago, suggested (controversially) that:

Pretence and equivocation are much used by schizophrenics. The reasons for doing this are, in any single case, likely to serve more than one purpose at a time. The most obvious one is that it preserves the secrecy, the privacy of the self against intrusion . . . Despite his longing to be loved for his

'real self', the schizophrenic is terrified of love. Any form of
understanding threatens his whole defensive system . . . If the
self is not known it is safe. [11]

Whatever the rights and wrongs of the application of Laing's
insights to schizophrenia, (and it has been widely criticized), the
pattern he describes is one we might nevertheless recognize to
some degree in ourselves or in others. Because truth is too painful,
we live in unreality.

David Smail makes the point much more generally than Laing
in his fascinating discussions of the meaning of anxiety, *Illusion and
Reality*.[12] He argues that human misery arises out of interactions
between a person and others and from the nature of the world we
have created. Part of this created world is a system of shared beliefs
about the nature of reality, which, Smail argues, are largely illusion.
There is, he says, a tacit belief to which most of us subscribe that
the majority of people are by and large pretty well adjusted,
contented, and lead conventionally well-ordered lives. 'In contrast
to this happy state of affairs – indeed, partly because of the belief
that it is so – it seems to me', Smail continues, 'that most people
keep the way they feel about themselves as a deep and shameful
secret.' [13]

Behind many of the symptoms of anxiety, Smail argues, lies an
injury to a person's self-esteem which is to do with failing to live
up to standards of adequacy 'which we are all complicit in setting.'

However banal it may seem, nothing holds up to us the nature
of our apirations better than television advertisements . . .
they confront us almost remorselessly with the ideals we
cannot live up to: the happy, loving family eating their
cornflakes against views of waving wheatfields, eagerly
waiting for the joys of the day to unfold; slim, beautiful
women whose smooth and unblemished limbs slide
effortlessly into blue denim skins, later to catch the strong
and approving gaze of confident young men who will cherish
them with just the right amount of lust; unwrinkled, middle-

aged couples, with lovely children, whose new washing machine unites them in a love burning only just less brightly than on their wedding night; mature, square-jawed men whose credit cards place the world of travel and technology instantly within their knowing grasp; beer-drinking workers who know how to be men in a man's world; wielders of power tools who cast contemptuous eyes over their neighbours' botched jobs; people who know the ropes and fit into the world, handle others with easy assurance, get what they want without ruffling any feathers, live their lives in material ease, basking in the admiration and affection of those around them, but being tough if they have to be . . . It is my contention, that the ideal world in which we profess belief is riddled with myth, and that the secret world of anxiety and pain in which we actually live our lives is the real one we truly share. [14]

Living in Untruth

From psychological fragility, perhaps, or from a mythical set of shared social beliefs, many of us do not live in the truth. And yet, as we said in Part 1, there is a deep human quest for meaning. The Logotherapy of Victor Frankl, writing from the experiences of surviving a concentration camp during the Second World War, is based on this fundamental human drive, what he calls 'the will to meaning'. [15, 16] And the Christian belief is that the 'meaning' of human life is inseparably bound up with the 'truth' as it is in Jesus.

A great deal of therapy misses the mark because it is geared to helping people adjust to their social world, as though that world were normal and their fears and fantasies were unreal. Smail thinks that it is the unreal and unhelpful standards in which we falsely often profess belief upheld by the institutions of our educational, political, social and therapeutic establishments which are a primary part of the problem. The real task is to expose the truth of the real world - both within and around us - in which we are struggling.

Of course, to face the truth may be too painful to contemplate.

Ezriel once wrote of 'the required relationship, the avoided relationship and the catastrophe'. By this he meant that we sometimes hold ourselves towards ourselves and others in 'required' relationships in order to avoid other things. What those other things are we may not be able to say. We may not even fully know that we are avoiding them. All we do know is that if we were to turn to face whatever it is we are avoiding, there would be a terrible catastrophe. We would go over the cliff; the world would come to an end in a cataclysmic explosion; a large hole would open in the universe and we would fall through. The sense of catastrophe may derive from real fears.

Liz, to whom we referred earlier, felt as soon as she began to become aware of her traumatic background, that she dare not say this or face that, because if she did, something utterly terrible would happen. No doubt this was an echo of her abuser's voice, threatening her to keep quiet about what he was doing to her. So she had to avoid the truth, because of the catastrophe. And she avoided it by holding on to her depression and anxiety; these were, for her, emotionally 'required'. As we mentioned before, it was the provision of a context of the love which can cast out fear, which opened up for her the possibility of even looking at the truth which can set free.

This is often the way round. We need an accepting environment of safety, in which we have learned to trust enough, before we can be enabled to face the truth.

But the time comes in caring and counselling when facing the truth is the appropriate next step, and at this point, many of the cognitive approaches to therapy have much to offer.

Irrational Ideas
One of the simplest and most used approaches is that derived from the work of Albert Ellis, called Ratio-Emotive Therapy.[16] By no means a Christian believer – quite the reverse, he is a militant atheist – Ellis's concepts have none the less been taken up and used fruitfully by many Christian workers. One of the clearest is Archibald Hart's book *Feeling Free*.[17]

Ellis's creative contribution lies in his suggestion that our emotional responses can be depicted by an A-B-C model. A stands for the Activating Event; C for the Consequential Emotion. We often think that A directly causes C.

If I am hooted at from behind by a very fast car which is trying to overtake me (A), I get annoyed, and indignant, (C), and tend to put the brakes on just a little bit more than I normally would. I might think that my annoyance (C), is *caused by* the following driver's impatience. Ellis's insight is to say that A does not cause C, but between A and C there is B, and B stands for my Beliefs. It is not the other driver that causes my annoyance; it is what I believe about him that leads to my consequential emotion.

The beliefs that lead to annoyance and indignation might be:

'It is ridiculous of him to want to go faster on a road this size';
'Some people have no patience';
'The road is slow for me as well, why shouldn't he have to wait?';
'At any rate I find it very rude to be hooted at from behind.'

These are my 'self-talk'; these are the thoughts going on in my head; these are part of my belief system, B. But let us suppose that I had reasons for other beliefs; let us suppose I knew that the driver behind had just heard that his daughter had been rushed into hospital and he wanted to get there fast; let us suppose that I knew that the car behind was a police car trying to catch a terrorist bomber. If these were my B thoughts, I would pull over, let him pass, and feel perhaps a sense of anticipation, perhaps of relief, perhaps I might say a prayer.

Or let us suppose that none of these are true, but that my self-talk went something like this: 'Gosh, this chap's in a hurry - I have no idea why, but I have nothing to lose from letting him past, so though I don't like being hooted like this, it will help everyone if I just give way.' I would then feel a glow of virtue, and perhaps satisfaction that I had somehow minimized someone else's anxiety just a little.

The point is that our beliefs affect our emotions. Ellis's Ratio-Emotive Therapy is based on the view that, by identifying inappropriate and destructive - what he calls irrational - beliefs, we can work on replacing these in our 'self-talk' with appropriate, constructive and rational ones. Among Ellis's list of beliefs which cause disturbances are:

I must be loved and approved by all 'significant others' in my life;

I must be thoroughly competent, adequate and achieving in everything;

When people act unfairly or obnoxiously, I should blame them, damn them, see them as bad;

I have to see things as awful and terrible whenever I am seriously rejected, frustrated or treated unfairly;

I cannot change or control my feelings because they are controlled from external pressures;

I can avoid facing life's difficulties more easily than undertaking self-discipline.[18]

Ungodly Ideas

We do not have to agree with Ellis's list of irrational ideas, though many of them are unexceptionable, to appreciate the insights of the A-B-C concept.

And we can see how the New Testament emphasis on the renewal of our minds (Romans 12:2), on bringing our thoughts captive to the obedience of Christ (2 Corinthians 10:5), of thinking on things that are true, honourable, just, pure, lovely and gracious (Philippians 4:8f), is another way of challenging our belief system (B), caught as it often is in thought patterns which are untrue, dishonourable, unjust and impure.

This following adaptation by Richard Mason[19] of Ellis's list of irrational ideas makes the point.

THE TEN COMMANDMENTS OF SELF-DEFEAT
And the devil saith unto his angels: 'Wreak havoc on the earth. Create unhappiness everywhere. Sow fear, worry, anger and depression in Jerusalem, in Judea and to the uttermost parts of the earth. For as I go, so send I you.'

And one of these angels, whose name was Blame, settled on the fertile valleys along the Ohio River. There he began to teach the ten commandments.

1 Thou shalt never make mistakes.
2 Thou shalt upset thyself when things go wrong.
3 Thou shalt blame thy neighbour as thyself.
4 Thou shalt neither love, nor forgive, nor accept thyself.
5 Thou shalt always expect things to be different than the way they are.
6 Thou shalt seek the love and approval of everyone for everything thou doest.
7 Thou shalt avoid facing life's difficulties, remembering that thou canst not change because thou are trapped by thy past.
8 Thou shalt be preoccupied with whatever bothers thee.
9 Thou shalt wait passively for happiness to come unto thee.
10 Thou shalt be dependent mostly on others for thy happiness.

And as Blame taught the people of the valleys, they believed him. In great numbers they came, and heard, and believed, so that the earth was truly filled with fear, worry, and anger and depression.

Clearly, if any or some of the above are part of our B Belief system, we can expect our C's in many situations to be miserable.

Through various techniques of rational self-analysis, noting down how we respond to painful situations, asking whether our self-talk is appropriate, is true, is Christian, asking what else we could have put into our belief system, B, which is more constructive, more in keeping with the mind of Christ, and noting down changes in our emotional responses, cognitive therapists can help clients nearer to living in the truth.

Gerald was a very bright boy. He was head and shoulders above everyone else in his year at school, and indeed probably in all the schools in his little town in Wales. His parents had given him every encouragement - pushed him, many people said. His school saw in Gerald the chance, at last, to get someone into Oxford. Everyone praised his work. His parents, who had never had the chance for higher education, set a lot of store by his A-level results. Doing well academically at school was the way Gerald's life was being framed. This was how he spent his time. This was where he received his affirmation. There was little else that his parents found to praise - the rest of life was really one of critical distance, complaining that he wasn't doing his homework, resenting the time he gave to his friends. Gerald learned that personal worth is something to do with achievement. The messages he received from home and school all added up to the equation: I am valued because of what I achieve. He made it to Oxford. And from being a very big fish in a rather small Welsh town pond, he suddenly found himself a tiny minnow in an ocean. No one now to pressurize him. No one to praise his every academic attainment. His essays and course work were adequate, but not nearly as good as many others'. Gerald's self-esteem took a knock. Gerald's quest for perfection led to one disappointment after another. Inevitably he got depressed.

In counselling Gerald, it was important to recognize the faulty self-talk that was going on in his head, 'tapes' which had played many times from his past home and school. 'If I get alpha grades, I am O.K.; if I don't achieve high grades, I am a no good person, worthless, hopeless, a failure.' The irrational - and indeed ungodly - 'self-talk' that was governing his mind, and thence his emotions, was the equation 'worth equals good works'. It did not need the use of any Christian language to challenge that false equation. To enable Gerald to see that there was another way of looking at himself, and his work, and to help him live on the basis that his personal worth was a gift (from God), not something he had to attain, was part of the counselling process. It is not very far from the Christian doctrine that we are justified by grace, not by works.

Changing Thought Habits

Of course, the changing of habits of thought is not an easy, overnight process. There are a number of difficulties. One is that many of our beliefs are long-standing habits of mind which are now virtually automatic responses. It is a long, slow business to identify and then to seek to change long-standing habits, as anyone trying to give up smoking will agree. But as many ex-smokers will also testify, it is possible, and when it happens it is liberating.

Another difficulty is that our emotions tend to drag behind our beliefs. Some people refer to this as 'limbic lag' – by which they mean that the limbic system in our brain, which deals with our emotions, seems to take longer to learn new habits than the 'rational' part of us.

A visitor from the USA came to visit in Oxford. He stayed in the centre of town, whereas his English friend lived beyond the ring road roundabout. Everytime the friend drove him from the lodgings to his house, the American visitor had to close his eyes at the roundabout. It was not just that he was used to driving on the left of the car and the right hand side of the road. It was not just that there are no roundabouts in his part of the States. It was that his whole system of emotional responses could not handle what for him was the total confusion of a busy traffic roundabout in rush hour. He believed firmly that the driver knew what he was doing. He believed he was safe in the car. He believed that there was a fair chance most other people were driving safely and the chances of an accident were slim. But emotionally he could not cope. His feelings had not caught up with his beliefs. However, it is probable that if he had stayed for three months, with practice his emotions would have caught up; he might even have been able to negotiate the roundabout himself.

Despite the difficulties, however, cognitive approaches to therapy are based on the view that liberating change in our fundamental attitudes is possible. In this sense, they are congruent with the Christian Gospel which tells us that living in the truth can set us free.

The Demonic

There is a further dimension to living in the truth which it is important for Christian carers and counsellors to be aware of and perhaps explore, namely what Christian theology has called 'the demonic'. M. Scott Peck published a strange, and rather extravagant book in 1983 called *People of the Lie*.[20] In it, he looked at the case studies of very ordinary people, and the bizarre destructiveness in which their lives can become enmeshed. Peck suggests that there is a particular category in human behaviour which we need to name as 'evil'. What characterises each of his case-studies is a web of lies, and Scott Peck relates this to the Satanic influences or what the writer of the Fourth Gospel called 'The Father of Lies' (John 8:44).

Although much of Scott Peck's work in this book seems overstated, there is some that corresponds with what the Christian Church has called Deliverance Ministry. John Richard's classic study *But Deliver Us From Evil*[21] is a major pastoral theological exploration of the demonic influences of human lives, and of approaches through prayer and sacraments which can liberate people from the demonic bondage, often resulting from deliberate involvement in the occult.

This ministry, though specialized, has been effectively used in alleviating mental disorders of various sorts, as Richards and others document. Main denominations in England have guidelines for pastoral ministers in approaching questions of the occult, or or deliverance from evil power. Within the Church of England, episcopal authority is needed for the exercise of exorcism, but many lesser ministries of deliverance (essentially using the petition in the Lord's Prayer) are increasingly widespread. This is an area of Christian caring and counselling fraught with dangers of misunderstanding, exploitation, manipulation and deceit. But it is one that cannot be ignored if part of our pastoral task is to enable one another to live more freely in the liberating truth of Christ.

Speaking the Truth in Love: Forgiveness

We have indicated that one of the causes of mental distress may be an emotional imbalance leading to despair. Whatever its causes, an appropriate pastoral caring response will include the provision of a facilitating environment in which love can be received, trust can be developed and eventually the fear can be faced and dealt with. The relational models of therapy have much to offer here.

Another cause may be a flight from the truth, the sufferer preferring to live in untruth and falseness because the truth is too painful to face. If the context of care is sufficiently loving and supportive, however, to face the truth and come to terms with it can be liberating and healing. The cognitive models of therapy contribute to our understanding of these processes.

A third factor in mental and emotional distress may be the pain of moral guilt. And the so-called 'moral approaches' to counselling may have things to offer in this area.

One of the causes of disquiet among some Christian counsellors about the use of 'secular' therapies is that many such therapies operate with what is called a 'medical model' of mental health and illness, which – so it is said – effectively denies the moral dimensions of personal responsibility in a suffering person. This is, in fact, by no means the case, but there have been a number of reactions over the recent decades, attempting to reassert the importance of moral responsibility in personal and social health.

Karl Mennigner's *'Whatever Became of Sin?'*[22] is one therapeutic approach which questions the alleged non-moral models of some psychoanalytic approaches. Mowrer's behaviourist approaches[23] on which Christians such as Jay Adams[24] have drawn, is another. Adams, for example, developed a directive model of counselling which he called 'nouthetic' (from the Greek *noutheteo* = to warn), in which counselling involves the confrontation of the client with the moral demands of the biblical text, by calling for repentance, and for a recognition that the sufferer's personal choices play a major part in their therapy. Many Christians would be unhappy to place sole reliance on the moral model, and Adams has received some justified criticism. It has been suggested that the nouthetic approach has too small a place for grace, places too much on the human will, and shows little regard for the emotional wounds and hurts which prevent many of us making the choices or the changes we would like. However, Christian faith must endorse the concerns of those therapies which seek to facilitate personal responsibility as part of the therapeutic task. Part of the Christian understanding of our human nature as reflecting the image of God, includes the recognition that we are responsible moral agents, living in a world in which choices between right and wrong, good and evil, are significant, even if those choices are necessarily constrained within limits.

One central Christian theological theme which holds together our earlier discussion of truth and love with the place of moral accountability and the pain of moral guilt, is forgiveness.

In his discussion, in *A Genuinely Human Existence*,[25] of what he calls the Three Great Enemies of the human race, fear, frustration and resentment, Bishop Stephen Neill commented:

> When I read technical books on psychology there is one word which I always look for in the index and rarely find. It is the word 'forgiveness'. If the absence of the word implies also an absence of this central idea from contemporary psychological thought, this may indicate a lacuna the filling of which would be greatly to the advantage of both psychological thought and psychiatric practice.[26]

This absence is particularly surprising when we reflect that forgiveness is one of the central words in Christian spirituality. There is a petition for forgiveness in the Lord's prayer; Jesus told parables on this theme (Matthew 18:25ff); St Paul urges his readers to forgive one another as God in Christ has forgiven us (Ephesians 4:32); St John remarks that God is faithful and just to forgive us our sins (I John 1:9). The liturgies of the Church frequently begin with, or include, a penitential section, asking for forgiveness. The Penitentials of the medieval church, the practice of confession and of penance, the therapeutic value of absolution: all of these play an important part in Christian self-understanding.

So what does 'forgiveness' mean? It means acknowledging that there is something wrong in a relationship, but refusing to allow the wrong for ever to stand in the way of the relationship being restored. Forgiveness seeks to use the wrong creatively to build something new for the future. It is to move beyond the law of retaliation, beyond the emotion of bitterness and resentment. It is to move beyond legalities altogether, into grace. Forgiveness is one way of acknowledging the value of the other person, even in a fallen world in which wrong has been done and people have been hurt.

Forgiveness reminds us of our accountability. We are moral persons with responsibility for our actions. However much the system or our environment diminishes our freedom to move and to choose, we cannot take refuge in fatalism.

Forgiveness breaks down idealizations. It reminds us that we are not perfect, and will not be this side of heaven. Nor are we utterly evil and irredeemable. There is an ambiguity about the human condition: created yet fallen, good and bad, neither devil nor angel. There are good things as well as bad things in others. Forgiveness seeks to recognize the work of grace in them; that they make mistakes; that they do evil, just as we do. They have hurt us, sometimes in deep and lasting ways. But forgiveness is about recognizing the wrong – not pretending that it did not happen, or did not hurt; not minimizing it, or hiding it – but deciding that we will not remain stuck in a response of resentment and retaliation, however justified such an attitude may feel.

The nearest psychoanalytic theory comes to the concept of forgiveness is in Melanie Klein's ideas about Reparation.[27] In Klein's understanding, a child needs to work through what she (confusingly) calls The Depressive Position. By this she means that a child has to come to terms with the ambiguity of the world, seeing the outside world – of mother, for example – as both satisfying and depriving. Part of that coming to terms with ambiguity will involve the child dealing with the powerful emotions aroused by the discovery that the person he has been screaming at is the very same person in whom sustenance and delight are found. This is what Klein calls the guilt which arises from having felt aggressive to the mother who cares. So there is a desire on the part of the child to make reparation - to make good the injuries the child in fantasy carried out upon its mother.

For reparation to happen, the mother needs to 'hold' the child psychologically in time so that this process of making good can proceed. Only if the environment is sufficiently facilitating - in other words, only if the mother can recognize the 'wrong', and provide a context in which it can be faced, acknowledged, and creatively left behind, can reparation happen. When that happens, the child is able to move into the stage of creativity - the 'stage of concern', the capacity to love.

That facilitating environment seems very close to what Christian theology means by forgiveness. The mother, in Klein's model, acknowledges that the child is seeking to make good a wrong, and in 'grace' offers it the assurance that the wrong will not destroy the relationship. The 'good enough parent' models grace.

Of course, no one can know objectively what a young child is feeling, but the model seems to be an insightful one, especially when replayed in terms of adult emotions. At other times later on in life, we can offer one another 'good enough' facilitating environments for the grace of forgiveness to be given and received.

This is not easy. Grace, as Bonhoeffer memorably put it, is not cheap.[28] Forgiveness is costly. The story of Hosea illustrates the cost of forgiveness - both in Hosea's own family life in relation to Gomer his runaway adulterous wife, and in the relationship between God and Israel, of which Hosea's family story is an analogy (Hosea 1-3). We see the costliness of grace most vividly in the Cross of Christ, where - as Nicholas Wolterstorff puts it - 'the tears of God are the meaning of history.'[29] The tender heart of God is broken open on the Cross, expressing the lengths God in forgiving love is prepared to go so that relationships might be restored.

But forgiveness heals. What does the abused child need to hear when she believes she was the cause of what happened? What does a sad and distorted adult need to hear, who has given in to the temptation to abuse a child? What does a social worker need to hear, when the case has gone wrong and mistakes have been made? Or when the Sunday tabloids elaborate the truth to load relatively innocent people with major guilt?

We need to hear from God, from others, from within our own hearts, that we can be forgiven and we need to learn to forgive. The past cannot be undone, but its wounds can be healed, and there is no need for all our sins to accumulate for ever against us. Guilt can be taken away. Wrong directions can be changed, not by pretending that everything was all right really, because it wasn't, but by building on the past creatively for the future. Not by living with the burdensome law of retaliation 'You owe, so you must pay', but by walking again in the fresh air of grace.

Forgiveness is not easy. It is not instant. It is not the same as forgetting – there are some things that we will not be able to forget. But it is allowing, over time, the grace of God to remove the emotional power and pain of the past, to set us again on the road to freedom.

And this involves our will, our choice, our taking responsibility. Forgiveness does not just happen, in the way that a wound may heal itself. Forgiveness is an action of the will.

Sarah, in her mid-twenties, came to the church after some years of different sorts of psychiatric care, some fruitful, some less so. She was still very disturbed. The most visible sign of disturbance was during the prayers in the service. When she reached the Lord's prayer, she would collapse in a heap at the phrase 'Our Father', with much clattering of hymn books, and concerned looks from those around.

Gradually she joined a small group of Christian friends who committed themselves to support her and pray for her. She did not pray with them herself: that was too hard. But after some months, she learned to trust this group enough to explore some of the painful memories of the past. Not surprisingly, many painful memories centred on her father, who had been extremely cruel, over demanding in setting unattainable standards, and physically abusive in his punishments. Sarah hated her father, and her depression and disturbance was to some large extent the 'frozen rage' of her anger towards him. It took a long time before she admitted to the group that she wanted to 'let her father go'. She decided, with much struggle and courage, that she wanted to pray for her father, and to forgive him. In a time of prayer set aside by the group, Sarah offered these thoughts to God. She said she felt warmed, and bathed in light. She said that she felt a great load taken off her shoulders. She smiled a most relaxed, tired, but satisfied smile.

It took a while before she could make contact with her father again. The relationship was by no means instantly easy. There were still areas of disturbance in her life. But she is now working on it creatively. She regards that time of prayer as a real step forward into emotional health. And now the hymnbooks stay on the pews.

The ministry of forgiveness is closely linked to the ministry which some call 'healing of memories', which we shall look at briefly in a later section. Forgiveness is that form of loving justice which becomes redemptive. It is part of the love which can cast out fear. It is part of the truth about the ambiguity of the world, which can set us free. It is the only means of alleviating true moral guilt (as opposed to subjective guilty feelings which may or may not be appropriate). But it is part of a process.

There is a gap, which T. F. Torrance calls the 'eschatological reserve'[30] between the word of forgiveness, and the word of complete healing. When the four friends brought the paralysed man to Jesus, and let him down through the roof, Jesus' first word was 'Your sins are forgiven'. The second word was 'Take up your bed and walk.'

In Christian discipleship this is often the order of progress, and sometimes the gap between the two words can be very long. Sometimes, it seems, we need to wait for the new heaven and the new earth, until 'there will be no more pain'. But forgiveness, though costly, painful and often a long struggle, can happen now.

The Social Expression of Love is Justice

Part of the meaning of the love of God is given expression in the quest for justice. God is proclaimed as one who 'executes justice' (Psalm 103:6), a quality which merges easily in Old Testament thought into the concepts of 'righteousness' and 'mercy'. The divine justice is seen in the punishment of evil, the vindication of the good, the victory over enemies, and the bias towards the poor and the disadvantaged. Divine justice gives more than human concepts of fairness require. Divine justice becomes redemptive – 'A just God and therefore a Saviour' (Isaiah 45:1). The NT speaks of God being 'faithful and just to forgive'.

Because of the grace of God in Christ, Christians are urged to take seriously the needs of others, and contribute to the welfare of the poor (2 Corinthians 8:9). In the coming 'new heaven and new earth', 'righteousness dwells' (2 Peter 3:13), and the NT writers use this fact to spur their readers on to lives of holiness in this present world. Human righteousness and justice should correspond with, and be transformed by, divine justice. Social justice is the political and social expression of neighbour love.

In Part I we concentrated on the inescapable significance of social context for all ministry, caring and counselling. A person, we have said, is not simply an isolated centre of choosing and of needs. A person is who he or she is in relation to other persons. We are all part of social networks, family, friends, community, colleagues, and so on, part of a network of dynamic interactions, in constant flux, constant change. Justice is a word which is concerned with the right and appropriate ordering of social contexts.

A carer and counsellor cannot operate in isolation from such a setting. Furthermore, it requires us not to bring specific situations of personal need under too many general headings. Thus, different people may come to us with help concerning their marriage breakdown. One person may be in difficulty because they married at 17, and everyone told them it was a mistake. Another because his wife has left him alone on the fifteenth floor of their council apartment wile she has accepted the offer of living with her richer boss in a wealthier part of town. Another because the wife cannot bear to see her drunken out-of-work husband being constantly cruel to the children. We cannot simply bring all such people under one heading 'divorcee'. The social context is an inseparable part of our moral evaluation and our pastoral response. The quest for social context and justice is part of the meaning of Christian ministry.

We noticed in the previous chapter how Jesus' ministry on occasion required a vindication of divine justice as part of the condition for *shalom*. In that he was not far from the stance of the Old Testament prophet Amos, whose call for justice is part of the meaning of the covenant of God's steadfast love. The Book of Amos gives us a vivid illustration of the ways in which injustices of various sorts diminish peoples' lives, and Amos' passion for justice in the name of God.

The world of Christian caring and counselling, cannot avoid the social, political and environmental context of peoples' lives, and there are themes in Amos which need to be reheard today. One of Amos's concerns was the growing gap between rich and poor and the powerlessness of poverty. The social leaders were living in pride and luxury, but rich houses were in fact robbers' dens. The rich celebrated their affluence with an insulation against the suffering of others. Amos delivers a stinging rebuke. The injustice makes him angry.

Another of Amos's frustrations was that the social institutions themselves were promoting injustice. The social system was actually preventing care being given to those who needed it. The courts at the city gate, which should have been places where justice was administered, were in fact places where the poor were even more enslaved.

A third concern was the fact that the religious institutions had become hijacked for political ends. Bethel had ceased to be the place where Yahweh was sought, but had instead become a shrine of the king. The processes of secularization and corruption meant that the people were beginning to look to God only for material success when it suited them, and for the rest, to look to Baal.

Yahweh was manipulated and kept just to a corner of their lives.

So Amos, affirming the Sovereignty of God over all things, affirming that God's holy and just nature stands behind His call for justice and righteousness, and recognizing that all human beings are precious to God, and that there is a common humanity to which he can appeal, thunders out his anger and his exhortation: 'Seek the Lord and Live!'; 'Let justice roll down like waters, and righteousness like an ever flowing stream!'(Amos 5:24).

He points to a God in whom justice and righteousness are the same, and are expressed in self-giving love to neighbour. He had very little political success. Samaria his capital fell to invaders; the kingdom of Israel was dismantled. In terms of immediate effects, Amos was a failure. But he stood in the breach at a crucial time and bore witness to God and to justice.

Christian pastoral care cannot ignore the fact that the social and political expression of neighbour love is justice. As Karl Barth memorably put it:

> The human righteousness required by God and established in obedience, the righteousness which according to Amos 5:24 should pour down as a mighty stream – has necessarily the character of vindication of right in favour of the threatened innocent, the oppressed poor, widows, orphans and aliens. For this reason, in the relations and events in the life of his people, God always takes His stand unconditionally and passionately on this side and on this side alone: against the lofty and on behalf of the lowly; against those who already enjoy right and privilege, and on behalf of those who are denied and deprived of it.[31]

If we are on the side of the poor, God is on our side.

Although justice will never be established in full this side of heaven, when justice and peace embrace (Psalm 86:10), we must move towards it. The Lord's Prayer enjoins on us the need to work and pray that God's will be done and his kingdom come on earth as it is in heaven. One of the expressions of love is that Christian people should look not only to their own interests, but also to the interests of others (Philippians 2:4). While Christian ministers, carers and counsellors must seek more than justice in human affairs, we may never seek less.

THE FELLOWSHIP
OF THE HOLY SPIRIT

We now need to set all that we have said concerning pastoral caring and counselling more firmly in the context of the ministry of the whole body of Christ, gifted by the Spirit of Christ, and moving to maturity in the fellowship of Christ.

As we have summarily said before, the metaphor of the Body of Christ, used in several places in the New Testament, indicates among other things that each member has needs and each has gifts. We noted how the Letter to the Ephesians draws a picture of the church as the Body of Christ, with each of the members of the Body gifted for ministry. The mutuality of such ministry within the Body is made very clear in Ephesians Chapter 4.

The members of the Body are called on to accept each other, with all their differences and even awkwardnesses ('putting up with one another in love' v.2), to minister to each other (v.7), and to seek to help one another towards maturity. 'Until we all attain to the unity of the faith and of the knowledge of the Son of God, to mature manhood, to the measure of the stature of the fulness of Christ'.

There is no distinction here between a 'professional' ministry and those who are ministered to. There is, however, a variety of gifts, all given for the common good (v.16). Those of us involved in pastoral caring and counselling, whatever 'professional' skills we may have learned, or indeed have been blessed with – and which can be used for the good of the Body – need first and foremost to recognize that we are all in this process of learning and growing, changing and maturing *together*, and that I need you and your gifts as much as you may need me and mine.

This paragraph in Ephesians 4 not only underlines the corporate nature of Christian ministry, it underlines also the dynamic nature of Christian living as a process of change. And the dynamic for Christian change, the power which energizes the gifts, is the Spirit of Christ. In the previous chapter in Ephesians, we read of being 'strengthened with might through his Spirit in the inner man' (3:16), and of the 'power at work within us' (3:20). Indeed, the word 'power', *dunamis*, is that used of God earlier in the Epistle, speaking of the 'greatness of his power which he accomplished in Christ . . . when he raised him from the dead' (2:19-20).

The energy of Christian ministry is the power of Christ's resurrection, made available within the Christian church through the gifts of the Holy Spirit. He is the resource for the carer, and the energy for change in all of us.

Paraklesis

Among the many spiritual gifts referred to in the New Testament, we must now underline the significance we noted earlier of the general word *paraklesis*, which connects up several of them. In the Fourth Gospel the Holy Spirit is described as the paraklete (John 14:16, 26; 15:26; 16:7). The concept of *paraklesis* covers many of the themes we looked at in our discussion in the previous chapters of pastoral caring and counselling. In the NT Epistles, *parakaleo* sometimes refers to coming alongside; just being there; encouragement; exhortation; comfort; warning. For example:

Encouragement - 1 Thessalonians 2:3; 1 Timothy 4:13; Hebrews 12:5;
Exhortation - 1 Corinthians 14:3;
Appeal - 2 Corinthians 8:4;
Comfort - 2 Thessalonians 2:16;
Consolation - Romans 15:4.

There is a range of fairly non-directive to fairly directive meanings of parakletic ministry. According to different needs, and in different circumstances, a Christian understanding of parakletic care and counselling may move between different styles and approaches.

Their common thread is that these are the ministries of the Spirit of Christ, and their goal is to enable the members of Christ's body to grow to maturity in Him.

Here is an example of how this range of approaches might be used in one particular situation.

A pastor may agree to set aside an hour each week for an initial period of, say, ten weeks, to work with a person, Sally, going through some personal anxieties. He will spend several of the initial sessions listening to Sally, trying to understand something of her story. These are the sorts of questions he will have in his mind:

How long has Sally been stressed like this?
Has this happened before in her life, and when?
Is she taking any medication?
Is there any particular precipitating cause for the present difficulties?
Why has she come to see me now? Why me? Why now?
Is there anything about her early life, her upbringing, parents, school, adolescence, medical history, that may be a contributory factor?
Is there anything about her spiritual history that is significant?
Has she or any of her family been involved in anything occult?
Is she someone who would say she has a firm religious faith?
Has this helped her emotionally, or made things harder?

Throughout the initial sessions the pastor will be seeking to provide space, attention, respect, understanding, empathy, warmth; to be the sort of person that Sally can learn to trust; to be someone who it is safe to share some, perhaps painful, perhaps embarrassing, perhaps shocking, things with, knowing that she will not be rejected for saying them. The quality of the interaction between Sally and the pastor will itself be therapeutic. During these sessions, the skills of relational therapies, listening and reflecting, will be vital.

The pastor will himself ideally be part of a supervision group, or peer group support team in which, within the bounds of strict confidentiality, he can check out his understanding of the therapeutic process, and receive sustenance and support for himself.

In due course, the pastor will need to judge whether this approach is sufficient. It might be the case that certain cognitive or behavioural patterns are emerging. Perhaps Sally always says things in a certain way, always responds to a particular reference in a certain way. Maybe there are unhelpful 'tapes' playing in her memory, or in her 'self-talk'. The time may perhaps also come when the pastor can best help Sally by indicating other ways of thinking, of helping her through cognitive therapeutic skills to accept the possibilities of seeing things another, more creative, way. There may come a time when it seems likely to the pastor that at the root of some of the anxiety and stress is an attitude of personal wrong, resentment, guilt or shame, for which Sally herself bears at least some of the responsibility. If the relationship is sufficiently strong, if the environment of their talking is sufficiently warm, if the pastor has earned the right to be heard, he may see it appropriate to take a more directive stance at this point. This can be done without condemnation or judgemental distance. It can be done without imposing the pastor's own views and values on Sally. There is a way of enabling Sally to understand where she has been in the wrong, and to explore with her possible ways of change: repentance, God's absolution, forgiveness, reconciliation.

Towards the end of the sessions, it could be that the pastor can offer another service of the Christian church: 'If you would like a group of Christian friends to pray about all this with you, please feel free to ask. What we could do is to invite one or two others of your special friends to join us. We don't need to go through all the confidential things we have discussed. They don't need to know all the details. We could simply set aside this time to bring all our anxieties to God, to present him with what we have been working at together, and to seek his grace and help for the future. Sometimes I do this in the setting of a small informal service of High Communion, just here in this room. We could say the prayer of Confession together, and hear God's absolution; we could read the Scriptures and share together any thoughts which come to mind.

Then we could pray for each other, and especially for you Sally, and take communion together as a symbol of God's love and grace. Sometimes people like us to use a little oil for annointing, and if you would find that helpful, we could talk about how we might do that at the end.'

If Sally later felt that this was a ministry she would like to ask for, that could be a fitting summing up of the work of caring and counselling for her for those particular stages of her journey.

Ministry: Individual and Corporate

The 'fellowship' of the Holy Spirit clearly implies a focus on the interconnectedness of the members of the Body of Christ with each other and with the Head. The covenant model of the OT holds together the importance of individual personal identity and growth and a sense of corporate identity and mutual accountability. So does the baptismal teaching of the NT. It is 'with all the saints' that we come to know the love of God (Ephesians 3:18). A Gospel-shaped pastoral care will not become so individually focused that it loses the importance of networks of relationships, of groups, of society, of political and environmental factors in human need and human growth, nor will it become so socially focused that the significance of each individual person's life journey becomes submerged. It will recognize the specific gifts which the Holy Spirit may give to a particular person, and encourage their use, but it will not neglect the importance of the place of those gifts within the wider ministry of the pastoral team of the church, and the Body of Christ as a whole. The covenantal model, rooted in an understanding of God as a Trinity of persons in relation, provides a way of thinking both these together.

One further aspect of pastoral ministry is worth noting at this point: the importance of the growth within Christian ministry of patterns of family therapy. Building on the psychological theories of group dynamics and systems approaches to networks of relationships, the importance of recognizing that the person we are seeking to help is necessarily part of a social network, and may, even unconsciously, be 'carrying' emotional feelings which more properly belong elsewhere in the family network, is being increasingly realized.

The importance for pastoral caring and counselling of recent advances in understanding of social and family systems needs to be underlined here. The work of Robin Skynner[1], or Edwin Friedman,[2], for example, or at the more accessible level of Sue Walrond-Skinner[3] are being used effectively in the training and work of Christian ministers.

The social, political and community aspects of care are also, as we have noted, of vital significance. In 1963, R. A. Lambourne, a medical practitioner and theologian in Birmingham, wrote *Community, Church and Healing* [4] in which he argued that the healing ministry of Jesus should be seen primarily not as instances of individually oriented compassion, but as community events. They were signs of a socio-political entity (the kingdom of God); they were acted parables; they functioned as disclosures of the judgement of God on the earthly communities of the time. Both the needs of the sick person and of their wider community must be thought through together.

In his provocative *Alive and Kicking*[5] Stephen Pattison also relates Christian concepts of healing to the wider concepts of justice in our society. Peter Selby's *Liberating God*[6] focuses on the political dimensions to and implications of counselling ministry. Issues of public health (preventative care, environmental pollution, social deprivation, epidemiology, long-term support for the chronic sick) are also part - though infrequently addressed - of Christian caring.

The wider community has a further function also. One of the features of the counselling covenant, is that a hurting person frequently transfers qualities or feelings about someone else onto the carer and counsellor. (This is often called transference.) There are feelings aroused in the counsellor in response to this (often called counter-transference). This can often be unconscious, and though when recognized it can be a powerful tool for developing insight, when unrecognized, it can get in the way of useful work. It is important, therefore, for the carer and counsellor to be able to check out their own reactions with some outside supervisory person. All professional counsellors are required to have regular supervisions - sometimes peer group supervisions - to aid this process. The Christian ministry has not been so good at seeing the importance of this. But there is considerable help to be had, and it can be done without the sharing and breaking of confidences, for the pastor, carer, or counsellor to meet on a regular basis with someone else, for support, supervision (in the technical sense), and prayer. In most counselling situations some supervision arrangements are essential. Some churches and Christian agencies are offering clergy support groups to help with this task. It is a denial in practice of the Christian belief in the every-member ministry of the Body of Christ, if pastor and clergy operate on a one-person ministry model. The provision of supervision, accountability and support is also part of the fellowship the Holy Spirit creates, and we ignore it at our cost.

Caring, Counselling, Spiritual Direction, Prayer

Counselling is a term that has tended to become identified with one-to-one individual ministry, usually problem-centred. Caring is a broader term, focussing not only on problems but on the on-going relationship between carer and cared-for in good times as well as critical times, and not only on an individual, but also in a social and family context.

Spiritual direction is a form of pastoral ministry particularly geared to developing the prayer life of the person - understood in the broadest sense.

Clearly these ministries will overlap and sometimes merge into one another.[7] Sometimes concern for a person's emotional well-being cannot be separated from the stage they have reached on their spiritual journey. Sometimes as we have indicated, it may be appropriate for a carer or counsellor to pray with a person they are seeking to help. As we have said, prayer may not be appropriate within a counselling session, though it can often be helpful to say, 'We are praying for you'. But if prayer arises naturally out of a conversation, or is requested by the person seeking help, prayer can often be a most natural way of offering all that has been spoken about, with the person's anxieties and hopes to God, and seeking his grace for the next step of the journey.

A word of caution is appropriate, however, for prayer, misused, can become unhelpfully manipulative. There can be a temptation to say in prayer what we feel uncomfortable saying face to face; there can be a temptation to give advice or moral direction in prayer which it would be inappropriate to give in a counselling conversation. It is a misuse of prayer to ask God to 'help Mary with the difficult task of forgiving her father' if that difficult task, the processes of forgiveness, the feelings for the father have not been adequately talked through. Even when they have, we need very great care not to place directive burdens on one another through prayer. Prayer is not a therapeutic technique. If prayer is primarily about seeking that our wills are brought more into line with God's will for us, prayer is often more about listening than speaking, about silently offering rather than requesting.

Some of these cautions need underlining in relation to the style of ministry that is sometimes called 'prayer counselling'. The James 5 pattern seems vital here: that it is for the one in need to request help, and not for the carers to impose it. It is also crucial to recall the basic rules of prayer - that we are coming to God with our perceived needs, our hopes, our fears, and we are not telling God what he has to do. We may ask, just as Paul asked God concerning his thorn in the flesh (2 Corinthians 12:7f). We may pray for one another 'that you may be in health', as in 3 John 2. But we need to be particularly aware that prayer can become inappropriately manipulative, especially as we are often in touch with people at their most vulnerable. Commanding God to act, calling down power from on high, refusing to cover all our prayer with 'nevertheless not my will but thine be done' both misuse this means of grace, and can also sometimes raise unrealistic expectations in those we seek to help.

Sometimes the prayer that is needed is a prayer of confession and absolution - a special ministry which the Christian church is able to give.

Michael was a graduate student finishing off his doctorate. He had been married two years, and they had a baby a few months ago. He was a strong Christian, the leader of the youth group at his local church, highly respected by everyone. He was clearly destined for work in the Church's ministry before long. He would be a bishop, everyone said. Michael was also a fine violinist and had toured abroad with the orchestra before he got married. Just recently he had another opportunity to go on a one-week tour to the continent, and his wife had encouraged him to do so. They were put up in a lovely hotel. He got on well with one particular young cellist. She was attractive, single, available. They ended up in bed.

Michael told his minister that he had always felt himself to be very sexually aware. He had always been attractive to women. Since the baby had been born, his wife had not been so interested, however. But nothing like this had ever happened before. Michael was clearly distraught. He had enjoyed himself, but felt ashamed that he had betrayed his wife, his faith, others' expectancies, his own standards. After a very long conversation, he simply asked for absolution. The minister took down the prayer book and invited Michael carefully to read the prayer of confession of sin, which he did with many tears. The minister then read the prayer of absolution, declaring the forgiveness and mercy of God. Then he laid his hands on Michael's head and asked God's blessing and grace for the future. Michael gave a deep sigh, and said he felt at last he was breathing cleaner air again. Then he had to face the question of what to say to his wife.

Inner Healing and Health

There are various styles of prayer which are often referred to as 'inner healing'. Ruth Carter Stapleton[8, 9] uses a process of guided meditation, 'faith-imagination', in which Jesus Christ, the same yesterday, today and for ever, is invited in prayer to go back into a person's past life to heal traumatic episodes. Francis MacNutt[10, 11] is another author working in this area. Building on the work of Agnes Sandford[12], MacNutt writes:

> The basic idea of inner healing is that Jesus can take the memories of our past and (i) heal them from wounds that still remain and affect our present lives and (ii) fill with his love all those places in us that have been empty for so long, once they have been healed and drained of the poison of past hurts and resentments . . . At times the healing is progressive and takes several sessions, but I believe that it is always God's desire to heal us of those psychological hurts that are unredemptive and that prevent us from living with the inner freedom that belongs to the children of God.

There are many who will testify to tremendous steps forward in emotional stability through prayer ministry of this sort. We referred earlier to the story of the person who found the image of the Cross of Christ, and His hand extended in love, filling her mind in place of a damaging memory of childhood cruelty. There are, however, others for whom God's word to Paul 'my grace is sufficient for you' needs to be received not as a promise of healing in this life, but of grace to cope with disabilities and sometimes deep wounds. While it is the case that, as Pentecostalist doctrine affirms[13], 'there is healing in the Cross', it is by no means clear that complete healing, anymore than complete sinlessness, is promised to us this side of heaven. A theology of suffering must always be part of our theology of healing.[14–16]

Deliverance ministries, and the ministry of 'healing the family tree' derived from the insights of Kenneth McAll, also need careful theological evaluation, but may with care become part of the caring and counselling ministry of the church.

A middle-aged lady came to the church from some distance away, to ask for help with her anorexic daughter. After several sessions of counselling with a member of the church, it was decided to hold a small informal communion service with her, to pray with her and for her and for her daughter. A group of half a dozen Christian people gathered for this informal service. Just before the prayer of confession was said, this lady said she needed to say something: she wanted to say that years before, she had had an abortion, had never told anyone about it, but it was now weighing on her conscience and she wished to say that to us all before we together confessed our sins and asked for God's forgiveness. The service proceeded. Prayer was offered for her and her family, and the little life that was lost was also remembered, and offered to God. At the end she went home. She determined to tell her anorexic daughter everything that had happened, including the fact of the abortion, which had taken place some while before this present daughter was born. 'Oh, that's who I must have been talking with all these years,' said the girl, to her mother's surprise. From that time, otherwise inexplicably, the anorexia began to clear up.

Such stories are hard to understand, hard to evaluate. There are more things in heaven and earth than we often dream of. Dr Kenneth McAll has written in medical journals of his belief in the importance of the link between ritual mourning (perhaps especially for situations of miscarriage, abortion and stillbirth) and emotional health. His written theology[17] is controversial and in places unorthodox even outlandish according to R. Hurding[18] when discussing McAll's 'Eucharist of the Resurrection' to deal with the restless spirits of the dead. However, apparently through the use of one of the special means of grace through which Christ wished us to remember him, peoples' anxieties are relieved, and health enhanced.

If *shalom* includes the sense of personal and relational well-being at all levels, i.e. health in the broad sense, all Christian ministries of healing will be understood to be concerned with individual cure from disease, the alleviation of the subjective pain of illness, and the processes of change needed to deal with social concepts of sickness. They will be concerned with medical, emotional, relational, spiritual, communal and environmental issues, relevant to human well-being and human flourishing at all levels of life.[19] Within this, the use of healing prayer, and sacramental ministries have their function and place.

Sacramental Ministry

We have referred to the Eucharist, or Holy Communion, as an appropriate context for prayer for healing. In some situations, and for some people, it can be a very helpful aspect of Christian ministry, to sum up several weeks of counselling in the context of a short, perhaps informal, service, at which the concerns which have been explored are offered to God. The Holy Communion is a marvellously powerful setting for such prayer. At the Eucharist, the natural and supernatural worlds meet in a special way. This is the means by which Jesus asked to be remembered. This is the service by which, as St Paul says, we 'show forth the Lord's death until he comes' (1 Corinthians 11:26). There is a reference to the past, in commemoration and remembrance, there is a reference anticipating God's future 'until he comes'. There is a shared action in the present, participating together in the tokens of Christ's promised grace. At the Eucharist we are in what Winnicott elsewhere calls 'transitional' space.[20] Two worlds, the inner and the outer, the physical and the spiritual meet together. Here the circle of God's grace and the circle of human need intersect in a special way.

The Holy Communion gives us a structure in which to say our prayers. There is confession for sin, in which we can include – as Nehemiah does – a prayer for 'my father's house' (Nehemiah 1:6); perhaps those who have sinned against us as well as our own shortcomings can be confessed and brought into the light of God's mercy.

There is a time for hearing and reflecting on the Scriptures. It can be very appropriate to use parts of 1 Peter 2 and 1 Peter 5 at this point:

To this you have been called, because Christ suffered for you, leaving you an example, that you should follow in His steps. He committed no sin; no guile was found on His lips. When He was reviled, He did not revile in return; when He suffered, He did not threaten; but He trusted to Him who judges justly. He himself bore our sins in His body on the tree, that we might die to sin and live to righteousness. By His wounds you have been healed.

Humble yourselves under the mighty hand of God, that in due time He may exalt you. Cast all your anxieties on Him, for He cares about you. Be sober, be watchful. Your adversary the devil prowls around like a roaring lion, seeking someone to devour. Resist Him, firm in your faith . . .

After you have suffered a little while, the God of all grace, who has called you to His eternal glory in Christ, will Himself restore, establish and strengthen you.

Then, as Morris Maddocks puts it, 'word and deed come together in the Eucharist, as they did in the life of Jesus and the Early Church.'[21] We offer ourselves to God, in our needs, and with our gifts. We seek the grace of Christ offered to us in His Body and His Blood. We can then pray especially for the healing touch of Christ, perhaps using laying on of hands, perhaps using oil for annointing. And the Eucharist closes with the prayer that God would send us out in the power of the Holy Spirit, that we may live and work to his praise and glory.

Bishop Maddocks quotes to good effect Archbishop Michael Ramsey's summary of the healing benefits of the Eucharist:

Nowhere more vividly than in the sacrament of the Eucharist do Christians find through Christ an openness to the past and to the present, to heaven and to the world. The sacrifice of Christ on Calvary is present in the here and now in its timeless potency, and the homely bread and wine of a contemporary meal are made the effectual signs of Christ's self-giving. The Christian community of earth is one with the saints in heaven. Blending past and present, earth and heaven, the Eucharist is a prophecy and a prayer for our coming to the vision of God and for the coming of God's reign in the world.[22]

This important part of the church's sacramental ministry can fruitfully be linked with counselling, confession, forgiveness, spiritual direction, and the ministry of reconciliation as a part of the jigsaw of healing.

The Church as a Community of Character

The Ephesian model of the church as a body describes a variety of gifts within the church 'for the equipment of the saints for their work of ministry' in order that 'we all attain to the unity of the faith and of the knowledge of the Son of God, to mature manhood, to the measure of the statute of the fulness of Christ' (Ephesians 4:13). The life of the Christian within the church is thus seen as one of progress, a journey of growth towards maturity. 'We are to grow up in every way into him who is the head, into Christ' (Ephesians 4:15). The church is a community of character.[23]

An essential part of Christian pastoral caring, therefore, will be a concern for mutual nurture. The faith-development psychology associated with the name of James Fowler, and also with some of his critics, is important in recognizing life, and the life of faith, as one of change, or growth towards maturity. The models of Christian instruction in some parts of the church called 'the catechumenate', Christian training schools, nurture groups, and so on, are all part of the mutual caring of the ministry of Christ's church. We have said before that much counselling is crisis-centred and problem-centred. Christian caring on a New Testament model is not episodic, but progressive.

Michael Jacobs' work *Towards the Fulness of Christ*[24] is one example of the way the world of Christian counselling and the world of Christian nurture are brought together. Craig Dykstra's

Vision and Character[25] is another. Arguing against the rules-orientated view of moral development which he finds in the work of Lawrence Kohlberg, and through Kohlberg in James Fowler, Dykstra believes instead in a 'visional ethics':

> 'Decisions, choices, particular actions are not the first consideration in visional ethics. The foreground is occupied by questions concerning what we see, and what it is that enables human beings to see more realistically. For visional ethics, action follows vision; and vision depends on character – a person thinking, reasoning, believing, feeling, willing and acting as a whole.'[26]

Dykstra goes on to argue, following Stanley Hauerwas, that character is formed in community, and that Christian character grows in a person, as that person learns from the experience and example of others. 'We learn from particular people who give themselves as a conduit for us into a vision of the community of which they and we together are a part.'[27]

At this point, pastoral care and counselling, and the educational tasks of the church, come close together. It is 'with all the saints' that we learn something of the love of God (Ephesians 3:18). It is within the community of Christian people learning together that character is formed in 'those who have their faculties trained by practice to distinguish good from evil (Hebrews 5:14).

Counselling: an Exploration of Meanings

What, then, is counselling in a Christian context? This is a form of Christian ministry which is less deep, less structured, less demanding, maybe, than psychotherapy, and yet is deeper, and more structured than simply 'being friends'. Counsellor and client, vicar and parishioner, member of house fellowship group and member of the church's pastoral team, member of a catechumenate group or church training session with their teacher, all are engaged in a particular form of covenanted relationship in which one is offering to try to understand the inner world of the other to try to help them find some sense, some meaning in it.

In the more structured forms of counselling, we are, for a particular time, setting aside everyday demands and assumptions, in order to work at certain tasks which, in due course, will enable us to handle the everyday more constructively. We are engaged in trying to help people deal with a reality that is sometimes too frightening to be faced, to handle anxieties which can be crippling, to find ways of dealing with guilt and shame which is not resentful and bitter.

The approach

The Christian carer and counsellor will be seeking to work with the Holy Spirit who guides into truth, and to learn from the Spirit who shows sin up to be what it is, who proves the ungodly world wrong with respect to what is good, and holy and righteous (John 16:8, 9).

Christian counsellors will work with a particular view of what it is to be human, informed by the nature of Jesus Christ, the Human Being. They will have a distinctive framework of moral values, believing these to liberate and not constrain. They will have goals set on the journey towards maturity in Christ, by whatever route, down whatever byways, through whatever rapids, over whatever obstacles, such a journey may take. As part of their resources, they will be armed not only with Christian convictions, but with theoretical and practical skills from the world of psychotherapy, counselling, and social work.

Given individual personalities and styles, what models work best? Counsellors will want to:

keep up to date with psychological understandings of human development;
nurture skills in making a good therapeutic relationship;
take care in diagnosis, and in what questions are asked;
be aware of how one's own personality and needs enter into the relationship, for good or ill;

provide a space, physical and emotional, in which the other
can grow, an environment which is facilitating, a resource of
grace.

The one-to-one here and now relationship is inevitably one part
of a wider network of human relationships; and if this wider
network can be a loving, supportive, Christian caring community,
it too contributes to the therapeutic environment: a 'culture to
grow in', to use Kegan's phrase. The Church as the whole body of
Christ, worshipping, praying, reconciling, caring, supporting,
giving, receiving, is the context for Christians to counsel.

Throughout the whole caring process we are seaching for truth,
searching for wisdom, searching for meaning. Alongside the secret
work of the Spirit in common grace, restraining evil and promoting
what is good, the ministry of Christian caring and counselling is
part of the Spirit's work healing wounds, establishing rationality,
making peace, furthering human harmony. And it is His work, with
which we may be allowed to cooperate. We do not take God into
situations where He was previously absent, as though we can
contain and manipulate God, and turn him on to order. God is
there. God is working. God's image is there in the hurting person
seeking our help. God's grace is already at work in that person's
life. God has a purpose for that person, and the carer is just one
part of an ongoing story, which began before this particular aspect
of counselling started, and will continue long after these
counselling sessions end. God is bringing all His creation towards
its completion in Christ.

So when we come into a situation in God's name, when we agree
to meet someone to talk things over with them, we take off our
shoes and we tread carefully, because we are already on holy
ground.

A Journey in Hope
The Holy Spirit is described as the 'earnest of our inheritance', as
a first down payment of divine blessing. This sort of language
reminds us of the dynamic of faith. We are part of a journey of

pilgrimage and change. There is a 'Not Yet' as well as a 'Now Already' in the story of salvation. Everything that is said about care, counselling, healing and political change has to be set in the eschatological context of being 'between the aeons'. We are still in Adam as well as now also being in Christ. All change is therefore incomplete this side of heaven.

The journey that we take, however, is also the journey that God has taken before us. Pastoral ministry is a taking part in the ministry of God, in which He is already engaged, taking His whole creation into the kingdom of His glory. Christian pastoral care looks for God's workings in people and in contexts, and seeks to cooperate with His already present work of grace.

The gifts of the Holy Spirit are given to the church to facilitate growth into maturity. For as Christ is formed in His Body, so the new humanity comes into its maturity. Ministry is not, then, only or even primarily for the sake of the Church. It is the ministry of Christ to the Father in the power of the Spirit for the sake of the whole world. It is our task to allow ourselves to be caught up into His work - to work, for He is at work within us for His good pleasure (Philippians 2:13). In Christ all the fullness of God was pleased to dwell, and through Him to reconcile to Himself all things (Ephesians 1:10; 2 Corinthians 5:19). From Him and through Him and to Him are all things (Romans 11:35). It is through Him that all the work of pastoral caring and counselling finds its meaning, its resources, its confidence, and its hope.

Part 3

A BASIS IN HOPE

THEOLOGY, HOPE AND COUNSELLING

Despairing World, Hopeless People

Purpose, meaning and hope at the end of the twentieth century are commodities in short supply. Shortly before he died, the French existentialist philosopher Jean Paul Sartre declared that 'the world seems ugly, bad and without hope.'[1] Sartre's contemporary and fellow existentialist, Albert Camus, spoke of 'that hopeless encounter between human questioning and the silence of the universe.'[2] The British philosopher Bertrand Russell wrote that, 'Only on the firm foundation of unyielding despair can the soul's habitation be safely built.'[3, 4]

Sartre and Camus are the twentieth century's leading exponents of a philosophy explicitly built on despair. John Hick accurately sums up the character and significance of existentialism:

Most of the writings which identify themselves as 'existentialist' are concerned with the description of human existence as it is immediately experienced. They stress its temporal character and make central use of themes such as anxiety, finitude, guilt, despair, dread of death and of 'non-being', doubt, meaninglessness, loneliness and self-estrangement. The language of existentialism tends to be the language of the soul's distress. It depicts twentieth-century urban life in the industrialized West as the spiritual nightmare that it can be for minds acutely sensitive to the decay of tradition, the collapse of cultural forms and the threat of a nuclear holocaust. Existentialist literature . . . expresses the neuroses of an age which finds itself being carried into the unknown on the wheel of immense and bewildering changes.[5]

What's more, when we move from the world of the despairing philosopher to the world of the ordinary person, we find the cry for hope ever present in the events and crises of human life:

- 'What hope is there doctor?' pleads the mother whose child has been run over in a car accident.
- 'What hope have I got?' asks the man who has been made redundant at the age of 49.
- 'I only hope a cure can be found in time,' says the AIDS patient.
- 'Is there *any* hope we can find somewhere to live?' begs the homeless couple speaking to the housing association.

The counsellor dealing with a troubled or distressed client is frequently found facing questions of deep despair and hopelessness: the person trapped by feelings of guilt; the person whose life seems implacably overshadowed by a sense of dread; the person who lives permanently in depression. All counsellees need some affirmation that hope exists not in the abstract or in theory alone but actually for *them*, in *their* world, faced with *their* problems. A major task of the counsellor is to enable them to discover such hope and to find resources for its sustenance.

The Christian counsellor has grounds for hope which go far beyond the ability of human beings to conjure up some kind of will o' the wisp optimism out of despair. In this final part of *Counselling in Context* we shall examine the theological foundation of hope as the counterpoint to existential despair and as the basis for effective counselling. Our analysis will divide into three parts:

Firstly, we shall observe the structure of hope: how the concept can be understood in such a way as to inform our counselling method.
Secondly, we shall consider the object and content of hope, namely God Himself.

Thirdly, we shall look at the resources of hope available to
   Christians as they seek to live in the light of hope.

The Structure of Christian Hope

The German theologian Jurgen Moltmann points out that hope
centres on promise: not any old promise but specifically the
promise of God.[6-8] It is this, he argues, which underwrites hope
and guarantees its vindication. So the despairing counsellee and
the Christian counsellor are immediately pointed away from the
source of despair to the source of hope - God. To see how this
works, we need to examine Moltmann's idea of promise more
closely.

   In his exposition of God's promise, Moltmann picks out six
features which undergird theological hope:

Firstly, we should note that a promise points to a situation which
   has yet to come into being. 'A promise is a declaration which
   announces the coming of a reality that does not yet exist.'[9]
   Moltmann is saying two things here: in the first place he is
   reminding us that the future is always open. It is not already
   specified like some blueprint which cannot be changed. It is
   there for the making, by us and by God. Indeed, when we speak
   of the purpose of God for our lives we should not think of only
   one already-determined pathway which we miss at our peril.
   Rather, we need to think in terms of several possible pathways
   which God holds out to us, all of which may be equally valid.
   As creatures made in His image and endowed with powers of
   choice and reason, we are invited to choose in good faith and
   to trust Him for whatever is to come. This means that we are
   not captives to the past. To be sure, the past does influence us
   and we are to some extent the children of our past. But, insists
   Moltmann, that does not mean that the future is completely
   controlled by the past. God can contradict the past. What
   seemed or seems impossible in human terms can be brought

about by the creative will of God. The divine promise can be 'something which by the standard of present experience appears impossible.' The resurrection of Jesus proves this.

Secondly, 'the promise binds man to his own future.' In other words, God's promise points us to the importance of what is to come rather than to what has already taken place. We need to understand our life histories – and this is where the insights of psychotherapy are crucial – but we must not regard ourselves as fundamentally backward looking. We must see ourselves as orientated toward the future which is *God's* future for us. The promise is a pledge of God's activity in and for our future. The future is linked to the past not by an inexorable law of history but by the promise of God which gives a unity of meaning to both: 'The meaning of the past and the meaning of the future come to light in the word of promise.'

Thirdly, we need to grasp that the promise *will* be fulfilled. Its guarantor is none other than God Himself. Whether we are speaking of the history and future of the world or of our own personal histories and futures, they are all underwritten not by 'the urge of vague forces' but by 'the word of direction that points us to the free power and faithfulness of God.' The person in distress finds hope, therefore, not in deterministic laws of cause and effect but in the divine promise whose fulfilment is guaranteed by Him whose word cannot be broken.

Fourthly, the divine promise always creates a tension between the 'now' and the 'not yet' – that is, between the life of God's kingdom as we presently experience it and the fulness which is to come. This is related to Moltmann's previous observation that the promise refers to a state of affairs not yet in being. The tension arises out of the fact that there is always an interval between the giving of a promise and its fulfilment. During this period, the fulfilment is awaited with eagerness and sometimes in pain but the end is assured: fulfilment of the promise. Part of this tension, however, is attributable to a second feature: the inherent nature of the divine promise as a contradiction of the present. The promise challenges and exposes the present for what it is - unfulfilled. The counsellee who feels the force of emptiness and pain, therefore, needs to see him or herself as living in an interval which will assuredly end in fulfilment. Pain is part and parcel of the unfolding of promise and although we may long to see it end, we can, by God's grace, embrace it (to borrow Paul's metaphor) as a birthpang preceding new life (see Romans 8:18-25).

Fifthly, God's promises are never comparable to fatalistic predictions which operate according to incontrovertible laws of history: 'There can be no burning interest in constructing a hard and fast juridical system of historic necessities according to a schema of promise and fulfilment.'[9] Although God can be trusted to bring about what He has promised, He is free as well as faithful. So 'the fulfilments can very well contain an element of newness and surprise over against the promise as it was received.' That God will fulfil His promise is not in doubt. How He will do so depends on His sovereign freedom.

Finally, Moltmann urges we remember that the nature of promise is that it has an ever-expanding horizon. When fulfilled, it is never wrapped up or completed in its fulfilment. For the fulfilment itself creates new horizons. Thus the promises of the Old Testament, although fulfilled, were never closed or written off. God fulfilled His promise to bring Israel to the Promised Land but this opened up a new horizon of obedience and blessing. God's promise of a Messiah was fulfilled in Christ but this in turn opened up the new horizon of Pentecost and the Second Coming. Each fulfilment leads to further hope: 'Hence every reality in which a fulfilment is already taking place now becomes the confirmation, exposition and liberation of a greater hope.'[9] In short, hope never ends.

How can the Christian counsellor appropriate these insights so as to help the troubled person? Three possibilities suggest themselves:

1 Remind the counsellee of the centrality of promise in the life of the believer. The activity of God and the experience of God's people are founded on promise. This will require the counsellor

to bring out the characteristics of promise as Moltmann has done. In this way, the counsellee can see that the counsellor is not simply trying to find comforting words or is resorting to theological evasion but is expounding a truth rooted in the activity of God. To quote Richard Bauckham, 'In His promises God is known . . . as one who pledges himself to do things in history - to implement his righteousness to accomplish his lordship in the world.'[10] Part of that lordship is the pouring of grace and love into the lives of agonized individuals.

2 The counsellee must be enabled to identify his own experience of pain, frustration and unfulfilment with the essential nature of the promised relationship. To the person who wonders whether there can be any point in the pain he is going through, this can be a liberating revelation. As he realizes that all God's promises carry with them an interval of pain prior to fulfilment, he can see how suffering may fit into the dynamics of the unfolding promise. 'If this is how God has worked in the past and how He works now, maybe my pain has purpose after all.'

3 We need to point to the faithfulness of God in honouring His promises in His dealings with His people throughout history. We are not preaching a God who makes grandiose promises that will never be fulfilled. Rather we are speaking of a God who has already enacted His promises in the experience of Israel and in the person of His Son. Promise is not another name for fancy dreams or pie in the sky but is a description of how God has worked and will work in the world. This leads us to our second major feature of hope, its *content*.

The Content of Hope

Hope without content is little more than mere sentiment. Those who come for counselling need more than wishful thinking. They need to be assured that Christian hope has a substantial content which will meet their needs. We can think of such content under three headings: hope in God; hope in God's faithfulness; and hope in Christ.

Hope in God

Christian hope is grounded in God. It turns outwards from the battered ego of the hoper to the object of hope, the Trinitarian God. In the Father, Son and Spirit we have the One who gives hope, the One who brings hope and the One who sustains hope. The Father of promise sends the Son as the fulfilment of His promise; the Son, in turn, is witnessed to by the Spirit of promise. In this way, hope is vouchsafed by the unity-in-action of the Godhead.

That hope is always orientated towards God is made clear throughout the Bible. In the 73 Old Testament passages in which the hope of Israel is expressed by the verb '*to hope*' or the noun '*hope*', the object is invariably Yahweh. This understanding is unique. As E. Hoffmann has pointed out, other nations did not equate their gods with hope. Only in Israel could Yahweh be addressed as Hope: 'Those Babylonians whose prayers have come down to us never called their gods their 'Hope'. But an Israelite could pray 'Thou, O Lord, art my hope (Psalm 71:5)'[11]

In consequence, despite the frequent temptation to despair, Israel knew her hope to be guaranteed by God: 'Thus Yahweh was the object, embodiment and guarantor of His people's hope.' Israel is therefore pictured as waiting for His name (Psalm 52:9), His word of forgiveness (Psalm 130:5), His mighty arm (Isaiah 51:5) and His salvation (Genesis 49:18). These are anticipations governed by hope.

We shall shortly see how this idea is picked up by the New Testament writers. For the moment we may note that the revelation of Christ creates a new situation so that Christian hope is grounded in the combination of God fulfilling his promise in Christ and the new horizons of promise opened up by the resurrection, the coming of the Spirit and the promised return of Jesus in glory.

In counselling terms, however, the key point about hope in God is that it removes both the counsellor and the counsellee from the realm of persistent introspection. The object of concern is no longer a preoccupation with self but instead becomes the promise of God. Moreover, since the fulfilment does not depend upon human efforts, but is solely in the hands of God, the striving for self-healing which characterizes so much counselling is negated. This is not to say that the inward journey of self-analysis is unnecessary. Far from it. The counsellee will need to understand his past in order to be open to the future and will need to face his own feelings if God is to bring about inner healing. But the focus and burden of hope is no longer solely the individual trying to effect change for himself by agonizing upon the past but is the God whose sovereign love will bring about the fulfilment of His promise.

To the troubled person we need therefore to say, 'Look, self-understanding is good. That way you will better come to terms with your pain. But it is God who will bring change, whether by therapy or by some other means. God's promise is to *you* and He will fulfil it.'

Hope in God's Faithfulness

How can we enable people in distress to trust God and thereby live in hope? Ultimately, this is a work of the Spirit who Himself is called 'the Counsellor'. But in His ministry He can use us as counsellors to disclose God's faithfulness to those who seek our (and God's) help. One crucial way in which we can do this is to show how God has been faithful to His people in the past. Here, as Lawrence Crabb rightly insists, a thorough knowledge of the Bible is vital. For it is in the Scriptures that we find the promises of God given and fulfilled. Two examples among many illustrate this truth.

Our first example is Abraham. He is significant both because the Old Testament portrays him as a man of faith trusting in God's faithfulness and because the New Testament pictures him as the supreme example of hope. Thus Paul speaks of Abraham's faith as 'hope against hope':

Against all hope, Abraham in hope believed and so became the father of many nations . . . Without weakening in his faith, he faced the fact that his body was as good as dead - since he was about a hundred years old - and that Sarah's womb was also dead. Yet he did not waver through unbelief regarding the promise of God but was strengthened in his faith and gave glory to God, being fully persuaded that God had the power to do what he promised (Romans 4:18-21 NIV).

Stephen Travis has argued that the significance of Abraham's hope lies in the fact that it serves as a paradigm first for the nation of Israel and later for the new Israel, the church. Both Old and New Testament writers see Abraham as the example *par excellence* of hope because in his person he receives and obeys the promise of God with the result that God is faithful and blesses him. What better picture could believers have of the dynamics of promise and hope?

'From their very beginning the Israelites were a people on a journey - a journey towards the destiny which God had set before them . . . With Abraham there began God's grand design to bring blessing to the whole world. And what began as the journey of a nomadic group became the pilgrimage through history of a people loaded with hope.'[12]

To understand how the story of Abraham brings together hope and faithfulness, we need to go back to the original incident in Genesis 12 in which God's promise is declared:

The Lord has said to Abram 'Leave your country, your people and your father's household and go to the land I will show you. I will make you into a great nation and I will bless you. I will make your name great and you will be a blessing. I will bless those who bless you and whoever curses you I will curse; and all the peoples on earth will be blessed through you (Genesis 12:1-3, NIV).

On what was Abraham's hope based? Travis identifies a threefold promise:

Firstly, God promised a land. To the nomadic Abraham this must have seemed stupendous. Here is a strange God promising not just blessing but a homeland. Later we learn that Abraham had his doubts and questions (Genesis 15:6) but God's promise remained secure: Abraham and his descendants were to inherit a land stretching from Egypt in the south-west to the Euphrates in the north-east (15:18).

Secondly, God promised Abraham descendants. At a time when Abraham was a hundred and his wife was ten years younger and barren, this at first seemed impossible. Indeed, Abraham's astonishment made him think God was joking: 'Abraham fell face down; he laughed and said to himself, "Will a son be born to a man a hundred years old? Will Sarah bear a child at the age of ninety?"' (Genesis 17:17). Significantly, God's reply is to reaffirm his promise of hope: 'Then God said, "Yes, but your wife Sarah will bear you a son and you will call him Isaac. I will establish my covenant with him as an everlasting covenant for his descendants after him"' (17:19).

Thirdly, God promised blessing. Not simply for Abraham but for his descendants; and through them for the nations. God's promise is only initially for Abraham. His covenant is ultimately a covenant for the world: 'As for me, this is My covenant with you: You will be the father of many nations . . . I will make you very fruitful; I will make nations of you and kings will come from you (Genesis 17:4-6).

When we put the Genesis account together with Paul's discussion in Romans we find that Abraham's story demonstrates exactly those features of promise and hope outlined by Moltmann:

- God's promise declared a reality which had not yet come to pass;
- it orientated Abraham to the future;
- it was fulfilled; it stood in contradiction to Abraham's present experience of landlessness and childlessness;

- it created a tension and disbelief in Abraham;
- it did not depend on Abraham for its fulfilment;
- and in fulfilling it, God opened up new horizons as Israel came to the Promised Land and struggled in its relationship with Yahweh.

So it is little wonder that Abraham features in the Bible as a prime example of hope.

How can this help counsellors and counsellees? Perhaps the most important point is that Abraham's doubts, fears, worries, disbelief and sense of unimportance echo precisely the feeling of those who come for counselling. This means that the dynamic of hope and promise is as relevant to modern humanity as it was to Abraham. Put simply, if God could be Abraham's secure hope, he can be ours. Although the work of healing may be long and tough, there can be no greater message of liberation than that.

Our second example of hope can be found in the writings of the Old Testament prophets. At first sight this might seem surprising since much of their message was concerned with pronouncing God's judgement. But the prophets illustrate well the truth that God's promises always create new horizons. For their condemnation of Israel was aimed at challenging the people of God to rediscover the horizon of God's will by honouring their covenant obligations: that is, they challenged their hearers to live in obedience to the promise of hope. The descendants of Abraham, having experienced the fulfilment of God's original promise by entering into the Promised Land, were now recalled to the conditions God had established for the continuing covenant relationship, the relationship of promise.

Paradoxically, the failure of Israel and Judah to accept the challenge delivered by the prophets vindicated the promise of God and thereby re-established the dynamic of hope. Even in failure, God's promise was upheld.

Living History
The prophets refused to allow God's people to introspect upon

their national past as if that were all that mattered in their relationship with God. The religion of Israel by the eighth century BC had become focused largely on the past. The prophets, however, did more than recall the nation to the chronicle of events which made up its history: they recalled it to its *living* history in which the experience of Yahweh's continuing and future presence was central. It was this presence which had been lost. The institutionalization of religion in the temple at Jerusalem had become a cover for apostasy and false promises. People had come to find their security not in a continuing relationship of hope but in military alliances. The relationship of promise had been reduced to lip service paid to God's deeds in history:

> People looked back to the exodus from Egypt, back to the reign of David and to the building of the temple in Jerusalem. Amos, in the middle of the eighth century BC, took them by the scruff of the neck and insisted that the event which they most needed to reckon with lay in the future – the day of the Lord. And that day would be darkness, not light.[13]

As we scan the writings of the prophets we see the same point emerging time and again: Yahweh will bring catastrophe unless the nation repents. They must not be fooled into a sense of false security. For in the end, nothing will save them from the God of promise determined to enact His judgement:

> The Lord has spoken: 'Woe to the obstinate children . . . who carry out plans that are not Mine, forming an alliance but not by My Spirit, heaping sin upon sin, who go down to Egypt without consulting Me, who look for help to Pharaoh's protection . . . The Sovereign Lord, the Holy One of Israel, says: 'In repentance and rest is your salvation, in quietness and trust is your strength, but you would have none of it. (Isaiah 30:1ff, 15ff NIV)
>
> Hear the word of the Lord, all you people who come through these gates (of the Temple) to worship the Lord. This

is what the Lord Almighty, the God of Israel says: 'Reform your ways and your actions and I will let you live in peace. Do not trust in deceptive words and say 'This is the Temple of the Lord, the Temple of the Lord, the Temple of the Lord.' If you really change your ways and your actions . . . I will let you live in this place, in the land I gave to your forefathers for ever and ever.' (Jeremiah 7:4-7 NIV).

Such passages make it clear that Yahweh's condemnation was not the result of divine caprice but of Israel's and Judah's abandonment of promise. How then can this be reckoned to be a feature of hope? It is important to realize that the judgement of God vindicates His promise every bit as much as does His blessing. For the essence of promise is consistency: God will achieve His purpose; He will not be thwarted or mocked. The integrity of God's promise is consequently tied to the integrity of His character. He could not be faithful to His promise unless He were prepared to act in judgement as well as blessing.

This is precisely what was at stake in the confrontation between Israel, Judah and Yahweh. They had flouted the covenant by presuming upon God's promise. They assumed that He would act mercifully no matter what sins His people committed and no matter how much they disregarded the promise relationship. The prophetic condemnations, therefore, safeguarded God's integrity. They declared that His promise could not be flouted at will without incurring His wrath.

We can see this yet more clearly by asking what integrity would have remained to God's promise had He chosen to ignore Israel's rebellion. Suppose He had not sent the prophets but had overlooked the breaking of the covenant. What then? The very basis of His promise would have collapsed: its fulfilment depended upon a God whose dealings were consistent. And a refusal to confront sin would have failed this test. The paradox of prophetic hope, therefore, is that in declaring the catastrophe yet to come God was at one and the same time imbuing the prophets with a message of despair and a message of hope. In Moltmann's words, 'His divinity consists in the constancy of His faithfulness, which becomes credible in the contradiction of judgement and grace.[14]

This is only one side of the paradox, however. The other feature of the prophetic hope was God's promise of restoration and a new start:

> 'At that time I will gather you; at that time I will bring you home. I will give you honour and praise among all the peoples of the earth when I restore your fortunes before your very eyes,' says the Lord (Zephaniah 3:20 NIV).

When we look at this hope we see it to be characterized by images of renewal and re-creation in which the pre-eminence of Israel and her God will shine forth to the world:

> In the last days the mountain of the Lord's temple will be established as chief among the mountains; it will be raised above the hills and all nations will stream to it. Many peoples will come and say, 'Come let us go up to the mountain of the Lord, to the house of the God of Jacob. He will teach us His ways so that we may walk in His paths. He will judge between the nations and will settle disputes for many peoples. They will beat their swords into ploughshares and their spears into pruning hooks. Nation will not take up sword against nation, nor will they train for war any more (Isaiah 2:2-4, NIV).

The promise of God will thus accomplish the impossible in contradiction of the present. The characteristics of hope are declared once more, this time for the whole earth:

> This judgement certainly means the annihilation of the people and of the history to which this people owes its existence, but it does not mean the annihilation of Yahweh's faithfulness to Himself. It can therefore be conceived as a judgement that paves the way for something finally new, and as annihilation for the sake of greater perfection.[15]

So where does this leave us *vis-à-vis* counselling? We can answer this by saying that as with the example of Abraham, the prophets serve to remind us that despite our feelings of failure, sinfulness, desertion and despair – whether they have arisen out of sinful behaviour or something else – the promise of God will be vindicated. He will fulfil His loving purpose. Moreover, we find the biblical writers giving expression to exactly those feelings which beset the troubled counsellee who feels he has failed God and that God has abandoned him:

> You (Yahweh) have covered yourself with anger and pursued us; you have slain without pity. You have covered yourself with cloud so that no prayer can get through. You have made us scum and refuse among the nations (Lamentations 3:43-45 NIV).

This sense of desolation is felt by many of those who come for counselling. The significance of the prophetic hope, therefore, must be that just as God acted out of promise to restore His people, even when they had sinned, so God will act out of that selfsame promise to restore the wounded soul today. This is the case whether we have sinned or not. God's *hesed*, his covenant love, remains true.

But we cannot leave the prophets without indicating one further dimension of their hope which is relevant to our theme. The prophets looked forward to a time when a Messiah, God's chosen servant, would accomplish His promise.

> Rejoice greatly, O Daughter of Zion! Shout, daughter of Jerusalem! See, your King comes to you, righteous and having salvation, gentle and riding on a donkey, on a colt, the foal of a donkey. He will proclaim peace to the nations. His rule will extend from sea to sea and from the River to the ends of the earth (Zechariah 9-10 NIV).

In these passages we see that the new horizon which is always present in the dynamic of promise and hope is to be fulfilled by a single man. The prophets saw this in terms of the warrior King, sent by God, who would establish God's rule over all the world with Israel restored to prominence. The New Testament writers, however, saw this somewhat differently as being fulfilled in the man Jesus Christ. It is therefore to His significance for a theology of hope we now turn.

Hope in Jesus Christ

The centre of Christian hope is Jesus Christ. In His incarnation, His inauguration of the kingdom, His death, His resurrection, the coming of His Spirit and the establishment of His body the church, we see divine promise enacted. Simply to recite this list shows how Christ is the all-encompassing fulfilment of the divine promise.

E. Hoffmann points out that for the writers of the New Testament the coming of Christ 'fundamentally altered' the situation of hope which had been promised but not yet fulfilled by the Old Testament.[16] The day of the Lord proclaimed by the prophets broke into history in the person of Christ. What was previously future became present in Him. And because of this, the concept of hope was radically reshaped.

This reshaping centred on the fact that God had come not in power and glory but in humility as 'one of us'. The visionary language of the prophets with its emphasis on God's seizing control of human affairs in majesty, might and dominion had to be reinterpreted to recognize the truth of the incarnation. The fulfilment of the divine promise could be seen not in the dramatic inbreaking of the cosmic king in glorious power but in the birth, life, death and resurrection of the God-man Jesus.

The all-encompassing nature of hope in Christ finds expression in a number of ways. Firstly, we may note that hope is one of the three virtues Paul refers to as characteristic of the Christian life. In his famous exposition of love in 1 Corinthians 13, he speaks of faith, hope and love as 'excellent ways' (vv.1,13). Together they form the triad essential to Christian discipleship. Moreover, none of them can exist without the others. There can be no hope without faith in Christ for He is the object and guarantor of our hope. There can be no faith without hope in the resurrected Christ for such faith would be empty and futile. And neither faith nor hope can truly embody the divine promise without embracing love. Thus faith, hope and love are bound up together.

Secondly, such is the centrality of hope that Peter speaks of it as 'new birth into a living hope':

> Praise be to the God and Father of our Lord Jesus Christ. In His great mercy He has given us new birth into a living hope through the resurrection of Jesus Christ from the dead and into an inheritance that can never perish, spoil or fade (1 Peter 1:3–4 NIV).

We see here once more the connection between hope and resurrection. Hope in Christ is not rooted in the example of His life or even His death. Still less it is to be found in our aspirations to be like Him. It is rooted in the fact of Christ's resurrection from the dead. This alone is the ground of our hope. In the words of St Paul:

> If Christ has not been raised, your faith is futile; you are still in your sins . . . If only for this life we have hope in Christ, we are to be pitied more than all men (1 Corinthians 15:17,19 NIV).

Thirdly, hope addresses the most fundamental questions of human existence. It lies therefore at the centre of the web of beliefs that comprises Christian faith. Issues of life, death, meaning and purpose converge on Christ. He is our hope because in Him these questions find their resolution. When we ask how we may know the hope of forgiveness from sin, the answer is in the death of the sin-bearer on the cross. If we inquire how we can be sure of eternal life, the answer lies in the resurrection. When we seek hope for power to live a new life by faith, our hope lies in the gift of the Spirit. When we look for hope for the world, such hope is found in the kingdom of the Christ who will make all things new. He is both the focus and the means of hope.

Fourthly, hope can be found only in Christ. In Ephesians 2:12, the writer reminds his audience that prior to their coming to Christ, they were devoid of hope. They were like the nations of old who, because they did not belong to God's chosen people, were excluded from the covenant relationship and its blessings. By contrast, their faith in Christ, made possible by His death, has brought them hope:

> Remember that at that time you were separate from Christ, excluded from citizenship in Israel and foreigners to the covenants of promise, without hope and without God in the world. But now in Christ Jesus you who were once far away have been brought near through the blood of Christ . . . Consequently, you are no longer foreigners and aliens but fellow-citizens with God's people and members of God's household (Ephesians 2:12,13,19 NIV).

Fifthly, hope is described as a gift. It is proclaimed by means of the gospel (Colossians 1:23) and is received freely. It cannot be worked for: it is a gift of God's grace. Thus Paul encourages the Thessalonians:

> May our Lord Jesus Christ Himself and God our Father, who loved us by His grace and gave us eternal encouragement and good hope, encourage your hearts and strengthen you in every good deed and word (2 Thessalonians 2:16–17 NIV).

This emphasis on grace is crucial. Paul is determined to make clear that the gospel of hope derives solely from divine promise and not from human goodness or strivings. It is only the objective grace of God which can guarantee our salvation. If we were to rely on ourselves we would be without hope. Christ alone is sufficient to ensure our righteousness before God and thereby our eternal life.

Having thus briefly surveyed ways in which hope is portrayed as Christocentric, we must now turn to a more detailed examination of how the God of promise revealed in the examples of Abraham and the prophets fulfils His promise in His Son. Once we have grasped the logic of this we shall be in a position to see how the counsellor is more adequately equipped to speak a word of authentic hope to the troubled person. To do this, we shall return to the writings of Jurgen Moltmann.

God in Christ: The Basis of Hope

Moltmann's theology is subtle and complex. But for our purposes we need only to understand how Moltmann traces the continuity of the divine promise from Abraham to Christ and then into the future. It is in this theology that we discover the richness of hope as a resource for counselling.

Moltmann's starting point is to affirm that the God who raised Jesus from the dead and thereby guaranteed *our* hope is the same God who revealed Himself in promise to Abraham and through him to Israel. 'It was Yahweh, the God of Abraham, of Isaac and of Jacob, the God of promise who raised Jesus from the dead.'[17] This leads logically to the conclusion that 'the God who reveals Himself in Jesus must be thought of as the God of the Old Testament, as the God of the exodus and the promise.'

Consequently, the God of the New Testament, the Father of our Lord Jesus Christ, is in His very Being, Promise.[18] 'It is peculiarly significant that in the New Testament God is known and described as the God of promise . . . The essential predicate of God accordingly lies in the statement: "Faithful is He that promised."' The God to whom we relate through Christ is a God of promise with all that the biblical conception of promise and hope entails.

Moltmann draws our attention to the fact that in Paul's exposition of the Christ-hope, Abraham is all-important. The Abraham/Christ connection lies at the heart of the gospel in Romans 1–4 and without it, the New Testament conception of hope collapses. Therefore we have to ask, 'What does this teach us about true hope?' As we reflect upon the question we observe significantly that

Paul does not return to Moses and the law as the example of promise but rather to Abraham. Why is this so?

The answer is twofold. In the first place, it is important to realize that Christ did not come to restore Israel as people of God but to create a *new* people of God. He therefore fulfils the promise not by renewing old life but by creating new. 'For Paul the Christ event is not a renewal of the people of God but brings to life a new people of God made up of Jews and Gentiles.'[19] He is the 'rebirth, liberation and validation' of promise. As Paul puts it, 'If anyone is in Christ he is a new creation; the old has gone the new has come' (2 Corinthians 5:17).

The second reason why Paul returns to Abraham rather than Moses is that he seeks to draw an analogy between the promise of life made to Abraham and the promise of life made to those who are in Christ. The crucial difference, however, is that 'Paul understands "life" no longer in the context of possessing the land, being fruitful and multiplying, but as "quickening of the dead"'[19] Christological hope is not hope of a new and or of some comparable material blessing but is hope of eternal life in which the power of death is broken and resurrection assured.

The God who fulfils His promise in Christ is thus the same God whose faithfulness is testified on every page of the Old Testament. From this we can discover two highly significant implications. Firstly, just as in Judaism there was a certainty in God's faithfulness to His promises, so the same is true of Christianity. The selfsame divine guarantor of hope is at work. Yet there is a radical difference – the ground of assurance is new: 'because God has the power to quicken the dead and call into being things that are not, therefore the fulfilment of His promise is possible; and because He has raised Christ from the dead, therefore the fulfilment of His promise is certain' according to Moltmann.

The second implication is concerned with the *scope* of God's promise. The movement of theological thought from citing the example of Abraham to Christ is a movement from the particular to the universal. The promise is expanded from the word of hope given to one man and through him to a single nation to being proclaimed to the whole of humanity. In Christ it is not simply a new nation that is created but a new human race:

> Through the raising of Jesus from the dead the God of the promises of Israel becomes the God of all men . . . It is the Christ event that first gives birth to what can theologically be described as 'man', 'true man', 'humanity' - 'neither Jew nor Greek, neither bond nor free, neither male nor female' (Galatians 3:28). Only when the real, historic and religious differences between peoples, groups and classes are broken down in the Christ event in which the sinner is justified, does there come a prospect of what true humanity can be and will be.[20]

This neatly illustrates one of the prime characteristics we have noted about divine hope: its capacity to open up new horizons even as it is being fulfilled. The fulfilment of the promise made to Abraham issues not only in salvation for the Jews but in salvation for the Gentiles. The coming of Christ creates a new horizon: hope for the world.

One further aspect must be noted. Moltmann insists that the essence of hope in Christ is its eschatological future. By this he means that the future is always present in the divine promise. Christian hope is never purely a matter of looking back to the action of God in the past. It can never be merely a recital of historical acts: this was the fatal mistake of Israel at the time of the prophets. We must understand that our hope lies not in the past fulfilment of promise but in the ways in which that fulfilment points to future promise. 'What the scripture that was "written before our time" offers must therefore contain possibilities and a future to which present hope can be directed.'[21]

The action of God in Christ consequently demonstrates the fulfilment of the promise made to Abraham (which was repeated in the prophets) but at the same time creates a new horizon for the promise of the future. Moreover, in fulfilling His promise God gives signs that the future has already begun. The resurrection is

evidence of the reversal of death which is to culminate in the
resurrection at the end of time. The coming of the Spirit is a
foretaste of heaven. The gifts of the Spirit are the firstfruits of the
new age. The church is the forerunner of the redemption of the
world. As the parables of Jesus make clear, the kingdom of heaven
has arrived. In George Ladd's memorable phrase, we have the
presence of the future.[22]

How, then, does all this help the Christian counsellor and the
counsellee? We have already noted a number of ways in which hope
can inform counselling; but we can perhaps best summarize these
by going back to one of the examples we saw in chapter one when
we considered the importance of contexts.

Michael Revisited

To summarize: Michael's situation is as follows. He is an officer
in the army who has been brought up and trained not to show his
feelings. He and his German wife Lisel, a Roman Catholic, have
had their baby aborted. Lisel is racked with guilt and Michael falls
into depression. He starts to drink heavily.

If Michael were to come to us in despair how would a theology
of hope help us and him? (or if Michael and Lisel were to come
together). The last thing he would be able to cope with is a lecture
on the theological concept of hope; so we would need to identify
points in his experience and self-understanding at which we could
share a word of hope. The most likely context for this would be
if Michael were to recount his life story. The telling of the past
would not only be therapeutic but would enable us to discover key
points of meaning.

Michael might, for example, reveal that he had experienced a
childhood in which emotional expression was frowned upon or
perhaps even forbidden. We would need to explore his feelings
about this as he recalled their impact at the time. But equally
important we would need to know how he feels about them now.
In this way, piece by piece, we would begin to build up a picture
of what makes Michael tick. This is important since our
understanding of his past would enable us to help him understand

it too. By means of such understanding Michael would hopefully start to discover God's healing as he became more able to reorient himself with Lisel towards the future.

At this point our theology of promise might begin to interact with Michael's interpretation of his past. His family relationships were no doubt only part of the formation of his psyche and we would need to look together at other areas too. But when we had built up a larger picture, the task of identifying points of hope could begin.

How might we do this? We might help Michael to see that in many respects his life corresponds to the pattern of promise contained in the Bible: the promise of a purposeful life held out by determined parents keen to see their son make an impression on others (hence the repression of emotion); the interval of waiting for this to be fulfilled with its pains and failures; the tension between the now and the not-yet, both before joining the army and then while moving up the career ladder within it; the initial sense of fulfilment as an officer; the new horizon of future promise as a senior officer, maybe even a Chief of Staff! This pattern corresponds closely to the structure of promise we have already noticed.

The same could apply, moreover, to Michael's marriage: the promise of courtship and the early years; the promise of a lifelong relationship of love (important to Michael given his upbringing) and acceptance; the hope of children. But at this point the pattern is destroyed. The promise turns into catastrophe.

A crucial point of meaning has now been identified in Michael's narrative. Up to this point the cycle of promise has been entirely hopeful (in the usual sense). The abortion and apparent collapse of his marriage, however, seem to invalidate the concept of promise. What kind of divine promise is it that ends up like this?

It is here that we might begin gently to introduce the paradox of promise: that in biblical terms it entails the possibility of pain as well as blessing and that the interim between the declaration of promise and its fulfilment contains both. The experience of Israel and even more of Jesus Himself are relevant here.

Great care would be needed in explaining this. For Michael blames himself for the loss of their baby and its effect on his marriage. It is true that he and Lisel must own responsibility for their decision to go ahead with abortion but the word which they long and need to hear at the moment is a word of forgiveness. They already are carrying an impossible burden of guilt and reproach for what they have done. What they need is a gospel which tells them that Christ can forgive and heal even their sense of shame and disvalue because of the promise held out in the Cross and the empty tomb.

They need also to come to terms with their pain in such a way that recognizes the force of the past but which does not make the future bound by it. This, as we have seen, is the essential nature of the promise/hope dynamic. Forgiveness is crucial but a sense of the future belonging to God is likewise important. The priority of gift and grace comes into play.

Michael and Lisel need to reorient their future through faith. We are back once more to the characteristics of the divine promise.

Enabling Michael and Lisel to see this would of course take time. The counsellor would have to live through their pain and despair with them. And these will periodically return, not least when they hear of other couples starting a family. Moreover, the counsellor would need all her skills to enable them to take hold of, and respond to, the gospel of promise. She may fail in this, in which case she would need to listen to the meaning of promise for herself. But the crucial thing is that in considering the hypothetical case of Michael and Lisel, we have seen that a theology of hope can inform the counselling process by offering an understanding of the past, present and future which does not depend wholly on the subjectivity of the counsellees but on the objective promise of God.

Resources for Hope

Michael and Lisel may grasp something of the meaning of divine promise but they will need help to sustain their faith in the future. We have seen in Part II the resources implicit within the Trinitarian grace formula. In this final section we shall summarize the range of distinctive resources which only the Christian churches can offer for the task of counselling. We have thus arrived once more at the point of our departure: counselling in context.

1. *The Holy Trinity* We have seen how hope is rooted in God. This must be our starting point for developing on one hand a theology of hope and on the other resources for the sustenance of hope. In the life of faith in the Trinity, we find immeasurable riches of love, grace and divine power. As we have seen, the Trinity is the foundation for all our hopes.

2. *The Body of Christ* Life in Christ is life in community. The fellowship of God's people is crucial to the sustaining of hope. It is in the life of the Body of Christ that Michael and Lisel will find support and nourishment.

3. *Worship* If God is the source of our hope then our relationship to Him must be governed by worship. The expression of our being in Christ is through worship and it is through worship that God renews our hope.

4. *The Eucharist* 'This is my body . . . this is my blood.' With these words Jesus instituted the meal by which our oneness with Him and our fellows is expressed. Our relationship to the risen Christ is fed and nurtured as we eat and drink the symbols of His death. In the Eucharist we are recalled to the centre of the divine promise, its enactment and its guarantee.

5. *Baptism* By baptism we are incorporated into the death and resurrection of Christ. Our symbolic dying and rising parallels the reality of His own. We carry with us the memory of our own symbolic participation in the events which both fulfilled God's promise of new life and which point to the future.

6. *The Word of God* This can be construed both as Christ Himself (the living Word) and as God's self-revelation through the Scriptures (the written Word). The latter witnesses to the former. It also gives rise to the preaching of God's truth, for how can hope be sustained unless we know about it? And how shall we

know unless it is expounded? The role of the Bible and of preaching in counselling is controversial but crucial.

7. *Prayer*   Prayer is the direct communion of believers with God. It is the lifeblood of the promise relationship without which the divine promise becomes another intellectual truth to be grasped as part of the web of belief. But to become a living hope it must be part of a living relationship with the One who is called Hope.

8. *Service*   It may seem strange to end a list of resources for hope with service. But service for God, our fellows and God's world safeguards us from seeing hope as solely self-centred. It helps us to avoid the temptation to introspect upon our troubled past or present. And in the act of self-giving we encounter the hopes of others to which our own experience of God's promise can bear witness.

Conclusion

It is apposite that this book should end with a discussion of hope. For above all things, the troubled person seeking help longs to be told there *is* hope. Without it, despair reigns and reality becomes an ever-decreasing spiral of bleakness and dread. But to be shown there is truly hope, not through our own efforts at self-improvement but through the gracious *shalom* of God, is the most liberating message a person can hear.

REFERENCES

CHAPTER 1

1. Richardson, Alan and Bowden, John (eds) *A New Dictionary of Christian Theology*, London: SCM (1983) pp 132-5.
2. Oden, Thomas, 'Recovering lost identity' in *The Journal of Pastoral Care* (March 1980) **34/1**, pp 4-19.
3. Oden, Thomas, *Pastoral Theology*, San Francisco: Harper & Row (1983).
4. Pattison, Stephen, *A Critique of Pastoral Care*, London: SCM (1988)
5. Tidball, Derek, *Skilful Shepherds: An Introduction to Pastoral Theology*, Leicester: IVP (1986) p. 223.
6. Hurding, Roger, *Roots and Shoots: A Guide to Counselling and Psychotherapy*, London: Hodder & Stoughton (1985).
7. Roberts, R. C., *Taking the Word to Heart: Self and Others in an Age of Therapies*, Grand Rapids: Eerdmans (1993).
8. Bridger, Francis, 'The past, present and future of pastoral theology' in *Anvil*, **6/3**, (1989) pp. 193-8.
9. Clinebell, Howard, *Contemporary Growth Theories: Resources for Actualizing Human Wholeness*, Nashville: Abingdon Press (1981) pp. 10-11.
10. Oden, Thomas, *The Care of Souls in the Classic Tradition*, Philadelphia: Fortress Press (1984).
11. Clebsch, W. A., and Jaekle, C., *Pastoral Care in Historical Perspective*, New Jersey: Prentice Hall (1964).
12. McNeill, J. T., *A History of the Cure of Souls*, New York: Harper & Row (1951).
13. Lake, Frank, *Clinical Theology*, abridged version by Martin Yeomans, London: Darton, Longman & Todd (1986).

14. Peters, John, *Frank Lake: The Man and His Work*, London: Darton, Longman & Todd (1989), ch. 5.
15. Wilson, Michael, *A Coat of Many Colours: Pastoral Studies in the Christian Way of Life*, London: Epworth Press (1988) p. 171.
16. Collins, Gary, *Helping People Grow: Practical Approaches to Christian Counseling*, Santa Ana, California: Vision House (1980) ch. 17, for further discussion of the distinctiveness of Christian counselling.

CHAPTER 2

1. Wilson, Michael, *A Coat of Many Colours: Studies of the Christian Way of Life*, London: Epworth Press (1988) p. 70.
2. Hurding, Roger, *Restoring the Image, An Introduction to Christian Caring and Counselling*, Exeter: Paternoster Press (1980) p. 10.
3. ibid.
4. Hurding, Roger, *Roots and Shoots: A Guide to Counselling and Psychotherapy*, London: Hodder & Stoughton (1985) p. 26.
5. Hansen, James C., Stevic, Richard R. and Warner, Richard W., *Counseling Theory and Process*, Boston: Allyn & Bacon (1978) p. vii.
6. Collins, Gary, *Christian Counselling: A Comprehensive Guide*, Waco: Word Books (1988) p. 26.
7. Crabb, Lawrence, *Effective Bible Counselling*, Basingstoke: Marshall Pickering (1985).
8. Clinebell, Howard, *Basic Types of Pastoral Care and Counselling*, London: SCM (1984) p. 26.
9. Adams, Jay, *More Than Redemption*, Phillipsburg: Presbyterian and Reformed Publications (1979) p. xiii.
10. Lake, Frank, *Clinical Theology*, (abridged version) London: Darton, Longman & Todd (1986) p. 10.
11. Halmos, Paul, *The Faith of the Counsellors*, London: Constable (1973) p. 2.
12. Guntrip, H., *Psychology for Minister and Social Workers*, (3rd edn) London: George Allen & Unwin (1971) p. 12.
13. Storr, Anthony, *The Art of Psychotherapy*, London: Heinemann (1979) p. vii.

14. Mathers, J.,'The accreditation of counsellors' in *British Journal of Guidance and Counselling*, VI 2 **vol. 1**, July 1978, pp. 129-39.

15. Hurding, *Roots and Shoots*, op. cit. pp. 24-27.

16. Martin, Bernice, *A Sociology of Contemporary Cultural Change*, Oxford: Blackwell (1981) p. 193.

17. Crabb, op. cit.

18. Ibid., pp 165,6.

19. Idem., pp. 176,7.

20. Idem. p. 182.

21. Wilson, Michael, op. cit., p. 170.

22. Clebsch, W. A. and Jaekle, C. R., *Pastoral Care in Historical Perspective*, New Jersey: Prentice-Hall (1964) pp. 4-10, 79-82; reprinted in Jacobs, Michael (ed.) *Faith or Fear? A Reader in Pastoral Care and Counselling*, London: Darton, Longman & Todd (1987) pp. 12-13.

23. Oden, Thomas, 'Recovering lost identity' in *Journal of Pastoral Care*, **34/1**, (March 1980) pp. 4-19, reprinted in Jacobs, ibid. p. 15.

24. Pattison, Stephen, *A Critique of Pastoral Care*, London: SCM (1988) p. 26.

25. McNeill, J. T., *A History of the Cure of Souls*, New York: Harper & Row (1951) p. 327.

26. Wilson, Michael, *Health is For People*, London: Darton, Longman & Todd (1975) p. 117.

27. Wilson, Michael, *The Church is Healing*, London: SCM (1967).

28. Maddocks, Morris, *The Christian Healing Ministry*, London: SPCK (1981) ch. 1.

29. Pattison, Stephen, *Alive and Kicking: Towards a Practical Theology of Illness and Healing*, London: SPCK (1989) ch. 4.

30. Clebsch & Jaekle, op. cit., reprinted in Jacobs, op. cit., p. 11.

31. Brown, Colin (ed.) *The New International Dictionary of New Testament Theology*, Vol. III, Exeter: Paternoster Press (1978), pp. 166ff.

32. Pattison, Stephen, *Critique*, op. cit., p. 7.

33. Clebsch & Jaekle, op. cit., in Jacobs, ibid., p. 10.

34. Oden, Thomas, art. cit., in Jacobs, ibid., p. 16.

35. Collins, Gary, *Helping People Grow: Practical Approaches to*

Christian Counseling, Santa Ana, California: Vision House (1980) ch. 17.

CHAPTER 3

1. Kirwan, William, *Biblical Concepts for Christian Counseling: A Case for Integrating Psychology and Theology*, Grand Rapids: Baker Book House (1984).
2. Spier, J. M., *An Introduction to Christian Philosophy*, Nutley NJ: Craig Press (1979) pp. 44–49 develops the idea of sphere sovereignty.
3. Kirwan, op. cit., p. 21.
4. Niebuhr, H. R., *Christ and Culture*, London: Faber & Faber (1952).
5. Carter, John and Narramore, Bruce, *The Integration of Psychology and Theology*, Grand Rapids: Zondervan (1979).
6. Carter and Narramore, op. cit., p. 85.
7. Hurding, Roger, *Roots and Shoots*, London: Hodder & Stoughton (1985) p. 265.
8. Crabb, Lawrence, *Principles of Biblical Counseling*, Grand Rapids: Zondervan (1975).
9. Crabb, Lawrence, *Effective Biblical Counseling*, Grand Rapids Zondervan (1977).
10. Crabb, Lawrence, *Understanding People: Deep Longings for Relationship*, Grand Rapids: Zondervan (1987).
11. Crabb, Lawrence, *Effective Biblical Counseling*, ibid., ch. 2.
12. Ibid., p. 49.
13. Farnsworth, Kirk E., *Wholehearted Integration: Harmonizing Psychology and Christianity Through Word and Deed*, Grand Rapids: Baker Book House (1985).
14. Ibid., pp. 93ff.
15. Idem., p. 97.
16. Stuart Van Leeuwen, Mary, *The Person in Psychology*, Grand Rapids: Eerdmans (1985).
17. Jeeves, Malcolm, *Psychology and Christianity: The View Both Ways*, Leicester: IVP (1976).
18. Mackay, D. M., *The Clockwork Image*, Leicester: IVP (1974) chs 4 & 9.

19. Evans, C. Stephen, *Preserving the Person*, Downers Grove: IVP (1979), chs 7-11.

20. Farnsworth, K. E., op. cit., p. 105.

21. Collins, Gary (ed) *Helping People Grow: Practical Approaches to Christian Counseling*, Santa Ana: Vision House (1980) pp. 17-18.

22. Holmes, Arthur, *All Truth is God's Truth*, Leicester: IVP (1979).

CHAPTER 4

1. Scruton, Roger, *A Short History of Modern Philosophy from Descartes to Wittgenstein*, London: Ark (1984) p. 6.

2. Mitchell, Basil, *How to Play Theological Ping Pong*, London: Hodder & Stoughton (1990) pp. 156-7.

3. Brown, Colin (ed.) *The New International Dictionary of New Testament Theology*, Vol. III, Exeter: Paternoster Press (1978) pp. 1023-38.

4. Cook, David, *Thinking About Faith*, Leicester: IVP (1986) p. 7.

5. Evans, Stephen, *Philosophy of Religion*, London: EUP (1965) p. 13.

6. Lewis, H. D., *Teach Yourself Philosophy of Religion*, London: EUP (1965), p. 1.

7. Holmes, Arthur, *All Truth is God's Truth*, Leicester: IVP (1979).

8. Brett, G. S., *History of Psychology*, London: Geo. Allen & Unwin (1953).

9. Brett, G. S., *Psychology Ancient and Modern*, London: Geo. Harrap (1928).

10. Thomson, R. (ed.) *The Pelican History of Psychology*, Harmondsworth: Penguin (1968) p. 21.

11. McNeil, Elton, *The Psychology of Being Human*, San Francisco: Cornfield Press (1974), p. 20.

12. Dennis, W. (ed.) *Readings in the History of Psychology*, New York: Appleton-Century-Crofts (1948).

13. Herrnstein, R. J. and Boring, E. G., *A Source Book in the History of Psychology*, Cambridge, Mass: Harvard University Press (1965).

14. Allen, Diogenes, *Philosophy For Understanding Theology*, London: SCM (1985) 1/iii.

15. Patterson, C. H., *Theories of Counseling and Psychotherapy*, New York: Harper & Row (1973), p. xx.

16. Corey, Gerald, *Theory and Practice of Counseling and Psychotherapy*, Monterey, California: Brooks/Cole Publishing Co. (1977) p. 185.

17. Dryden, Windy, 'Rational-emotive therapy and cognitive therapy: a critical comparison' in Reda, M. and Mahoney, M. J. (eds) *Cognitive Psychotherapies*, Cambridge, Mass: Ballinger Publishing Co. (1984) p. 83.

18. Lyon, David, *Sociology and the Human Image*, Leicester: IVP (1983) p. 39.

19. Ibid., p. 40.

20. Corey, op. cit., pp. 184-5.

21. Collins, Gary, *Helping People Grow*, Santa Ana, California: Vision House (1980) p. 24.

22. Ibid., p. 26.

23. Guntrip, Harry, *Personality Structure and Human Interaction*, New York: International Universities Press (1961) p. 121.

24. Clinebell, Howard, *Contemporary Growth Therapies*, Nashville: Abingdon Press (1981) p. 34 comments that Freud's reductionism 'led him to a mechanistic model of human beings reflecting nineteenth-century physics'.

25. Guntrip, op. cit., p. 125.

26. May, Rollo, *Existence: A New Dimension in Psychiatry and Psychology*, New York: Basic Books (9158) p. 3.

27. Clinebell, ibid., p. 113.

28. May, ibid., p. 7.

29. Idem., p. 8.

30. Jeeves, Malcolm, *Psychology and Christianity: The View Both Ways*, Leicester: IVP (1976) pp. 129-30.

31. Dryden, Windy, Issues in the eclectic practice of individual therapy, in Dryden (ed.) *Individual Therapy in Britain*, London: Harper & Row (1984) ch. 14 esp. p. 351.

32. Dryden, ibid., pp. 341-43.

33. Dryden, loc. cit.

34. Clinebell, ibid., p. 18.

CHAPTER 5

1. Berger, Peter, 'Towards a sociological understanding of psychoanalysis' in Berger, *Facing up to Modernity: Excursions in Society, Politics and Religion*, Harmondsworth, Penguin (1977) p. 49.
2. Bolger, A. W. (ed.) *Counselling in Britain: A Reader*, London: Batsford (1982) p. 14.
3. Berger, ibid., p. 14.
4. Marx and Engels, *The Communist Manifesto*, Part I, reprinted in Mendel, Arthur, (ed.) *Essential Works of Marxism*, New York: Bantam Books (1971) pp. 13-25.
5. Berger, Peter, Berger, Brigitte and Kellner, Hansfried, *The Homeless Mind*, Harmondsworth: Penguin (1973) chs. 1 & 3.
6. Ibid., pp. 74, 77.
7. Berger, *Facing up to Modernity*, op. cit., p. 59.
8. Appleyard, Brian, *Understanding the Present: Science and the Soul of Modern Man*, London: Picador (1992).
9. Midgley, Mary, *Science as Salvation: A Modern Myth and its Meaning*, London: Routledge (1992).
10. Berger, *Facing up to Modernity*, op. cit., p. 60.
11. North, Maurice, *The Secular Priests*, London: Allen & Unwin (1972) p. 185.
12. Ibid., p. 188.
13. Leech, Kenneth, *The Social God*, London: SPCK (1981) p. 80.
14. Leech, Kenneth, *Spirituality and Pastoral Care*, London: Sheldon Press (1986) p. 55.
15. Padover, Saul L., *The Essential Marx: The Non-Economic Writings*, New York: Mentor (1978) pp. 286-7.
16. Selby, Peter, *Liberating God: Private Care and Public Struggle*, London: SPCK (1983) p. 52.
17. Ibid., p. 100.
18. Pattison, Stephen, *A Critique of Pastoral Care*; and *Alive and Kicking: Towards a Practical Theology of Illness and Healing*, London: SCM (1988/9).
19. Thiselton, A. C., *The Two Horizons*, Exeter: Paternoster Press (1980) p. 8.

20. Thiselton, A. C., *New Horizons in Hermeneutics*, London: HarperCollins (1992) ch. XVI.

21. Palmer, Richard, E., *Hermeneutics*, Evanston: Northwestern Universities Press (1969) ch. 3.

22. Capps, Donald, *Pastoral Care and Hermeneutics*, Philadelphia: Fortress Press (1984) p. 15.

23. Gerkin, Charles V., *The Living Human Document: Re-Visioning Pastoral Counseling in a Hermeneutical Mode*, Nashville: Abingdon Press (1984).

24. Patton, J., 'Clinical Hermeneutics: Pastoral Counseling in Soft Focus' in *Journal of Pastoral Care*, **35/3**, (Sept 1981).

25. Ricoeur, Paul, *Hermeneutics and the Human Sciences: Essays on Language, Action and Interpretation*, (trans. Thompson, J. B.) Cambridge: Cambridge University Press (1981) p. 253.

26. Habermas, Jurgen, *Knowledge and Human Interests*, London: Heinemann (1972) p. 214.

27. Brockelman, Paul, *Time and Self: Phenomenological Explorations*, New York: Crossroad Publishing Co. and Scholars Press (1985) pp. 65-6.

28. Berger, Peter and Luckmann, Thomas, *The Social Construction of Reality: A Treatise in the Sociology of Knowledge*, Harmondsworth: Penguin (1981).

29. Halmos, Paul, *The Faith of the Counsellors*, London: Constable (1965).

30. North, Maurice, *The Secular Priests*, London: Allen & Unwin (1972).

31. Halmos, ibid., p. 13.

32. North, ibid., p. 90.

33. Berger, *Facing up to Modernity*, op. cit., pp. 60-1.

34. Guinness, Os, *The Dust of Death*, London: IVP (1973) p. 276.

35. Berger, ibid., p. 50.

36. Ibid., p. 48.

CHAPTER 6

1. Perry, Ralph B., 'The Individual as the Seat of Value' in Munitz, Milton K. (ed.) *A Modern Introduction to Ethics*, New York: The Free Press (1961) p. 476.

2. Ibid., p. 496.
3. MacIntyre, Alasdair, *After Virtue: A Study in Moral Theory*, London: Duckworth (1981). But the Robinson Crusoe scenario is illusory - even Crusoe had to have his Man Friday.
4. Cottingham, John, *The Rationalists*, Oxford: OUP (1988) pp. 11ff.
5. Descartes, René, *Meditations on the First Philosophy*, Meditation **II**, (trans. Lindsay, A. D.) London: J. M. Dent (1934) p. 87.
6. Descartes, René, *The Principles of Philosophy*, **Part I**, Principle **VII**, in Lindsay, op. cit., p. 167.
7. Ryle, Gilbert, *The Concept of Mind*, Harmondsworth: Penguin (1988) p. 17.
8. Lyon, David, *Sociology and the Human Image*, Leicester: IVP (1983) p. 127.
9. Peters, Richard, *Hobbes*, Harmondsworth: Penguin (1967) pp. 87-8.
10. Woolhouse, R. S., *The Empiricists*, Oxford: Oxford University Press (1988) p. 99.
11. Locke, John, *An Essay Concerning Human Understanding*, **II.1.2**, Nidditch, P. (ed.) Oxford: Oxford University Press (1975).
12. Graham, Gordon, *Contemporary Basic Philosophy*, Oxford: Basil Blackwell (1988) p. 29.
13. de Wulf, Maurice, 'Medieval Philosophy Illustrated from the System of Thomas Aquinas' quoted in Munitz, op. cit., p. 476.
14. Plamenatz, John, *Man and Society*, Vol. 1, London: Longman (1963) chs. 6, 10.
15. Locke, John, *Second Treatise on Civil Government*, ch. VIII, para. 99, reprinted in Barker, E. (ed.) *Social Contract*, Oxford: Oxford University Press (1970) p. 83.
16. Ibid., pp. 80-81.
17. Ibid., p. 255.
18. Ibid., p. 257.
19. Ibid., ch. XIX.
20. Sulloway, Frank, *Freud, Biologist of the Mind*, London: Fontana (1980) p. 3.
21. Habermas, Jurgen, *Knowledge and Human Interests*, London: Heinemann (1972) p. 246.

22. Berne, Eric, *A Layman's Guide to Psychiatry and Psychoanalysis*, Harmondsworth: Penguin (1978) p. 271.

23. Habermas, ibid., p. 247.

24. Ibid., p. 249.

25. Hare-Duke, Michael, *Sigmund Freud*, London: Lutterworth (1972).

26. Hall, Calvin S., *A Primer of Freudian Psychology*, New York: Mentor Books (1970), chs. 2, 3.

27. Dilman, Ilham, *Freud and the Mind*, Oxford: Basil Blackwell (1986), ch. 7.

28. Berne, loc. cit.

29. Dominian, Jack, *Make or Break*, London: SPCK (1982) p. 61.

30. Clinebell, Howard, *Basic Types of Pastoral Care and Counselling*, London: SCM (1984) p. 97.

31. Jacobs, Michael, *Still Small Voice*, London: SPCK (1982) p. 12.

32. North, Maurice, *The Secular Priests*, London: Allen & Unwin (1972) p. 63.

33. Hurding, Roger, *Roots and Shoots: A Guide to Counselling and Psychotherapy*, London: Hodder & Stoughton (1985) p. 22.

34. Collins, Gary, *Christian Counselling: A Comprehensive Guide*, Waco: Word Books (1988) p. 26.

35. Bolger, A. W. (ed.) *Counselling in Britain: A Reader*, London: Batsford (1982) p. 43.

36. Anderson, Ray S., *On Being Human*, Grand Rapids: Eerdmans (1982).

37. McFadyen, Alistair, I., *The Call To Personhood*, Cambridge: Cambridge University Press (1990).

38. Peacocke, Arthur and Gillet, Grant, (eds) *Persons and Personality: A Contemporary Enquiry*, Oxford: Basil Blackwell (1987).

39. Zizioulas, John D., *Being as Communion: Studies in Personhood and the Church*, London: Darton, Longman & Todd (1985), pp. 29-30.

40. Ibid., p. 32.

41. Ibid., p. 33.

42. Ibid., p. 34.

43. Anderson, Ray S., op. cit., pp. 4-6.

44. Ibid., pp. 6-7.

45. North, ibid., p. 77.

46. O'Donovan, Oliver, op. cit.

47. Ibid., p. 51.

48. Macquarrie, John, 'A theology of personal being' in Peacocke and Gillet, op. cit., p. 178.

49. Ware, Kallistos, 'The unity of the human person according to the Greek fathers' in Peacocke and Gillet, ibid., p. 206.

50. MacMurray, John, *Persons in Relation*, London: Faber and Faber (1961) p. 17.

CHAPTER 7

1. Heaton, E. W., *The Hebrew Kingdoms*, Oxford: Oxford University Press (1968) p. 165ff.

2. McNeil, J. T., *A History of the Cure of Souls*, New York: Harper & Row (1951) chs 1-5.

3. *Pensées*, Harmondsworth: Penguin p. 64.

4. Evans, Stephen, *Preserving the Person*, Leicester: IVP (1977).

5. Jaki, Stanley, *Angels, Apes and Men*, Illinois: Sherwood, Sugden & Co. (1983).

6. Dawkins, R., *The Selfish Gene*, Oxford: Oxford University Press (1976).

7. Skinner, B. F., *Beyond Freedom and Dignity*, London: Jonathan Cape (1972).

8. Evans, op. cit.

9. Fromm, Erich, *You Shall be as Gods*, New York: Holt, Reinhart & Winston (1966).

10. Shakespeare, W., *The Merchant of Venice*.

11. Berger, Peter, *A Rumour of Angels*, Harmondsworth: Penguin (1969).

12. Becker, E., *The Denial of Death*, New York: Macmillan (1973).

13. Allen, Diogenes, *Christian Belief in a Post-Modern World*, Philadelphia: Westminster/John Knox (1989).

14. *Pensées*, Harmondsworth, Penguin, p. 60.

15. Fromm, Erich, *Man for Himself*, London: Routledge/Kegan Paul (1949) p. 210.

16. Rogers, C., *On Becoming a Person*, Boston: Houghton Mifflin Co. (1961) p. 61f.

17. Maslow, A., *Motivation and Personality*, New York: Harper & Row (1954) p. 124.

18. Hobbes, T., *Leviathan*, (1651).

19. Skinner, B. F., *Beyond Freedom and Dignity*, Harmondsworth: Penguin (1971).

20. Storr, A. (ed.) *Jung: Selected Writings*, London: Fontana (1983), drawing on the 18 volumes of C. J. Jung's *Collected Works*.

21. Rogers and Marlow, *Toward a Psychology of Being*, Princeton: Van Nostrand (1968) p. 28 (quoted in Hurding, R., *Roots and Shoots*, London: Hodder & Stoughton (1985) p. 151.

22. Browning, D., *Religious Ethics and Pastoral Care*, Philadelphia: Fortress Press (1983).

23. Storr, Anthony, *The Integrity of the Personality*, Harmondsworth, Penguin (1960) p. 28.

24. Rowley, H. H., *The Faith of Israel*, London: SCM (1956) p. 149.

CHAPTER 8

1. Torrance, T. F., *The Trinitarian Faith*, Edinburgh: T&T Clark (1988) and *The Ground and Grammar of Theology*, Belfast: Christian Journals (1980).

2. Zizioulas, J. D., *Being as Communion*, London: Darton, Longman & Todd (1985).

3. Moltmann, J., *The Trinity and the Kingdom of God*, London: SCM (1981).

4. Gunton, C. E., *The One, the Three and the Many*, Cambridge: Cambridge University Press (1933), and *The Promise of Trinitarian Theology*, Edinburgh: T&T Clark (1991).

5. McFadyen, Alistair, *The Call to Personhood*, Cambridge: Cambridge University Press (1991).

6. Moltmann, op. cit.

7. cf. Anderson, Ray, *On Being Human*, Grand Rapids: Eerdmans (1982). He refers to Richard of St Victor on p. 6.

8. Ramsey, Paul, *Basic Christian Ethics*, New York: Scribners (1950).

9. Hughes, P. E., *The Divine Image*, Leicester: IVP (1989).

10. Leech, K., *The Social God*, London: Sheldon Press (1981) pp. 6ff.

11. Macmurray, John, *Persons in Relation*, London: Faber & Faber (1961) p. 17.

12. MacFayden, op. cit., p. 29.

13. Atkinson, D., *The Message of Genesis 1-11*, Leicester: IVP (1990) pp. 85ff.

14. MacQuarrie, J., 'A theology of personal being' in Peacocke, Arthur and Gillet, Grant (eds) *Persons and Personality*, Oxford: Blackwell (1987).

15. Leech, Ken, op. cit.

16. Warfield, B. B., *The Person and Work of Christ*, Philadelphia: Presbyterian and Reformed Publishing Company (1956).

17. James, W., *The Varieties of Religious Experience*, London: Longman (1952).

18. Jung, C. G., *Psychological Types* (1921).

19. Briggs Myres, Isobel, *Gifts Differing*, Palo Alto, CA: Consulting Psychologists Press (1980).

20. Eysenck, H. J., *The Maudsley Personality Inventory*, London: University of London Press (1959).

21. Myers, D., *Psychology*, drawing on McCrae, R. and Costa, P. T., Jr., *American Psychologist*, (1986) 41, p. 1002.

22. Piaget, J., *The Child's Conception of the World*, (1929).

23. Donaldson, Margaret, *Children's Minds*, London: Fontana (1978).

24. Erikson, E., 'The eight ages of man' in *Childhood and Society*, London: Imago Publishing (1951).

25. Kohlberg, L., 'Stage and sequence: the cognitive-developmental approach to socialization' in Goslin, D. A., (ed.) *Handbook of Socialization Theory and Research*, Skokie, Illinois: Rand McNally (1969).

26. Gilligan, Carol, *In a Different Voice*, Boston: Harvard University Press (1982).

27. Jantzen, Grace, 'Connection or competition: identity and personhood in Christian ethics' in *Studies in Christian Ethics*, **5/1**, Edinburgh: T&T Clark (1992).

28. Dykstra, Craig, *Vision and Character*, New York: Paulist Press (1981).

29. Fowler, James, *Stages of Faith*, New York: Harper & Row (1981).

30. Fowler, James, *Becoming Adult, Becoming Christian*, San Francisco: Harper & Row (1984).
31. General Synod Board of Education, *How Faith Grows*, London: The National Society/Church House Publishing (1991).
32. Bridger, Francis, *Children Finding Faith*, London: Scripture Union (1988).
33. Dykstra, Craig and Parks, Sharon, *Faith Development and Fowler*, Birmingham, Alabama: Religious Education Press (1986).
34. Astley, Jeff, and Francis, Leslie (eds) *Christian Perspectives on Faith Development*, Leominster/Grand Rapids: Gracewing Books/Eerdman's (1992).
35. Jacobs, Michael, *Towards the Fulness of Christ: Pastoral Care and Christian Maturity*, London: Darton, Longman & Todd (1988).
36. Capps, Donald, *Life Cycle Theory and Pastoral Care*, Philadelphia: Fortress Press (1983).
37. Fowler, James, *Faith and the Structuring of Meaning*, in Dykstra and Parks, ibid., p. 26.
38. Fowler, ibid., p. 31.
39. Fowler, *How Faith Grows*, op. cit., p. 50.
40. Donaldson, Margaret, *Children's Minds*, London: Fontana (1978).
41. Donaldson, Margaret, *Human Minds: An Exploration*, Harmondsworth: Penguin (1993).

CHAPTER 9
1. Oden, T., *Kerugma and Counseling*, New York: Harper & Row (1966) p. 50.
2. Ibid., p. 51.
3. Ibid., p. 57.
4. Ibid., p. 55.
5. Taylor, John, *The Go-Between God*, London: SCM (1972) p. 243.
6. Hauerwas, S., *Suffering Presence*, Edinburgh: T&T Clark (1988).
7. Warfield, B. B., *The Person and Work of Christ*, Philadelphia: Presbyterian and Reformed Publishing Company (1956).
8. Ibid.
9. Lake, Frank, *Clinical Theology*, abridged edition, London: Darton, Longman & Todd (1986).

10. Lambeth Conference Report, *The Truth Shall Make You Free*, London: ACC (1988) p. 31.

11. Lambourne, R. A., *Community, Church and Healing*, London: Darton, Longman & Todd (1963) p. 36.

12. Hurding, Roger, *Roots and Shoots*, London: Hodder & Stoughton (1985) p. 34.

13. Erikson, E., 'Eight ages of man' in *Childhood and Society*, London: Imago (1951) ch. 7.

14. Klein, Melanie, 'Our adult world and its roots in infancy' (1959) in *Envy and Gratitude*, London: Hogarth (1975).

15. Laing, Ronald, *The Divided Self*, London: Tavistock Publications (1960).

16. Browning, D., *The Moral Context of Pastoral Care*, Philadelphia: Westminster Press (1976).

17. Browning, D., *Religious Thought and Modern Psychologies*, Philadelphia: Fortress Press (1987).

CHAPTER 10

1. Peck, M. S., *The Road Less Traveled*, New York: Simon & Schuster (1978) pp. 81ff.

2. Williams, Margery, *The Velveteen Rabbit*, London: Heinemann (1922).

3. Laing, R. D., *The Divided Self*, London: Tavistock Publications (1960).

4. Truax, C. B. and Carkhuff, R. R., *Towards Effective Counseling and Psychotherapy: Training and Practice*, Aldine (1967).

5. Winnicott, D. W., *The Maturational Processes and the Facilitating Environment*, London: Hogarth Press (1976).

6. Kierkegaard, S., *Sickness Unto Death*, Princeton: Princeton University Press (1980).

7. Augsburger, D., *Pastoral Counseling Across Cultures*, Philadelphia: Westminster Press (1986) p. 338.

8. Winnicott, D. W., op. cit., p. 145-6.

9. Winnicott, ibid., ch. 12.

10. Eliot, T. S., *The Wasteland*.

11. Laing, R. D., *The Divided Self*, London: Tavistock Publications (1960) p. 163.
12. Smail, David, *Illusion and Reality: The Meaning of Anxiety*, London: J. M. Dent (1984).
13. Ibid., p. 4.
14. Ibid., p. 5,7.
15. Frankl, V., *The Doctor and the Soul*, New York: Knopf (1955) and *Man's Search for Meaning*, Boston: Beacon Press (1959).
16. Ellis, A., *Reason and Emotion in Psychotherapy*, Secaucus, New Jersey: Lyle Stuart (1973).
17. Hart, A., *Feeling Free*, Old Tappan, New Jersey: Felming H. Revel (1979).
18. Ellis, op. cit., ch. 3.
19. Mason, Richard L. (I have been unable to trace this publication.)
20. Scott Peck, M., *People of the Lie*, New York: Simon & Schuster (1983).
21. Richards, John, *But Deliver us From Evil*, London: Darton, Longman & Todd (1974).
22. Menninger, K., *Whatever Became of Sin?* New York: Hawthorn Books (1973).
23. Mowrer, O. H., *The Crisis in Religion and Psychiatry*, Princeton: Van Nostrand (1961).
24. Adams, J. E., *Competent to Counsel*, Grand Rapids: Baker Book House (1970).
25. Neill, S., *A Genuinely Human Existence*, London: Constable (1959).
26. Ibid., p. 209.
27. Klein, M., *Love, Hate and Reparation*, London: Hogarth Press (1953).
28. Bonhoeffer, D., *The Cost of Discipleship*, London: SCM (1959) ch. 1.
29. Wolterstorff, N., *Lament for a Son*, Grand Rapids: Eerdmans (1987) p. 90.
30. Torrance, T. F., *Space, Time and Resurrection*, Edinburgh: Handsel (1976).
31. Barth, K., *Church Dogmatics*, Edinburgh: T&T Clark, **11/1**, p. 386.

CHAPTER 11

1. Skynner, R., *One Flesh, Separate Persons*, London: Constable (1976).
2. Friedman, E. H., *Generation to Generation: Family Process in Church and Synagogue*, New York: the Guilford Press (1985).
3. Walrond-Skinner, Sue, *Family Matters*, London: SPCK (1988).
4. Lambourne, R. A., *Community, Church and Healing*, London: Darton, Longman & Todd (1963).
5. Pattison, S., *Alive and Kicking*, London: SCM (1989).
6. Selby, P., *Liberating God*, London: SPCK (1983).
7. Leech, K., *Soul Friend*, London: Sheldon Press (1977).
8. Stapleton, Ruth Carter, *The Experience of Inner Healing*, London: Hodder & Stoughton (1977).
9. Stapleton, Ruth Carter, *The Gift of Inner Healing*, London: Hodder & Stoughton (1976).
10. MacNutt, F., *Healing*, Notre Dame: Ave Maria Press (1974).
11. MacNutt, Francis, *The Power to Heal*, (1977).
12. Sanford, A., *Healing Gifts of the Spirit*, Evesham, Arthur James (1966).
13. Gee, Donald, *Wind and Flame*, incorporating *The Pentecostal Movement*, Nottingham: Assemblies of God (1967).
14. Israel, M., *The Pain that Heals*, London: Hodder & Stoughton (1981).
15. Tournier, Paul, *Creative Suffering*, London: SCM (1982).
16. Atkinson, David, *The Message of Job*, Leicester, IVP (1991).
17. McAll, K., *Healing the Family Tree*, London: Sheldon Press (1982).
18. Hurding, R., *Roots and Shoots*, London: Hodder & Stoughton (1985) pp. 379ff.
19. Lambourne, R., 'Models of health and salvation' in Lambourne, R., *Explorations in Health and Salvation*, Birmingham: Institute of the Study of Worship and Religious Architecture, University of Birmingham (1983) (paper edited by M. Wilson).
20. Winnicott, D. W., *Playing and Reality*, London: Tavistock Publications (1971) based on 'Transitional objects and transitional phenomena' (1951).
21. Maddocks, M., *The Christian Healing Ministry*, London: SPCK (1981) p. 115f.

22. Maddocks, op. cit., p. 115, quoting Ramsey, A. M., *God, Christ and the World*, London: SCM (1969) p. 116.
23. Hauerwas, S., *A Community of Character*, Notre Dame, Notre Dame Press (1980).
24. Jacobs, M., *Towards the Fulness of Christ*, London: Darton, Longman & Todd (1988).
25. Dykstra, C., *Vision and Character*, New York: Paulist Press (1981).
26. Dykstra, op. cit., p. 59.
27. Ibid., p. 129.

CHAPTER 12

1. Sartre, J. P., in Travis, Stephen, *I Believe in the Second Coming of Jesus*, London: Hodder & Stoughton (1988) p. 227.
2. Camus, Albert, in Travis, ibid., p. 46.
3. Russell, B., in Travis, Stephen, *The Jesus Hope*, Leicester: IVP (1980) p. 16.
4. Travis, Stephen, *Christian Hope and the Future of Man*, Leicester: IVP (1980).
5. Hick, John, *Philosophy of Religion*, Engelwood Cliffs: Prentice-Hall (1963) p. 2.
6. Moltmann, Jurgen, *A Theology of Hope*, New York: Harper & Row (1967).
7. Hebblethwaite, Brian, *The Christian Hope*, Basingstoke: Marshall, Morgan & Scott (1984).
8. Macquarrie, John, *Christian Hope*, Oxford: Mowbray (1978).
9. Moltmann, ibid., pp. 103-106 for quotations in this section.
10. Bauckham, Richard, *Moltmann: A Messianic Theology in the Making*, Basingstoke: Marshall Pickering (1987) p. 31.
11. Brown, Colin (ed.) *The New International Dictionary of New Testament Theology*, Vol. 2, Exeter: Paternoster Press (1978) p. 239.
12. Travis, Stephen, *I Believe in the Second Coming of Jesus*, op. cit., p. 12.
13. Ibid., p. 15.
14. Moltmann, op. cit., p. 143.

15. Ibid., p. 129.
16. Brown, ibid., p. 242.
17. Moltmann, ibid., p. 141.
18. Ibid., pp. 143ff.
19. Ibid. p. 145.
20. Ibid., p. 142.
21. Ibid., p. 153.
22. Ladd, George, *The Presence of the Future*, London: SPCK (1980)

HANDBOOKS OF PASTORAL CARE
General Editor: Marlene Cohen

This series is an aid for all involved in the pastoral
ministry. Informed by biblical theology, the series offers
practical resources for counselling while emphasizing
the importance of a wider context of care in which
the Christian community, prayer, preaching and
nurture are essential
to wellbeing and growth.
Details of the first volumes are given on the
following pages.

Handbooks of Pastoral Care Series

GROWING THROUGH
LOSS AND GRIEF
Althea Pearson

All of life involves loss. Whether great or small, reactions to loss frequently follow a common pattern. From even minor experiences of loss, counsellors can gain valuable insights into major traumas such as redundancy, sexual abuse, marriage failure, declining health or bereavement.

From her extensive experience as a counsellor and trainer, Dr Althea Pearson also demonstrates that loss, however traumatic, always brings some measure of gain in its wake. Therefore, though tackling a subject which requires the greatest sensitivity on the part of the counsellor, *Growing Through Loss and Grief* helps to show the way to new understandings, fresh hopes and new beginnings.

Handbooks of Pastoral Care Series

SETTING CAPTIVES FREE
Bruce A. Stevens

Setting Captives Free is based on the assumption that all truth is God's truth, and freely draws on the insights and therapy techniques from counselling theories, clinical psychology and psychiatry to inform and equip all who are involved in the pastoral ministry of the Church. Differentiating between individual, marital and group counselling, and the skills appropriate to each, Dr Stevens demonstrates the many opportunities for healing and growth that these varying styles offer.

Illustrated throughout with case studies on grief, depression, incest, marital conflict and self-esteem, and including a supplement on the complementary role of psychiatric medicine by Dr Ian Harrison, this highly practical guide will prove an invaluable resource.

Handbooks of Pastoral Care Series

FREE TO LOVE
Margaret Gill

Sexuality lies at the heart of our deepest human needs for companionship, intimacy and acceptance, yet through fear, ignorance and emotional hurts, it is often regarded as a sleeping snake, best left untouched. Many counsellors and pastoral carers are not sufficiently at ease with their own sexuality to help those experiencing sexual difficulties to the place of healing and freedom to which a full recognition of the God-givenness of sexuality can lead.

Free To Love brings together Margaret Gill's extensive experience as a medical doctor working in psychosexual medicine and as a Christian counsellor. Her deeply sensitive, wise and professional approach will be an invaluable guide to all aspects of sexual identity and experience encountered in pastoral care today.

DECEMBER 1994

Handbooks of Pastoral Care Series

FAMILY COUNSELLING
John and Olive Drane

The Christian Church's lofty teaching on family life all too often imposes unrealistic ideals, which tend to magnify the normal stresses felt by any family. A sense of guilt for failing to achieve perceived Christian standards often compounds other problems. When those problems are serious, denial is commonplace and yet another family is well on the way to being screwed-up.

John and Olive Drane first question the evangelical definition of a family, looking beyond the Western nuclear family for a better model. Biblical characters who are often held up as shining examples are honestly appraised, and the stereotypic advice sometimes given by clergy is brought under critical review.

Sweeping these unhelpful, burdensome attitudes aside, the authors suggest a more realistic and compassionate way that the Church can affirm and support families.

John Drane is Director of the Centre for Christian Spirituality and Contemporary Society at the University of Stirling. The place of the family in the Church has long been a concern of John and his wife Olive, and they have co-authored several published articles on the subject.

SPRING 1995

Handbooks of Pastoral Care Series

FOR BETTER, FOR WORSE
Mary and Bruce Reddrop

An extremely wise, sensitive and informed guide for
Christian counselling dealing with marriage problems.
Emphasis is given to the counsellors' own categories of
thinking, Christian belief about marriage, appropriate
and inappropriate psychological strategies, etc., with
the goal of increasing counsellors' competence and
self-understanding. Practical chapters deal with
identifying root problems and their origins, biblical
anthropology (and its various interpretations), the
nature of marital breakdown, feelings and behaviour,
causes of conflict, sexual difficulties, separation and
divorce, counselling for change,
and much more.

The Reddrops are a highly experienced team. Mary
trained as a teacher and social worker and was
Director of Family Life Education for the Marriage
Guidance Council of Victoria before establishing her
own private practice as a psychotherapist. She is also
supervisor and trainer for the Anglican Marriage
Guidance Council in Melbourne, of which her
husband, Bruce, was Director for almost thirty years.
He is also Founding President of the Australian
Association of Marriage and Family Counsellors.

SPRING 1995

Handbooks of Pastoral Care Series

Other titles already planned

DEVELOPING PASTORAL GIFTS
Penny Nairne

PASTORAL CARE OF THE DYING AND NEWLY BEREAVED
Patrick Dixon

UNDERSTANDING PERSONALITY TYPES
Mark Pearson